Directory of Global Professional Accounting and Business Certifications

Lal Balkaran

BICENTENNIAL
1807
WILEY
2007
BICENTENNIAL

JOHN WILEY & SONS, INC.

For general information on our other products and services, or technical support, please contact our Customer Care Department within the United States at 800-762-2974, outside the United States at 317-572-3993 or fax 317-572-4002.

Wiley also publishes its books in a variety of electronic formats. Some content that appears in print may not be available in electronic books.

For more information about Wiley products, visit our Web site at http://www.wiley.com.

Library of Congress Cataloging-in-Publication Data:

Balkaran, Lal.
   Directory of global professional accounting and business certification / Lal Balkaran.
      p. cm.
   Includes index.
   ISBN-13: 978-0-470-12486-4 (pbk.)
  1. Accountants—Certification—Directories. 2. Accounting—Societies, etc.—Directories. I. Title.
   HF5630.B25 2007
   657.025—dc22
                                         200636784

10 9 8 7 6 5 4 3 2 1

CONTENTS

PREFACE

If you happen to be reading the profiles of people in the corporate world, or dealing with qualified business persons or even undertaking some activity in the world of business, chances are that you will inevitably come across certain designations and designatory letters used after peoples' names that will baffle you. You will ask yourself: "What are those? What do they mean? Where were they obtained?" Where can I get some information on them?" Ever wonder where you can start looking for the answers? You would think that such information is readily available only to find out that it is not. In the past, you would certainly have been at the mercy of libraries and professional associations only to discover that they, too, were in the dark. Not anymore.

This guide covers over 2,000 of the known professional designations and designatory letters in accounting, auditing, finance, investment, insurance, logistics, management, purchasing, marketing, actuarial science, consulting, corporate governance, information technology, information technology security, supply management, banking, real estate, taxation, inventory management and other related disciplines. Over 980 professional bodies from 147 countries around the world are in this handy reference. It is certainly not an exhaustive one as some organizations might have been unintentionally omitted, but, it represents a good start for information on professional designations.

Why such a directory in the first place? Several reasons propel me to research the material for this book, the more important of which are

- **Globalization.** As the world is rapidly becoming one big global village, there is a great need to understand information on professional organizations around the world.
- **Multinationals.** Qualified personnel from their corporate staff headquarters are sent to the branches of these giants all over the world where they are also required to recruit local staff.
- In **both** cases, professionals will need to know what the local and foreign professional qualifications are in order to determine peer acceptance, reciprocity and compliance with any local laws.
- **Career guidance.** College and university students, career guidance counselors and others will find that this is a good starting point in seeking or advising on a career in the world of business. This book will save valuable time and resources that would otherwise be spent rummaging through voluminous sources for information leading up to the designations listed here.
- **Clarification.** Human Resources (HR) and other corporate departments are sometimes at a loss as to the nature and meaning of certain designations. While some credentials like the Certified Internal Auditor (CIA) and Certified Information Systems Auditor (CISA) pose no problem since each is the only of its kind administered by a single body worldwide, the same is not true for others. For instance, the Certified Public Accountant (CPA) and Chartered Accountant (CA) designations are not solely restricted to the United States and Scotland, respectively. There are now scores of professional administering bodies that award CPAs and CAs all over the world. Each varies in terms of scope, objective, experience requirement, and depth of technical knowledge.
- **Information.** In the academic world, there is a range of material such as individual university calendars, the Commonwealth Universities Yearbook, Higher Education Directory, International Handbook of Universities, World Guide to Higher Education, and so forth on degree programs given by colleges, universities and other institutions of higher learning. But have you ever wondered where to initially look for information

on the CPA, CMA, CIA, CPM, ASIA, CFA, FLMI, FCIA, CA, or ACCA, just to name a few? Until this guide was produced, there was no material in this area.
- **Research.** Accounting firms, members of academe, libraries, professional accounting and business organizations and researchers will all find this directory helpful in pinpointing certain designations and what they mean. Contact can also be made with the professional bodies listed for sharing knowledge on common issues. It is hoped that they will all contribute towards harmonizing the various professions on a global basis.

What then does this directory set to prove? It can be used to track organizations around the world to provide further material on the programs leading up to the qualifications they offer which are listed here. The descriptions obtained can then be evaluated to measure their worth, coverage, and in-depth level to determine comparability for peer acceptance.

The book is organized alphabetically by countries. Each entry listed has 11 fields as follows:

Designation:	Address:
Designatory Letters:	Telephone:
Administering Body:	E-mail:
Membership:	Fax:
Profession:	Web:
Established:	

Certain fields do not apply to some organizations, for example, the International Federation of Accountants that grants no designation or designatory letters or the Financial Accounting Standards Board that has no membership. These are denoted as 'NA.' For others, especially the non-English speaking countries, it was difficult obtaining information for these fields and others. A dash (--) has therefore been inserted in a particular field where the information sought was not obtained. It is hoped that there will be an improvement in this area in a future edition of the guide.

Designations and designatory letters are spelled out. In some instances, the professional bodies insist on this distinction. Memberships are rounded and approximate. Some professional bodies keep their membership a closely guarded secret refusing to divulge the information while others willingly provide the numbers. For some organizations, the membership numbers refer to the amount of certification holders. The year the organization was established will be useful for those who have an interest in business history and the impact of professional associations on business trends. In this era of technology, most organizations have e-mail addresses and Web sites of their own. However, some do not have any contact details at all but they can be tracked through umbrella organizations to which they belong.

Please note that the mentioning of a professional body in this guide does not validate or endorse that particular administering body and where applicable, the certification/s it offers. That was not the intention of the book. Rather, it was put together to help clarify the meaning of designatory letters and provide the contact details of their administering bodies.

Finally, readers are encouraged to provide information on any professional body that has not been listed in this guide for a future revised edition.

Lal Balkaran

Toronto, Canada

January 2007

ABOUT THE WEB SITE

A companion Web site has been created to accompany this book. This site will contain updated information. Please visit this site periodically to get current data:

www.wiley.com/go/directory

The password to enter the site is: global

ABOUT THE AUTHOR

Lal Balkaran is self-taught and is a Certified Internal Auditor (CIA), Certified General Accountant (CGA), Fellow of the Chartered Institute of Management Accountants of the UK (FCMA), and Fellow of the Institute of Chartered Secretaries and Administrators in Canada (FCIS). He also holds an MBA from Heriot-Watt University of Edinburgh, Scotland.

Mr. Balkaran has had over 25 years of senior finance and varied internal auditing experience obtained in a wide range of industries in the Caribbean and North America. He has had articles published in several international journals including four in the Institute of Internal Auditor's (IIA) own prestigious *Internal Auditor*. On top of this, he has authored the following six reference books on international professional accounting and business certification programs:

- *A Practical Guide to Auditing and Related Terms* [World's first dictionary of auditing]
- *Accountants & Related Professionals: Reciprocal Memberships & Peer Acceptance*
- *Handbook of Global Professional Accounting Programs*
- *Handbook of Global Professional Business Programs*
- *Managerial Control Techniques* and
- *Professional Accounting & Business Programs: Effective Study and Examination Techniques*

He also wrote five reference books on his native Guyana. Mr. Balkaran taught courses in Internal Auditing, Management Accounting, and Quantitative Techniques, and was an external examiner to two Commonwealth universities.

He is a past President of the Toronto Chapter of the IIA and was recently made an Honorary Member of the chapter. Mr. Balkaran has also done several seminars in North America and the Caribbean on internal auditing related topics. He is a member of the IIA's Global Board of Research and Education Advisors, the *Internal Auditor* Editorial Advisory Board, and the Internal Audit Advisory Committee of the Treasury Board of Canada. Mr. Balkaran is also the founder of IIA-Guyana.

He currently works as a Senior Manager in the Advisory Practice of KPMG in Toronto.

Professional Bodies and Designations and Designatory Letters

A

ALBANIA

Institute of Authorized Chartered Auditors of Albania (IEKA)

Designation:	--	**Address:**	Ruruga Nikolla Tupe, Tirana, Albania
Designatory Letters:	--		
Profession:	Accounting/Auditing	**Telephone:**	355-42-34187
Membership:	--	**Fax:**	355-42-34187
Established:	--	**E-mail:**	cela hysen@yahoo.com
		Web:	--

ANDORRA

Centre Nacional d'Informatica d'Andorra (CNIA)

Designation:	--	**Address:**	Av. Santa Coloma, 91, Andorra La Vella, Andorra
Designatory Letters:	--		
Profession:	Information Technology	**Telephone:**	376-822-400
Membership:	--	**Fax:**	376-828-218
Established:	--	**E-mail:**	dbastida@andorra.ad
		Web:	www.andorra.ad

ANGOLA

The Association of Economists, Technicians, Professionals of Accounting of Central Plateau of Angola (AETPC)

Designation:	--	**Address:**	PO Box 645, Luanda, Republic of Angola
Designatory Letters:	--		
Profession:	Accounting/Economics	**Telephone:**	244-2-264-651
Membership:	--	**Fax:**	244-2-395-393
Established:	--	**E-mail:**	wachimanda@yahoo.co.uk
		Web:	--

The Association of Experts on Finance, Auditing, Management, and Accounting of Angola

Designation:	--	**Address:**	Street Higino Aires nr.22, 2nd Floor door nr. 15 TV-Radio Building, PO Box 645, Luanda, Republic of Angola
Designatory Letters:	--		
Profession:	Accounting/Mangement/ Auditing		
Membership:	--		
Established:	--	**Telephone:**	244-923-406-777
		Fax:	--
		E-mail:	muhongo@snet.co.ao
		Web:	--

ARGENTINA

Federación Argentina de Consejos Profesionales de Ciencias Económicas (FACPE)

Designation:	Contador Público Licenciado en Administración	**Address:**	Av. Córdoba 1367, Piso 6, Casilla Postal 1055, Buenos Aires-CF 1053, Argentina
Designatory Letters:	CP (Contador Público)		
Profession:	Accounting		
Membership:	--	**Telephone:**	54-11-4813-2613
Established:	--	**Fax:**	54-11-4813-8911
		E-mail:	facpe@facpe.com.ar
		Web:	www. facpe.com.ar

Federación Argentina de Graduados de Ciencias Económicas

Designation:	--	**Address:**	Viamonte 1592, Piso 3, OF
Designatory Letters:	--		410, C1055ABD, Buenos
Profession:	Accounting		Aires, Argentina
Membership:	--	**Telephone:**	54-374-1260
Established:	--	**Fax:**	54-374-1260
		E-mail:	federacion@cgce.org
		Web:	www.ciencias-economicas.com

Consejo Profesional de Ciencias Económicas de la Ciudad Autónoma de Buenos Aires

Designation:	--	**Address:**	Viamonte No. 1549 – (1055)
Designatory Letters:	--		Ciudad Autónoma de
Profession:	Actuarial Science		Buenos Aires, Argentina
Membership:	--	**Telephone:**	5382-9200
Established:	--	**Fax:**	--
		E-mail:	consejo@consejo.org.ar
		Web:	www.cpcecf.org.ar

Instituto Actuarial Argentino

Designation:	--	**Address:**	Suipacha 1111, Piso 5, 1368
Designatory Letters:	--		Buenos Aires, Argentina
Profession:	Actuarial Science	**Telephone:**	--
Membership:	--	**Fax:**	--
Established:	1943	**E-mail:**	--
		Web:	--

Instituto de Auditores

Designation:	--	**Address:**	Intoros de Argentina, Ave.
Designatory Letters:	--		Corrientes, 385- 5º Piso,
Profession:	Internal Auditing		Buenos Aires 1327,
Membership:	--		Argentina Argentina
Established:	--	**Telephone:**	54-1317-2805/371-5573
		Fax:	54-1317-2841
		E-mail:	--
		Web:	--

Instituto Argentino de Ejecutivos de Finanzas (IAEF)

Designation:	--	**Address:**	Tucuman, 612, Piso 4
Designatory Letters:	--		(1049AAN), Buenos
Profession:	Investment Management		Aires, Argentina
Membership:	--	**Telephone:**	54-11-4322-6222
Established:	--	**Fax:**	54-11-4322-4710
		E-mail:	webmaster@iaef.org.ar
		Web:	www.iaef.org.ar

Consejo Asesor de Empresas Consultoras

Designation:	--	**Address:**	Leando N. Alem 465 4 "g",
Designatory Letters:	--		1003 Buenos Aires,
Profession:	Management Consulting		Argentina
Membership:	--	**Telephone:**	54-11-4311-6299
Established:	--	**Fax:**	54-11-4311-2722
		E-mail:	mz@lvd.com.ar
		Web:	--

Asociación Argentina de Marketing

Designation:	--	**Address:**	Viamonte 723, Piso 7 of 27,
Designatory Letters:	--		1053 Buenos Aires,
Profession:	Marketing		Argentina
Established:	--	**Telephone:**	4322-3149
		Fax:	4888-4326-7702
		E-mail:	AAM@AAMAR.com
		Web:	www.aam-ar.com

ARMENIA

Association of Accountants and Auditors in Armenia

Designation:	--	**Address:**	31 K. Ulnetsu, Yerevan
Designatory Letters:	--		375037, Republic of
Profession:	Accounting		Armenia
Membership:	--	**Telephone:**	374-10-2416-63
Established:	--	**Fax:**	347-10-2416-20
		E-mail:	hharutyunyan@aaa.am
		Web:	www.aaaa.am

AUSTRALIA

Accounting and Finance Association of Australia and New Zealand

Designation:	--	**Address:**	Level 1, AFAANZ, 156
Designatory Letters:	--		Bouverie Street, Carlton,
Profession:	Accounting		Victoria, VIC 3053,
Membership:	--		Australia
Established:	--	**Telephone:**	61-03-9349-5074
		Fax:	61-03-9349-5076
		E-mail:	info@afaanz.org
		Web:	www.aanz.org

Association of Accounting Technicians Australia Ltd.

Designation:	--	**Address:**	P.O. Box 18204, Collins St.
Designatory Letters:	MAAT (Member of the Association of Accounting Technicians)		E., Melbourne, VIC 8003, Australia
	FMAAT (Fellow Member of the Association of Accounting Technicians)	**Telephone:** **Fax:** **E-mail:** **Web:**	61-03-8665-3100 61-03-8665-3130 natoffice@aat.org.au www. aat.org.au
Profession:	Accounting		
Membership:	--		
Established:	2002		

Association of Taxation and Management Accountants

Designation:	Taxation and Management Accountant
Designatory Letters:	AMATMA (Affiliate Member of the Association of Taxation and Management Accountant)
	ATMA (Associate Member of the Association of Taxation and Management Accountant)
	MTMA (Member of the Association of Taxation and Management Accountant)
	FTMA (Fellow Member of the Association of Taxation and Management Accountant)
	IMATMA (International Member of the Association of Taxation and Management Accountant)
Profession:	Accounting
Membership:	--
Established:	1985

Address:	Suite 2E, 9 Burwood Road, Burwood, NSW 2134, Australia
Telephone:	61-2-9744-3153
Fax:	61-2-9744-3154
E-mail:	enquiries@atma.com.au
Web:	www.atma.com.au

Australian Accounting Standards Board

Designation:	NA
Profession:	Accounting
Designatory Letters:	NA
Established:	1989

Address:	PO Box 204, Collins St. W, VIC 8007 or Level 7, 600 Bourke Street, Melbourne, VIC 3000, Australia
Telephone:	61-03-9617-7600
Fax:	61-03-9617-7606
E-mail:	standard@aasb.com.au
Web:	www.aasb.com.au

CPA Australia (formerly the Australian Society of Practising Accountants or ASCPA)

Designation:	Certified Practising Accountant
Designatory Letters:	ASA (Associate of the Australian Society of Certified Practising Accountants)
	CPA (Certified Practising Accountant)
	FCPA (Fellow of the Australian Society of Certified Practising Accountants)
Profession:	Accounting
Membership:	108,000
Established:	Incorporated in 1952 although its orgins date back to the 1880s

Address:	GPO Box 2820AA, Melbourne, Victoria 3000, Australia
Telephone:	61-3-9606-9689
Fax:	61-3-9602-1163
E-mail:	cpaonline@cpaaustralia.com.au
Web:	www.cpaaustralia.com.au

Financial Reporting Council

Designation:	NA	**Address:**	Charles Macek, Chairman, c/o The Treasury Corporations and Financial Services Division, Langton Crescent, Canberra, ACT 2600, Australia
Designatory Letters:	NA		
Profession:	Accounting		
Established:	--		
		Telephone:	--
		Fax:	--
		E-mail:	chairman@frc.gov.au
		Web:	www.frc.gov.au

The Institute of Chartered Accountants in Australia

Designation:	Chartered Accountant	**Address:**	37 York Street, Sydney, NSW 2000, Australia
Designatory Letters:	ACA (Associate Member of the Institute of Chartered Accountants in Australia)	**Telephone:**	61-2-9290-1344
		Fax:	61-2-9262-5469
	FCA (Fellow Member of the Institute of Chartered Accountants in Australia)	**E-mail:**	stephen@icaa.org.au
		Web:	www.icaa.org.au/
Profession:	Accounting		
Membership:	44,000		
Established:	1928		

National Institute of Accountants (NIA)

Designation:	--	**Address:**	Level 8, 12-20 Flinders Lane, Melbourne, Victoria 3000, Australia
Designatory Letters:	ANIA (Associate of the National Institute of Accountants)		P O Box 18204, Collins St., East Melbourne, Victoria 8003, Australia
	MNIA (Member of the National Institute of Accountants)	**Telephone:**	03-8665-3100
	FNIA (Fellow of the National Institute of Accountants)	**Fax:**	03-8665-3130
		E-mail:	natoffice@nia.org.au
Profession:	Accounting	**Web:**	www.nia.org.au
Membership:	14,000		
Established:	1923		

The Institute of Actuaries of Australia

Designation:	--	**Address:**	Level 7, Challis House, 4 Martin Place, Sydney, NSW 2000, Australia
Designatory Letters:	AIAA (Associate of the Institute of Actuaries of Australia)	**Telephone:**	612-9233-3466
	FIAA (Fellow of the Institute of Actuaries of Australia)	**Fax:**	612-9233-3446
		E-mail:	actuaries@actuaries.asn.au
Profession:	Actuarial Science	**Web:**	actuaries.asn.au/
Membership:	3,200		
Established:	1897		

Financial Services Institute of Australasia (FINSIA)

(FINSIA is the new face of the merger of the Securities Institute of Australia established in 1966 and the Australian Institute of Banking and Finance established in 1886)

Designation:	--	**Address:**	Level 3, NAB House, 255 George Street, Sydney, NSW 2000, Australia
Designatory Letters:	A Fin (Associate Member of the Financial Services Institute of Australasia)		
		Telephone:	02-8248-6799
	SA Fin (Senior Associate Member of the Financial Services Institute of Australasia)	**Fax:**	02-8248-7696
		E-mail:	info@finsia-edu.au
		Web:	www.finsia-edu.au
	F Fin (Fellow Member of the Financial Services Institute of Australasia)		
	SF Fin (Senior Fellow Member of the Financial Services Institute of Australasia)		
Profession:	Banking		
Membership:	--		
Established:	2005		

Chartered Institute of Company Secretaries in Australia
(the Australian Division of the Institute of Chartered Secretaries and Administrators [ICSA]).

Designation:	Chartered Secretary	**Address:**	GPO Box 1594, Sydney, New South Wales 2001, Australia
Designatory Letters:	ACIS (Associate Member of both the Chartered Institute of Company Secretaries in Australia Ltd and the Institute of Chartered Secretaries and Administrators)		
		Telephone:	612-223-5744
		Fax:	612-232-7174
		E-mail:	info@csaust.com
		Web:	www.csaust.com
	FCIS (Fellow Member of both the Chartered Institute of Company Secretaries in Australia Ltd and the Institute of Chartered Secretaries and Administrators)		
Profession:	Corporate Governance		
Membership:	--		
Established:	1891 in London, England and 1914 in Australia		

Australian Institute of Credit Management

Designation:	--	**Address:**	Suite 202, 619 Pacific Highway, St. Leonards, NSW 2065, Australia
Designatory Letters:	AICM (Associate of the Australian Institute of Credit Management)		
		Telephone:	61-02-9906-4563
	MICM (Member of the Australian Institute of Credit Management)	**Fax:**	61-02-9906-5686
		E-mail:	aicm@aicm.com.au
		Web:	www. aicm.com.au
	CCE (Certified Credit Executive)		
Profession:	Credit Management		
Membership:	--		
Established:	--		

Financial Planning Association of Australia Ltd (FPA)

Designation:	Certified Financial Planner	**Address:**	PO Box 109, Collins Stret West, Melbourne, VIC 8007, Australia
Designatory Letters:	CFP (Certified Financial Planner)		
	AFPA (Associate Member of the Financial Planning Association of Australia Ltd.)	**Telephone:**	800-337-301
		Fax:	--
		E-mail:	--
	FPA (Aff) (Affiliate of the Financial Planning Association of Australia Ltd.)	**Web:**	www.fpa.asn.au
Profession:	Financial Planning		
Membership:	12,000		
Established:	1992		

Institute of Financial Services

Designation:	--	**Address:**	PO Box 489, Darlinghurst, NSW 1300, Australia
Designatory Letters:	AIFS (Associate of the Institute of Financial Services)	**Telephone:**	02-9283-5999
		Fax:	02-9283-5993
Profession:	Financial Services	**E-mail:**	IFSoffice@ifs-inc.com.au
Membership:	--	**Web:**	www.ifs-inc.com.au
Established:	1955		

Australian Human Resource Institute

Designation:	--	**Address:**	Level 10, 601 Burke Street, Melbourne, VIC 3000, Australia
Designatory Letters:	AHRI (Affiliate of the Australian Human Resource Institute)		
	MAHRI (Member of the Australian Human Resource Institute)	**Telephone:**	61-03-9918-9200
		Fax:	61-03-9918-9201
		E-mail:	enquiries@ahri.com.au
	CAHRI (Certified Professional of the Australian Human Resource Institute)	**Web:**	www.ahri.com.au
Profession:	Human Resources Management		
Membership:	--		
Established:	--		

The Australian Computer Society Inc. (ACS)

Designation:	--	**Address:**	PO Box Q534, Queen Victoria Building, Sydney, NSW 1230, Australia.
Designatory Letters:	--		
Profession:	Information Technology		
Membership:	--	**Telephone:**	02-9299-3666
Established:	1966	**Fax:**	02-9299-3997
		E-mail:	info@acs.org.au
		Web:	www.acs.org

Association of Financial Advisers Ltd.

(formerly the Australian Lifewriters Association established in 1946)

Designation:	--	**Address:**	PO Box 132, Deakin West, ACT 2600, Australia.
Designatory Letters:	--		
Profession:	Insurance	**Telephone:**	06-285-1986/800-656-009
Membership:	--	**Fax:**	06-285-2022
Established:	1997	**E-mail:**	info@afa.asn.au
		Web:	www.afa.asn.au

Australia and New Zealand Institute of Insurance and Finance

Designation:	Certified Insurance Professional	**Address:**	Level 17, 31 Queen Street, Melbourne, VIC 3000, Australia
Designatory Letters:	CIP (Certified Insurance Professional)	**Telephone:**	61-03-9629-4021
	(Aff.) ANZIIF (Affiliate Member of the Australian and New Zealand Institute of Insurance and Finance)	**Fax:**	61-03-9629-4204
		E-mail:	ceo@institute.com.au
		Web:	www.theinstitute.com.au
	(Assoc.) ANZIIF (Associate Member of the Australian and New Zealand Institute of Insurance and Finance)		
	(Snr. Assoc.) ANZIIF (Senior Associate Member of the Australian and New Zealand Institute of Insurance and Finance)		
	(Fellow) ANZIIF (Fellow Member of the Australian and New Zealand Institute of Insurance and Finance)		
Profession:	Insurance/Finance		
Membership:	--		
Established:	--		

Institute of Internal Auditors–Australia (IIA--Australia).

Designation:	NA	**Address:**	Level 7, 133 Castlereagh St., Sydney, NSW 2000, Australia
Designatory Letters:	NA		
Profession:	Internal Auditing		
Membership:	2,600	**Telephone:**	61-02-9267-9155/800-236-366
Established:	1952	**Fax:**	61-02-9264-9240/800-644-380
		E-mail:	enquiry@iia.org.au
		Web:	www.iia.org.au

Australian-Asian Institute of Civil Leadership (AAICL)

Designation:	--	**Address:**	P.O. Box 7577, Garbutt, QLD 4814, Australia
Designatory Letters:	AAICL(Associate of the Australian-Asian Institute of Civil Leadership)	**Telephone:**	--
		Fax:	--
	MAICL (Member of the Australian-Asian Institute of Civil Leadership)	**E-mail:**	--
		Web:	www.uk-geocities.com/ instituteofcivilleadership. institute.html
	FAICL (Fellow of the Australian-Asian Institute of Civil Leadership)		
	HonFAAICL (Honourary Fellow of the Australian-Asian Institute of Civil Leadership)		
Profession:	Management		
Membership:	--		
Established:	--		

Australian Institute of Management

Designation:	NA	**Address:**	181 Fitzroy Street, St. Kilda, VIC 3182, Australia
Designatory Letters:	NA		
Profession:	Management	**Telephone:**	61-03-9534-8181
Membership:	25,000	**Fax:**	61-03-9534-5250
Established:	1941	**E-mail:**	enquiry@aim.com.au
		Web:	www.aim.com.au

Institute of Certified Management Accountants of Australia

Designation:	Certified Management Accountant	**Address:**	CMA House, Monash Corporate Centre, Unit 5, 20 Duerdin Street, Clayton North, VIC 3168, Australia
Designatory Letters:	CMA (Certified Management Accountant)		
	AMA (Associate Management Accountant)	**Telephone:**	61-03-9544-7913
		Fax:	61-03-9544-7299
	GMA (Graduate Management Accountant)	**E-mail:**	info@cmawebline.org
		Web:	www.cmawebline.org
	MAA (Management Accountant Affiliate)		
Profession:	Management Accounting		
Membership:	--		
Established:	1996		

Institute of Management Consultants in Australia Inc. (IMC)

Designation:	Certified Management Consultant	**Address:**	PO Box 193, Surrey Hills, VIC 3127, Australia
Designatory Letters:	CMC (Certified Management Consultant)	**Telephone:**	800-800-719
	AIMC (Associate Member of the Institute of Management Consultants)	**Fax:**	613-3989-1986
		E-mail:	imc@imc.org.au
		Web:	www.management-consultants.com.au
	MIMC (Member of the Institute of Management Consultants)		
	FIMC (Fellow Member of the Institute of Management Consultants)		
Profession:	Management Consulting		
Membership:	987		
Established:	1969		

Australian Marketing Institute (AMI)

Designation:	Certified Practising Marketer	**Address:**	P.O. Box 7443, Melbourne, VIC 3004, Australia
Designatory Letters:	CPM (Certified Practising Marketer)	**Telephone:**	61-1-800-240-264
Profession:	Marketing	**Fax:**	61-1-800-211-284
Membership:	--	**E-mail:**	membership@ami.org.au
Established:	1933	**Web:**	www.ami.org.au

Marketing Association of Australia and New Zealand (MAANZ).

Designation:	Chartered Professional Practitioner*	**Address:**	PO Box 369, Ormond, VIC 3204, Australia
Designatory Letters:	CPP (Chartered Professional Practitioner)	**Telephone:**	61-3-9578-8610
	MMA (Member of the Marketing Association of Australia and New Zealand)	**Fax:**	61-3-9578-7365
		E-mail:	info@marketing.org.au
	AFMA (Associate Fellow of the Marketing Association of Australia and New Zealand)	**Web:**	www.marketing.org.au
	FAMA (Fellow of the Marketing Association of Australia and New Zealand)		
	Granted by MAANZ and the Institute of Chartered Practicing Professionals		
Profession:	Marketing		
Membership:	--		
Established:	--		

Australian Institute of Project Management

Designation:	--	**Address:**	Level 9, 139 Macquarie St., Sydney, NSW 2000, Australia
Designatory Letters:	AAIPM (Associate of the Australian Institute of Project Management)	**Telephone:**	61-02-8288-8700
		Fax:	61-02-8288-8711
	MAIPM (Member of the Australian Institute of Project Management)	**E-mail:**	info@aipm.com.au
		Web:	www. aipm.com.au
	FAIPM (Fellow of the Australian Institute of Project Management)		
Profession:	Project Management		
Membership:	--		
Established:	1976		

Risk Management Institution of Australasia (RMIA)

Designation:	Certified Practising Risk Manager	**Address:**	PO Box 93, Box Hill, VIC 3128, Australia
Designatory Letters:	CPRM (Certified Practising Risk Manager)	**Telephone:**	03-9899-7100
	MRMIA (Member of the Risk Management Institution of Australasia)	**Fax:**	03-9890-6310
		E-mail:	admin@rmia.org.au
		Web:	www.rmia.org.au
	AFRMIA (Associate Fellow of the Risk Management Institution of Australasia)		
	FRMIA (Fellow of the Risk Management Institution of Australia)		
Profession:	Risk Management		
Membership:	--		
Established:	2003		

Taxation Institute of Australia

Designation:	--	**Address:**	Australia
Designatory Letters:	ATIA (Associate of the Taxation Institute of Australia)	**Telephone:**	61-02-8223-0000
		Fax:	--
		E-mail:	--
	FTIA (Fellow of Taxation Institute of Australia)	**Web:**	www. taxinstitute.com.au
Profession:	Taxation		
Membership:	--		
Established:	--		

The Finance and Treasury Association Ltd.
(formerly The Australian Society of Corporate Treasurers or ASCT)

Designation:	Corporate Treasurer	**Address:**	Level 5, 22 William Street, Melbourne, Victoria 3000, Australia
Designatory Letters:	MFTA (Member of the Finance and Treasury Association)		
	CFTP (Certified Finance and Treasury Professional)	**Telephone:**	613-9616-0200
		Fax:	613-9629-7881
		E-mail:	info@fta.asn.au
	CFTP (Snr.) (Senior Certified Finance and Treasury Professional)	**Web:**	www.finance-treasury.com
	FFTP (Fellow Finance and Treasury Professional)		
Profession:	Treasury Management		
Membership:	--		
Established:	1982		

AUSTRIA

Kammer der Wirtschaftstreuhänder

Designation:	Wirtschaftstreuhaender	**Address:**	Schönbrunner Str. 222-228, (U4Center), Stiege 1/Top 2, A-1120 Wien, Austria
Designatory Letters:	--		
Profession:	Accounting		
Membership:	--	**Telephone:**	43-1-81173-0
Established:	1947	**Fax:**	43-1-81173-100
		E-mail:	office@kwt.or.at
		Web:	www.kwt.or.at/index.html

Institut Österreichischer Wirtschaftprüfer

Designation:	--	**Address:**	Schwarzenbergplatz 4, A-1050, Wien, Austria
Designatory Letters:	--		
Profession:	Accounting	**Telephone:**	43-1-71135-2623
Membership:	--	**Fax:**	43-1-71135-2625
Established:	1947	**E-mail:**	office@iwp.or.at
		Web:	www.iwp.or.at/uebersicht.html

Aktuarvereinigung Österreichs (AVÖ) (Actuarial Association of Austria)

Designation:	--	**Address:**	Schwarzenbergplatz 7, A-1030, Wien, Austria
Designatory Letters:	--		
Profession:	Actuarial Science	**Telephone:**	--
Membership:	--	**Fax:**	--
Established:	1971	**E-mail:**	sekretariat@avoe.att
		Web:	www.avoe.at

Austrian Computer Society

Designation:	--	**Address:**	Wollzeile 1-3, A-1010,
Designatory Letters:	--		Vienna, Austria
Profession:	Information Technology	**Telephone:**	43-1-512-0235
Membership:	--	**Fax:**	43-1-512-02359
Established:	--	**E-mail:**	ocg@ocg.or.at
		Web:	www.ocg.or.at

Österreichische Vereinigung für Finanzanaluse und Asset Management (OVFA)

Designation:	--	**Address:**	Esslinggasse 17/5, A-1010
Designatory Letters:	--		Wien, Austria
Profession:	Investment Management	**Telephone:**	431-533-5050-15
Membership:	--	**Fax:**	431-533-5050-33
Established:	--	**E-mail:**	office@ovfa.at
		Web:	www.ovfa.net

Fachverband Unternehmensberatung und Datenverarbeitung
(Professional Association of Management Consulting and Technology or UBIT)

Designation:	--	**Address:**	Wiedner Haupstrasse 63,
Designatory Letters:	--		1045 Vienna, Austria
Profession:	Management Consulting	**Telephone:**	430-590-900-3760
Membership:	--	**Fax:**	43-05-90-900-285
Established:	--	**E-mail:**	ubit@wk.at
		Web:	www.ubit.at

Projektmanagement Austria

Designation:	--	**Address:**	WRK Road, 25-2-3-21,
Designatory Letters:	--		A-1090 Vienna, Austria
Profession:	Project Management	**Telephone:**	1319-29-210
Membership:	--	**Fax:**	1319-29-2129
Established:	--	**E-mail:**	--
		Web:	www.p-m-a.at

Austrian Society of Corporate Treasurers

Designation:	--	**Address:**	Rockhgasse 6, Vienna
Designatory Letters:	--		A-1014, Austria
Profession:	Treasury Management	**Telephone:**	253-386-3631
Membership:	--	**Fax:**	253-386-3973
Established:	--	**E-mail:**	office@finanz.opwz.com
		Web:	www.opwz.com

AZERBAIJAN

The Chamber of Auditors of Azerbaijan Republic

Designation:	--	**Address:**	S.Y. Bakuvi Street 14, Baku,
Designatory Letters:	--		Az 1072, Azerbaijan
Profession:	Auditing		Republic
Membership:	94	**Telephone:**	99412-498-2855
Established:	1996	**Fax:**	99412-498-2855
		E-mail:	audit-azerbaijan@
			azeurotel.com
		Web:	www.audit.gov.az

Azerbaijan Project Management Association (AZPAIA)

Designation:	--	**Address:**	AZ 1005, Baki, Azerbaijan
Designatory Letters:	--	**Telephone:**	99-412-492-9582
Profession:	Project Management	**Fax:**	--
Membership:	--	**E-mail:**	info@ipma.org
Established:	--	**Web:**	www.azpma.net

B

BAHAMAS

The Bahamas Institute of Chartered Accountants (BICA)

Designation:	Chartered Accountant	**Address:**	South Wing, The Plaza, Mackay Street, Nassau, Bahamas
Designatory Letters:	CA (Chartered Accountant)	**Telephone:**	242-394-3439
Profession:	Accounting/Auditing	**Fax:**	242-394-3629
Membership:	--	**E-mail:**	bica@batelnet.bs
Established:	1971	**Web:**	www.bica.bs

BAHRAIN

Bahrain Accountants Association (BAA)

Designation:	--	**Address:**	PO Box 1119, Manama, Bahrain
Designatory Letters:	--	**Telephone:**	973-727433
Profession:	Accounting	**Fax:**	973-727201
Membership:	--	**E-mail:**	--
Established:	--	**Web:**	--

The Bahrain Society of Accountant and Auditors

Designation:	--	**Address:**	PO Box 50, Manama, Bahrain
Designatory Letters:	--	**Telephone:**	--
Profession:	Accounting	**Fax:**	--
Membership:	--	**E-mail:**	--
Established:	--	**Web:**	--

BANGLADESH

The Institute of Chartered Accountants of Bangladesh (ICAB)

Designation:	Chartered Accountant	**Address:**	Chartered Accountant Bhaban, 100 Kazi Nazral Islam Avenue, Kawran Bazar, Dhaka-1215, Bangladesh.
Designatory Letters:	ACA (Associate Member of the Institute of Chartered Accountants of Bangladesh)		
	FCA (Fellow Member of the Institute of Chartered Accountants of Bangladesh)	**Telephone:**	880-2-911-7521
		Fax:	888-2-811-9399
		E-mail:	icab@icab-bd.org
		Web:	icab-bd.org
Profession:	Accounting		
Membership:	--		
Established:	1973		

The Institute of Cost and Management Accountants of Bangladesh (ICMA)

Designation:	Accountant	**Address:**	ICMA Bhaban, Nilkhet, Dhaka,
Designatory Letters:	ACMA (Associate		Bangladesh.
	Member of the Institute	**Telephone:**	880-2-861-9645
	of Cost and	**Fax:**	880-2-865703
	Management	**E-mail:**	icmab@citechco.net
	Accountants)	**Web:**	www.icmab.org.bd
	FCMA (Fellow Member		
	of the Institute of Cost		
	and Management		
	Accountants)		
Profession:	Accounting		
Membership:	--		
Established:	1972		

Institute of Management Consultants of Bangladesh (IMCB)

Designation:	--	**Address:**	396 New Eskaton Road, PO Box
Designatory Letters:	--		7092, Dhaka 1000, Bangladesh.
Profession:	Management Consulting	**Telephone:**	880-2-9351102-935-3350
Membership:	--	**Fax:**	880-2-9351103
Established:	1987	**E-mail:**	imcb@consultant.com
		Web:	www.imcbangladesh.net

BARBADOS

The Institute of Chartered Accountants of Barbados

Designation:	Chartered Accountant	**Address:**	Room 29, 1ˢᵗ Floor, Hastings Plaza,
Designatory Letters:	CA (Chartered		Christ Church, Barbados
	Accountant)	**Telephone:**	246-429-5678
Profession:	Accounting	**Fax:**	246-426-0970
Membership:	--	**E-mail:**	admin@icab.bb
Established:	1974	**Web:**	www.icab.bb

BELGIUM

Association Nationale des Comptables de Belgique

Designation:	--	**Address:**	Avenue Legrand 62, B-1050
Designatory Letters:	--		Bruxelles, Belgium.
Profession:	Accounting	**Telephone:**	32-71-886-160
Membership:	--	**Fax:**	--
Established:	--	**E-mail:**	--
		Web:	www.ancb.be

Fédération des Experts Comptables Européens (FEE)

Designation:	--	**Address:**	83 Rue de La Loi, 1040 Brussels
Designatory Letters:	--		Belgium
Profession:	Accounting	**Telephone:**	322-231-0555
Membership:	--	**Fax:**	322-231-1112
Established:	1986	**E-mail:**	--
		Web:	--

Institut des Experts-Comptables et des Conseils Fiscaux

Designation:	Experts-Comptables	**Address:**	Rue de Livourne, 41, 1050
Designatory Letters:	--		Brussels, Belgium
Profession:	Accounting	**Telephone:**	32-2-543-7490
Membership:	--	**Fax:**	32-2-543-7491
Established:	--	**E-mail:**	info@iec-iab.be
		Web:	www.iec-iab.be-fra/

Institut des Reviseurs d'Entreprises

Designation:	--	**Address:**	Avenue Marnix 22, B 1050,
Designatory Letters:	--		Brussels, Belgium
Profession:	Accounting	**Telephone:**	32-2-512-5136
Membership:	--	**Fax:**	32-2-512-7886
Established:	--	**E-mail:**	info@ibr-ire.be
		Web:	www.ibr-ire.be

Association Royale des Actuaires Belges-Koninklijke Vereniging van Belgische Aktuarissen

Designation:	--	**Address:**	Rue Fossé-aux Loups 48,
Designatory Letters:	--		Wolvengracht 48, 1000
Profession:	Actuarial Science		Brussels, Belgium
Membership:	--	**Telephone:**	--
Established:	1895	**Fax:**	--
		E-mail:	webmaster@actuaweb.be
		Web:	www.actuaweb.be

The European Governance Institute

Designation:	--	**Address:**	Avenue des Statuaires 120, 1180
Designatory Letters:	--		Bruxelles, Belgium
Profession:	Corporate Governance	**Telephone:**	--
Membership:	622	**Fax:**	--
Established:	2004	**E-mail:**	--
		Web:	www.ecgi.org

Fed.des Assoc. Informat.de Belgique (FAIB-FBVI)

Designation:	--	**Address:**	Bloesemlaan 17, BE-3360,
Designatory Letters:	--		Korbeek-Lo, Belgium
Profession:	Information Technology	**Telephone:**	32-16-46-2841
Established:	--	**Fax:**	
		E-mail:	ads@faib.org
		Web:	www.bfia.be

Association Belge des Analystes Financiers (ABAF)

Designation:	--	**Address:**	Palais de la Bourse, B-1000
Designatory Letters:	--		Brussels, Belgium
Profession:	Investment Management	**Telephone:**	32-2-514-43-13
Membership:	--	**Fax:**	32-2-511-75-27
Established:	--	**E-mail:**	info@abaf.be
		Web:	www.abaf.be

Association Belge des Conseils en gestion et Organisation

Designation:	--	**Address:**	60 Rue de Tongres, B-1040
Designatory Letters:	--		Brussels, Belgium
Profession:	Management Consulting	**Telephone:**	32-2-251-2996
Membership:	--	**Fax:**	32-2-251-2996
Established:	--	**E-mail:**	ascobel@skynet.be
		Web:	www.ascobel.be

Stichting Marketing

Designation:	--	**Address:**	Research Park Zellik, De Haak 1,
Designatory Letters:	--		B-1731, Zellik, Belgium
Profession:	Marketing	**Telephone:**	32-2-467-5959
Membership:	--	**Fax:**	32-2-467-5956
Established:	--	**E-mail:**	--
		Web:	--

Association des Tresoriers d'Entreprises en Belgique

Designation:	--	**Address:**	74 AV. Armand Huysmans, B-
Designatory Letters:	--		1050 Brussells, Belgium
Profession:	Treasury Management	**Telephone:**	32-2-645-4816
Membership:	--	**Fax:**	32-2-645-4848
Established:	--	**E-mail:**	ateb@ateb.be
		Web:	www.ateb.be

BELIZE

Institute of Chartered Accountants of Belize (ICAB)

Designation:	Chartered Accountant	**Address:**	Suite # 107, Blake Building,
Designatory Letters:	CA (Chartered Accountant)		Hudson & Eyre Streets, PO Box 1223, Belize City, Belize
Profession:	Accounting	**Telephone:**	501-223-2455
Membership:	50	**Fax:**	501-227-6012
Established:	1984	**E-mail:**	secretariat@icab.bz
		Web:	www.icab.bz

BERMUDA

Institute of Chartered Accountants of Bermuda (ICAB)

Designation:	Chartered Accountant	**Address:**	Boyle Building, PO Box HM
Designatory Letters:	CA (Chartered Accountant)		1625, Hamilton HM GX,
Profession:			Bermuda
Membership:	FCA (Fellow of the Institute of Chartered Accountants of Bermuda)	**Telephone:**	441-292-7479
Established:		**Fax :**	441-295-3121
	Accounting	**E-mail:**	icab@northrock.bm
	--	**Web:**	--
	1973		

BOLIVIA

Colegio de Contadores de Bolivia (School of Accounting of Bolivia)

Designation:	--	**Address:**	Calle Republiquetas N. 696 – 2do,
Designatory Letters:	--		Of. Floor 2B, Square 4386,
Profession:	Accounting		Cochabamba, Bolivia
Membership:	--	**Telephone:**	(591) 333-8816
Established:	--	**Fax:**	--
		E-mail:	contadores@contadoresbolivia.org.bo
		Web:	www.contadoresbolivia.org.bo

Colegio de Auditores de Bolivia

Designation:	Licenciado en Auditoria	**Address:**	Calle Don Bosco, #154,
Designatory Letters:	--		Santa Cruz, Bolivia
Profession:	Auditing	**Telephone:**	591-3-339-1257
Membership:	--	**Fax:**	591-3-339-1258
Established:	--	**E-mail:**	caub@cotas.com.bo
		Web:	www.caub-bo.com

BOSNIA and HERZEGOVINA

Association of Accountants and Auditors of Republic of Srpska

Designation:	--	**Address:**	Mirka Kovacevica 13a, 78000
Designatory Letters:	--		Banja Luka, Bosnia and
Profession:	Accounting/Auditing		Herzegovina
Membership:	--	**Telephone:**	387-51-43-1260
Established:	--	**Fax:**	387-51-43-02-00
		E-mail:	sr-rrs@inecco.net
		Web:	--

Association of Business Consultants in Bosnia and Herzegovina

Designation:	--	**Address:**	Branilaca grada 47-3, Sarajevo,
Designatory Letters:	--		Bosnia and Herzegovina
Profession:	Management Consulting	**Telephone:**	387-33-222-854
Membership:	25	**Fax:**	387-33-442-567
Established:	2001	**E-mail:**	lespnet@lespnet.ba
		Web:	www.lespnet.ba

BOTSWANA

The Botswana Institute of Accountants (BIA)

Designation:	--	**Address:**	Plot 50676 Block B, Second Floor,
	L.B.I.A. (Licentiate		Fairground Office Park,
	Member of the Botswana		Gabarone, Botswana
Designatory Letters:	Institute of Accountants)	**Telephone:**	267-397-2992
	R.B.I.A. (Registered	**Fax:**	267-397-2982
	Member of the Botswana	**E-mail:**	tsen@bia.org.bw
	Institute of Accountants)	**Web:**	www.bia.org
	A.C.P.A. (Bots) (Associate		
	Member of the Botswana		
	Institute of Accountants)		
	F.C.P.A. (Bots) (Fellow		
	Member of the Botswana		
	Institute of Accountants)		
Profession:	Accounting		
Membership:	910		
Established:	1990		

Botswana Information Technology Society (BITS)

Designation:	--	**Address:**	Private Bag BO 262, Gabarone,
Designatory Letters:	--		Botswana
Profession:	Information Technology	**Telephone:**	--
Membership:	--	**Fax:**	--
Established:	--	**E-mail:**	--
		Web:	www.bits.bw

BRAZIL

Conselho Federal de Contabilidade

Designation:	--	**Address:**	SAS Quadra 5, Bloco J, Lote 03,
Designatory Letters:	--		CEP 70070-500, Brasilia DF
Profession:	Accounting	**Telephone:**	55-61-322-2052
Membership:	--	**Fax:**	55-61-322-2033
Established:	--	**E-mail:**	cfc@cfc.org.br
		Web:	www.cfc.org.br

Instituto dos Auditores Independentes do Brasil (IBRACON)

Designation:	--	**Address:**	Rua Bela Cintra, 952-4th Floor,
Designatory Letters:	--		CEP 01415-000, Sao Paulo,
Profession:	Accounting		Brazil
Membership:	--	**Telephone:**	55-11-231-0595
Established:	--	**Fax:**	55-11-258-0210
		E-mail:	ibracon@ibracon.com.br
		Web:	www.ibracon.com.br

Instituto Brasileiro de Atuaria (Brazilian Institute of Actuaries)

Designation:	--	**Address:**	Rua da Assembleia 10, Sala 1304,
Designatory Letters:	--		20119-001, Rio de Janeiro, R.J.,
Profession:	Actuarial Science		Brazil
Membership:	--	**Telephone:**	55-21-2531-0267
Established:	1969	**Fax:**	--
		E-mail:	iba@atuarios.org.br
		Web:	www.atuarios.org.br

Brazilian Computer Society – SBC (Instituto de Informatica – UFRGS)

Designation:	--	**Address:**	C.P. 15064, CEP 91501-970 Porto
Designatory Letters:	--		Alegre, Brazil
Profession:	Information Technology	**Telephone:**	55-351-316-6835
Membership:	--	**Fax:**	55-351-319-1576
Established:	--	**E-mail:**	sbc@sbc.org.br
		Web:	www.sbc.org.br

Associação dos Analistas E Professionals de Investimient o do Mercado de Capit (APIMEC)

Designation:	--	**Address:**	Rua São Paulo, SP, Brazil CEP
Designatory Letters:	--		01011-904, Brazil
Profession:	Investment Technology	**Telephone:**	55-11-3107-1571
	Investment Management	**Fax:**	55-11-3242-7842
Membership:	--	**E-mail:**	apimec@uol.com.br
Established:	--	**Web:**	www.apimec.com.br

Instituto Brasileiro dos Consultores de Organização (IBCO) (Brazilian Institute of Management Consultants)

Designation:	--	**Address:**	Av. Paulista, 326, 7° andar - cj.77-
Designatory Letters:	--		Bela Vista CEP 01310-90,
Profession:	Management Consulting		São Paulo, Brazil
Membership:	--	**Telephone:**	55-11-3289-4152
Established:	--	**Fax:**	--
		E-mail:	ibco@ibco.org.br
		Web:	www.ibco.org.br

Associação dos Dirigentes de Vendas e Marketing do Brasil

Designation:	--	**Address:**	São Paulo-SP, Brazil
Designatory Letters:	--	**Telephone:**	11-3372-3800
Profession:	Marketing	**Fax:**	11-3372-3820
Membership:	--	**E-mail:**	advb@advbfbm.org.br
Established:	--	**Web:**	www.advbfbm.org.br

Associação Brasileira de Gerenciamento de Projetos – ABGP (Project Management Association of Brazil)

Designation:	--	**Address:**	Brazil
Designatory Letters:	CPMA (Certified Project Management Associate)	**Telephone:**	--
		Fax:	--
	CPM (Certified Project Manager)	**E-mail:**	abgp@abgp-org.br
		Web:	www.abgp.org.br
	CSPM (Certified Senior Project Manager)		
	CPD (Certified Project Director)		
Profession:	Project Management		
Membership:	--		
Established:	--		

BRUNEI DARUSSALAM

Brunei Darussalam Institute of Certified Public Accountants (BICPA)

Designation:	--	**Address:**	1st Floor (Left Wing), ASEAN-EC,
Designatory Letters:	--		Management Centre, Sunpang
Profession:	Accounting		347, Jalan Pesar Baru, Gadong,
Membership:	--		BE 1318, Brunei Darussalam
Established:	1987	**Telephone:**	673-245-4945
		Fax:	673-245-4946
		E-mail:	bicpa@brunet.bn
		Web:	www.bicpabrunei.com

BULGARIA

Institute of Certified Public Accountants of Bulgaria

Designation:	Certified Public Accountant	**Address:**	22 Iskar St, 2nd Floor, 1000 Sofia,
Designatory Letters:	CPA (Certified Public Accountant)		Bulgaria
		Telephone:	359-2-950-0777
Profession:	Accounting	**Fax:**	359-2-950-0777
Membership:	--	**E-mail:**	ides@ides.bg
Established:	--	**Web:**	--

Bulgarian Actuarial Society

Designation:	--	**Address:**	Laboratory of Computer
Designatory Letters:	--		Stochastics, Institute of
Profession:	Actuarial Science		Mathematics, Bulgarian
Membership:	--		Academy of Sciences, PO Box
Established:	1993		373, 1090 Sofia, Bulgaria
		Telephone:	--
		Fax:	359-2-718878
		E-mail:	--
		Web:	--

Bulgarian Academy of Sciences–Institute of Parallel Processing

Designation:	--	**Address:**	1, "15th November" Street, Sofia
Designatory Letters:	--		1040, Bulgaria.
Profession:	Information Technology	**Telephone:**	359-2-883-575
Membership:	--	**Fax:**	359-2-880-448
Established:	--	**E-mail:**	boyanov@bgcict.avad.bg
		Web:	www.acad.bg-ifip

Bulgarian Association of Management Consultants (BAMC)

Designation:	--	**Address:**	BAMCO, 1 Macedonia Square,
Designatory Letters:	--		17th Floor, 1040 Sofia, Bulgaria
Profession:	Management Consulting	**Telephone:**	359-2-4010-506
Membership:	--	**Fax:**	359-2-986-1291
Established:	1996	**E-mail:**	bamco@delin.org
		Web:	www.delin.org-bamco

Institute of Marketing

Designation:	--	**Address:**	2K Shapkarov ul, 1130 Sofia,
Designatory Letters:	--		Bulgaria
Profession:	Marketing	**Telephone:**	359-220-6727
Membership:	--	**Fax:**	--
Established:	--	**E-mail:**	--
		Web:	--

Bulgaria Project Management Association (BPMA)

Designation:	--	**Address:**	Sofia, Bulgaria
Designatory Letters:	--	**Telephone:**	02-983-5324
Profession:	Project Management	**Fax:**	02-983-1094
Membership:	--	**E-mail:**	--
Established:	--	**Web:**	www.project.bg

C

CAMEROON

Institute of Chartered Accountants of Cameroon

Designation:	Chartered Accountant	**Address:**	BP 12 850, Doula, Cameroon
Designatory Letters:	CA (Chartered Accountant)	**Telephone:**	237-428-093
		Fax:	237-431-825
Profession:	Accounting	**E-mail:**	onecca@camnet.com
Membership:	--	**Web:**	www.cica.ca
Established:	--		

CANADA

Accounting Standards Board AcSB)

Designation:	NA	**Address:**	277 Wellington Street West,
Designatory Letters:	NA		Toronto, Ontario M5V 3H2,
Profession:	Accounting		Canada
Established:	--	**Telephone:**	416-977-3222
		Fax:	416-977-8585
		E-mail:	--
		Web:	www.acsb.ca

Accounting Standards Oversight Council (ASOC)

Designation:	NA	**Address:**	277 Wellington Street West,
Designatory Letters:	NA		Toronto, Ontario M5V 3H2,
Profession:	Accounting		Canada.
Membership:	NA	**Telephone:**	416-977-3222
Established:	2000	**Fax:**	416-977-8585
		E-mail:	--
		Web:	www.acsoc.ca

Association of Filipino Canadian Accountants

Designation:	NA	**Address:**	4800 Sheppard Ave., East, Unit
Designatory Letters:	NA		125, Scarborough, Ontario M1S
Profession:	Accounting		4N5, Canada
Membership:	400	**Telephone:**	416-609-8912
Established:	1978	**Fax:**	--
		E-mail:	afcatoronto@gmail.com
		Web:	www.afcatoronto.org

The Canadian Academic Accounting Association (CAAA)

Designation:	NA	**Address:**	3997 Cheswood Drive, Toronto,
Designatory Letters:	NA		Ontario M3J 2R8, Canada
Profession:	Accounting	**Telephone:**	416-486-5361
Membership:		**Fax:**	416-486-6158
Established:	1976	**E-mail:**	admin@caaa.ca
		Web:	www.caaa.ca

Canadian Institute of Chartered Accountants (CICA)

Designation:	Chartered Accountant	**Address:**	277 Wellington Street West, Toronto, Ontario M5V 3H2, Canada
Designatory Letters:	CA (Chartered Accountant)		
	FCA (Fellow of the Institute of Chartered Accountants)	**Telephone:**	416-977-3222
		Fax:	416-977-8585
		E-mail:	--
	Specialist Designations	**Web:**	www.cica.ca
	CF (Corporate Finance)		
	CA·IFA (Chartered Accountant [Investigative and Forensic Accounting])		
	CA·IT (Chartered Accountant [Information Technology])		
	CA·CBV (Chartered Accountant [Business Valuation])		
	CA·CIA (Chartered Accountant [Internal Auditing])		
	CA·CISA (Chartered Accountant [Information Systems Auditing])		
	CA·CIRP (Chartered Accountant [Insolvency and Restructuring])		
Profession:	Accounting		
Membership:	71,000		
Established:	1902		

The Canadian Institute of Professional Accountants

Designation:	Professional Accountant	**Address:**	102 10516-100 Avenue, Westlock, Alberta T7P 2J9, Canada
Designatory Letters:	PA (Professional Accountant)	**Telephone:**	780-349-3601
	PATC (Professional Accountant-Tax Consultant)	**Fax:**	780-349-5823
		E-mail:	info@icpa-canada.org
	PABV (Professional Accountant-Business Valuator)	**Web:**	www.icpa-canada.org
	PAFC (Professional Accountant-Forensic Consultant)		
	PAFP (Professional Accountant-Financial Planner)		
Profession:	Accounting		
Membership:	--		
Established:	--		

The Certified General Accountants' Association of Canada

Designation:	Certified General	**Address:**	700-1188 West Georgia Street,
Designatory Letters:	Accountant		Vancouver, BC V6E 4A2,
	CGA (Certified General		Canada
	Accountant-	**Telephone:**	604- 669-3555 800-663-1529
	FCGA (Fellow Certified	**Fax:**	604-689-5845
	General Accountant)	**E-mail:**	public@cga-canada.org
Profession:	Accounting	**Web:**	www.cga-canada.org
Membership:	42,000		
Established:	1913		

Guild of Industrial, Commercial and Institutional Accountants

Designation:	Industrial, Commercial	**Address:**	Admin Office, 36 Tandian Court,
	and Institutional		Woodbridge, Ontario L47 8Z9,
	Accountant		Canada
Designatory Letters:	ICIA(Industrial,	**Telephone:**	--
	Commercial and	**Fax:**	--
	Institutional	**E-mail:**	iciaguild@aol.com
	Accountant)	**Web:**	www.guildoficia.ca
	FICIA (Fellow,		
	Industrial, Commercial		
	and Institutional		
	Accountants)		
Profession:	Accounting		
Membership:	525		
Established:	1961		

Public Accountants Council for the Province of Ontario

Designation:	NA	**Address:**	1200 Bay St, Ste 901, Toronto,
Designatory Letters:	NA		Ontario M5R 2AJ, Canada
Profession:	Accounting	**Telephone:**	416-920-1444
Established:	1950	**Fax:**	416-920-1917
		E-mail:	generalenquiries@pacont.org
		Web:	webhome.idirect.com

Registered Professional Accountants Association

Designation:	--	**Address:**	PO Box 306, Station Main,
Designatory Letters:	--		Edmonton, Alberta T5J 2J6,
Profession:	Accounting		Canada.
Membership:	--	**Telephone:**	780-448-9692
Established:	1980	**Fax:**	780-448-9698
		E-mail:	info@rpaa.org
		Web:	www.rpaa.org

The Society of Professional Accountants of Canada (SPAC)

Designation:	Registered Professional	**Address:**	250 Consumers Road, Suite 1007,
	Accountant		Ontario M2J 4V6, Canada.
Designatory Letters:	RPA (Registered	**Telephone:**	416-350-8145
	Professional	**Fax:**	416-350-8146
	Accountant)	**E-mail:**	--
Profession:	Accounting	**Web:**	www.professionalaccountant.org
Membership:	--		
Established:	1978		

The Society of Management Accountants of Canada (CMA-Canada)

Designation:	Certified Management Accountant	**Address:**	Mississauga Executive Center, 1 Robert Speck Parkway, Suite 1400, Mississauga, Ontario L4Z 3M3, Canada
Designatory Letters:	CMA (Certified Management Accountant)		
	FCMA (Fellow of the Society of Management Accountants of Canada)	**Telephone:**	905-949-3100
		Fax:	905-949-0058
		E-mail:	info@cma-canada.org
	CPFA (Chartered Public Finance Accountant) (A new dual professional designation between the CIPFA of the United Kingdom and the CMA Canada)	**Web:**	www.cma-canada.org
Profession:	Accounting/Financial/Strategic Management		
Membership:	37,000		
Established:	1920		

Association of Professional Accounting and Tax Consultants

Designation:	--	**Address:**	4025 Dorchester Road, Suite 310, Niagara Falls, Ontario L2E 7K8, Canada
Designatory Letters:	--		
Profession:	Accounting/Taxation		
Membership:	--	**Telephone:**	888-621-1005/905-354-1856
Established:	1981	**Fax:**	905-374-0600
		E-mail:	--
		Web:	www.apatcinc.com

Canadian Institute of Actuaries and the Society of Actuaries

Designation:	--	**Address:**	800-150 Metcalfe Street, Ottawa, Ontario 2P1 1P1, Canada
Designatory Letters:	FCIA (Fellow of the Canadian Institute of Actuaries)		
		Telephone:	613-236-8196
		Fax:	613-233-4552
Profession:	Actuarial Science	**E-mail:**	secretriat@actuaries.ca
Membership:	2,807	**Web:**	www.actuaries.ca
Established:	1965		

Auditing and Assurance Standards Council (AASOC)

Designation:	NA	**Address:**	277 Wellington Street West, Toronto, Ontario M5V 3H2, Canada
Designatory Letters:	NA		
Profession:	Auditing		
Membership:	NA	**Telephone:**	416-977-3222
Established:	2002	**Fax:**	416-977-8585
		E-mail:	jan.burns@cica.ca
		Web:	www.aasoc.ca

Canadian Comprehensive Auditing Foundation (CCAF)

Designation:	NA	**Address:**	291 Olmstead Vanier), Ottawa, Ontario K1L 7J9, Canada
Designatory Letters:	NA		
Profession:	Auditing	**Telephone:**	613-241-6713
Membership:	--	**Fax:**	613-241-6900
Established:	1980	**E-mail:**	info@icaf-fcvi.com
		Web:	www.ccaf-fcvi.com

Canadian Public Accountability Board

Designation:	NA	**Address:**	150 York Street, Suite 200, Box
Designatory Letters:	NA		90, Toronto, Ontario M5H 3S5,
Profession:	Auditing/Accounting		Canada
Membership:	2002	**Telephone:**	416-913-8260
Established:		**Fax:**	416-850-9235
		E-mail:	info@cpab-ccrc.ca
		Web:	www.cpab-ccrc.ca

Institute of Canadian Bankers ICB)

Designation:	--	**Address:**	4 King Street West, Ste. 1500,
Designatory Letters:	AICB (Associate,		Toronto, Ontario M5H 1B6,
	Institute of Canadian		Canada
	Bankers)	**Telephone:**	800-361-7339 416-304-1828
	FICB (Fellow, Institute of	**Fax:**	--
	Canadian Bankers)	**E-mail:**	icb.info@icb.org
	MTI (Member, Trust	**Web:**	www.icb.org
	Institute)		
	PFP (Personal Financial		
	Planner)		
	STI (Specialist Trust		
	Institute)		
Profession:	Banking		
Membership:	100,000		
Established:	--		

The Canadian Bookkeepers Association

Designation:	--	**Address:**	Suite 465, 7360-137 Street, Surrey,
Designatory Letters:	--		British Columbia V3W 1A3, Canada
Profession:	Bookkeeping	**Telephone:**	604-664-7576
Membership:	--	**Fax:**	--
Established:	1998	**E-mail:**	info@canadianbookkeepersassociation.ca
		Web:	www.c-b-a.ca

The Canadian Institute of Bookkeeping

Designation:	Certified Bookkeeper	**Address:**	PO Box 963, 31 Adelaide Street
Designatory Letters:	CB (Certified		East, Toronto, Ontario M5L 2K3,
Profession:	Bookkeeper)		Canada
Membership:	Bookkeeping	**Telephone:**	416-925-9420
Established:	--	**Fax:**	416-929-8815
	--	**E-mail:**	info@cibcb.com
		Web:	www.cibcb.com

The Canadian Society of Association Executives CSAE)

Designation:	Certified Association	**Address:**	10 King Street East, Suite#1100,
Designatory Letters:	Executive		Toronto,Ontario M5C 1C3,
	CAE (Certified		Canada
	Association Executive)	**Telephone:**	800-461-3608/416-363-3555
Profession:	Corporate Governance	**Fax:**	416-363-3630
Membership:	2,000	**E-mail:**	csae@csae.com
Established:	1951	**Web:**	www.csae.com

Institute of Chartered Secretaries and Administrators (ICSA)
The Canadian division of ICSA in the United Kingdom

Designation:	Chartered Secretary and Professional Administrator	**Address:**	55 St Clair Avenue Wst, Suite 255, Toronto, Ontario M4V 2Y7, Canada
Designatory Letters:	ACIS (Associate Member of the Institute of Chartered Secretaries and Administrators)	**Telephone:**	416-944-9727/ 800-501-3440
		Fax:	416-967-6320
		E-mail:	icsa@icsacanada.org
		Web:	www.icsacanada.org
	FCIS (Fellow Member of the Institute of Chartered Secretaries and Administrators)		
	P. Adm (Professional Administrator Applies to Canada only)		
Profession:	Corporate Governance		
Membership:	1,000		
Established:	1891 in the United Kingdom; 1920 in Canada		

Institute of Corporate Directors

Designation:	Institute Certified Director	**Address:**	40 University Avenue, Suite 602, Toronto, Ont. M5J 1T1, Canada
Designatory Letters:	ICD.D (Institute Certified Director)	**Telephone:**	416-593-7741
		Fax:	416-593-0636
Profession:	Corporate Governance	**E-mail:**	admin@icd.ca
Membership:	2,300	**Web:**	www.icd.ca
Established:	1981		

Credit Institute of Canada

Designation:	--	**Address:**	Ste 216 C, 219 Dufferin Street, Toronto, Ontario M6K 3J1, Canada
	ACI (Associate of the Credit Institute)		
Designatory Letters:	FCI (Fellow of the Credit Institute)	**Telephone:**	416-572-2615
Profession:	Credit Management	**Fax:**	416-572-2619
Membership:	3,000	**E-mail:**	--
Established:	1928	**Web:**	www.creditedu.org

Canadian Environmental Auditing Association

Designation:	Environmental Auditor	**Address:**	1-6820 Kitimat Road, Mississauga, Ontario L5N 5M3, Canada
Designatory Letters:	CEA (Certified Environmental Auditor)		
		Telephone:	905-814-1160
	CEA SFM-(Certified Environmental Auditor Sustainable Forest Management)	**Fax:**	905-815-1158
		E-mail:	admin@ceaa-acve.ca
		Web:	www.ceaa-acve.ca
	EMS A-(Environmental Management System Auditor)		
	EMS LA-(Environmental Management System Lead Auditor)		
Profession:	Environmental Auditing		
Membership:	400		
Established:	1991		

The Canadian Association of Financial Consultants

Designation:	Chartered Certified Financial Consultant	**Address:**	1090 West Pender Street, Ste 420, Vancouver, BC V6E 2H7, Canada
Designatory Letters:	CCFC (Chartered Certified Financial Consultant)	**Telephone:**	--
		Fax:	604-687-1221
Profession:	Financial Consulting	**E-mail:**	info@thecafc.org
Membership:	--	**Web:**	www.thecafc.org
Established:	--		

The Institute of Financial Consultants

Designation:	Certified Financial Consultant	**Address:**	Suite 420, 1090 West Pender Street, Vancouver, BC V6E 2N7, Canada
Designatory Letters:	CFC (Certified Financial Consultant)	**Telephone:**	--
Profession:	Financial Consulting	**Fax:**	604-687-1221
Membership:	--	**E-mail:**	info@ifconsultants.org
Established:	--	**Web:**	www.ifconsultants.org

Aboriginal Financial Officers Association

Designation:	Certified Aboriginal Financial Manager	**Address:**	1066 Somerset W., Ottawa, Ste 301, Ottawa, Ontario K1Y 4T3, Canada
Designatory Letters:	CAFM (Certified Aboriginal Financial Manager)	**Telephone:**	613-722-5543
		Fax:	613-722-3467
Profession:	Financial Management	**E-mail:**	afoa@afoa.ca
Membership:	--	**Web:**	www.afoa.ca
Established:	2000		

Financial Management Institute of Canada

Designation:	NA	**Address:**	PO Box 613, Station B, Ottawa, K1P 5P7, Canada
Designatory Letters:	NA		
Profession:	Financial Management	**Telephone:**	613-569-1158
Membership:	2000	**Fax:**	613-569-4532
Established:	1962	**E-mail:**	national@fmi.ca
		Web:	www.fmi.ca

Canadian Institute of Financial Planners

Designation:	--	**Address:**	3660 Hurontario Street, 8th Floor, Mississauga, Ontario L5B 3C4, Canada
Designatory Letters:	--		
Profession:	Financial Planning		
Membership:	--	**Telephone:**	905-803-0167/866-933-0233
Established:	1995	**Fax:**	905-803-0167
		E-mail:	cifps@cifps.ca
		Web:	www.cifps.ca

Institut Québecois de Planification Financière (IQPF)

Designation:	Financial Planner Planificateur Financier	**Address:**	4 Place du Commerce, Suite 420, Île-des-Soeurs, Verdun, Quebec
Designatory Letters:	F.Pl. (Financial Planner) Pl.Fin.(Planificateur Financier)	**Telephone:** **Fax:**	H3E, 1J4, Canada 800-640-4050/514-767-2845 514-767-2845
Profession:	Financial Planning	**E-mail:**	ctrudeau@iqpf.org
Membership:	--	**Web:**	www.iqpf.org
Established:	--		

Institute on Governance

Designation:	NA	**Address:**	122 Clarence Street, Ottawa,
Designatory Letters:	NA		Ontario K1N 5PG, Canada
Profession:	Governance	**Telephone:**	613-562-0090
Membership:	--	**Fax:**	613-562-0097
Established:	1990	**E-mail:**	info@iog.ca
		Web:	www.iog.ca

Board of Canadian Registered Safety Professionals

Designation:	Canadian Registered Safety Professional	**Address:**	6519-B Mississauga Road, Mississauga, Ontario L5N 1A6,
Designatory Letters:	CRSP (Canadian Registered Safety Professional)	**Telephone:**	Canada 905-567-7198 888-279-2777
Profession:	Health and Safety	**Fax:**	905-567-7091
Membership:	--	**E-mail:**	bcrsp@sympatico.a
Established:	1976	**Web:**	www.bcrsp.ca

Canadian Society of Safety Engineering (CSSE)

Designation:	Certified Health and Safety Consultant	**Address:**	39 River Street, Toronto, Ontario M5A 3P1, Canada
Designatory Letters:	CHSC (Certified Health and Safety Consultant)	**Telephone:** **Fax:**	416-646-1600 416-646-9460
Profession:	Health and Safety	**E-mail:**	csseinfo@associationsfirst.com
Membership:	2,500	**Web:**	www.csse.org
Established:	1949		

Human Resources Professional Association of Ontario

Designation:	Certified Human Resources Professional	**Address:**	2 Bloor St., W., Ste 1902, Toronto, Ontario M4W 3E2, Canada
Designatory Letters:	CHRP (Certified Human Resources Professional)	**Telephone:** **Fax:**	416-923-7264/800-387-1311 416-923-7214
Profession:	Human Resources Management	**E-mail:** **Web:**	info@hrpao.org www.hrpao.org
Membership:	15,500		
Established:	1936		

The Canadian Institute of Internal Auditors (CIIA)

(At the time of compiling this directory, the CIIA is about to be established and will be based in Toronto. The contact details of the Toronto Chapter of the IIA are therefore used)

Designation:	NA	**Address:**	173 Homewood Avenue, Toronto,
Designatory Letters:	NA		Ontario M2M 1K4, Canada.
Profession:	Internal Auditing	**Telephone:**	416-223-5326
Membership:	5,000	**Fax:**	416-222-1041
Established:	2006	**E-mail:**	iia@homewoodave.com
		Web:	www.theiia.org/chapters/toronto/

Audit Command Language (ACL)

Designation:	ACL Data Analyst	**Address:**	1550 Alberni Street, Vancouver, BC VG 1A5, Canada
Designatory Letters:	ACDA ACL (Certified Data Analyst)	**Telephone:**	604-669-4225
Profession:	Information Technology	**Fax:**	604-669-3557
Established:	--	**E-mail:**	info@acl.com
		Web:	www.acl.com

Canadian Information Processing Society (CIPS)

Designation:	Information Systems Professional of Canada	**Address:**	2800 Skymark Avenue, Suite #402, Mississauga, Ontario L4W 5A6, Canada
Designatory Letters:	ISP (Information Systems Professional of Canada)	**Telephone:**	905-602-1370
Profession:	Information Technology	**Fax:**	905-602-7884
Membership:	6,000	**E-mail:**	info@cips.ca
Established:	1958	**Web:**	www.cips.ca

Canadian Association of Insolvency and Restructuring Professionals CAIRP)

Designation:	Chartered Insolvency and Restructuring Professional	**Address:**	277 Wellington St., W., Toronto, Ontario M5V 3H2, Canada
		Telephone:	416-204-3242
Designatory Letters:	CIRP (Chartered Insolvency and Restructuring Professional)	**Fax:**	416-204-3410
		E-mail:	info@cairp.ca
		Web:	www.cairp.ca
Profession:	Insolvency		
Membership:	922		
Established:	1979		

Canadian Independent Adjusters' Association CIAA)

Designation:	--	**Address:**	Centennial Centre, 5401 Egliinton Avenue W., Suite 100, Etobicoke, Ontario M9C 5K6, Canada
Designatory Letters:	CIAA (Canadian Independent Adjuster) CLA Chartered Loss Adjuster) FCIAA (Fellow of the Canadian Independent Adjusters' Association)	**Telephone:**	416-621-6222/877-255-5589
		Fax:	416-621-7776
		E-mail:	info@ciaa-adjusters.ca
		Web:	www.ciaa-adjusters.ca
Profession:	Insurance		
Membership:	1,400		

The Insurance Institute of Canada (IIC)

Designation:	Chartered Insurance Professional	**Address:**	18 King Street East, 6th Floor, Toronto, Ontario M5C 1C4, Canada
Designatory Letters:	CIP (Chartered Insurance Professional) FCIP (Fellow Chartered Insurance Professional) LLQP (Life Licensing Qualification Program)	**Telephone:**	416-362-8586/1-866-362-8585
		Fax:	416-362-4239
		E-mail:	iicmail@insuranceinstitute.ca
		Web:	www.iic-iac.org
Profession:	Insurance		
Membership:	30,000		
Established:	1952		

Independent Financial Brokers of Canada (IFBC)

Designation:	--	**Address:**	4284 Village Centre Court, Suite 200, Mississauga, Ontario L4Z 1S2, Canada
Designatory Letters:	CFSB (Chartered Financial Services Broker)		
		Telephone:	905-279-2727
Profession:	Insurance	**Fax:**	905-276-7295
Membership:	--	**E-mail:**	admin@ifbc.ca
Established:	1906	**Web:**	www.ifbc.ca

Insurance Brokers Association of Canada

Designation:	--	**Address:**	1230-155 University Ave.,Toronto, Ontario M5H 3B7, Canada
Designatory Letters:	CCIB (Canadian Certified Insurance Broker)		
		Telephone:	416-367-1831
	CPIB (Canadian Professional Insurance Broker)	**Fax:**	416-367-3687
		E-mail:	ibac@ibac.ca
	CAIB (Canadian Accredited Insurance Broker)	**Web:**	www.ibac.ca
	CSIP (Customer Service for the Insurance Professional)		
Profession:	Insurance		
Membership:	25,000		
Established:	--		

LOMA Canada–Life Insurance Institute of Canada

Designation:	--	**Address:**	1155 North Service Road W, Ste #11, Oakville, Ontario L6M 3E3, Canada.
Designatory Letters:	--		
Profession:	Insurance		
Membership:	--	**Telephone:**	905-847-8966
Established:	--	**Fax:**	905-847-8897
		E-mail:	liic@loma.org
		Web:	www.liic.ca

Forum for International Trade Training (FITT)

Designation:	International Trade Professional	**Address:**	30 Metcalfe St., 4th Floor, Ottawa, Ontario K1P 5L4, Canada
Designatory Letters:	CITP (Certified International Trade Professional)	**Telephone:**	613-230-3553/800-561-3488
		Fax:	613-230-6808
		E-mail:	info@fitt.ca
Profession:	International Trade	**Web:**	www.fitt.ca
Membership:	625		
Established:	--		

The Canadian Securities Institute (CSI)

Designation:	--	**Address:**	Suite 1550, 121 King Street West,
Designatory Letters:	Canadian Securities Course [No designatory letters]		Toronto, Ontario M5H 3T9, Canada
		Telephone:	866-866-2601
	DMS (Derivatives Market Specialist)	**Fax:**	866-866-2660
	Ch.P (Chartered	**E-mail:**	customer_support@csi.ca
	Professional *Strategic Wealth)*	**Web:**	www.csi.ca
	FMA (Financial Management Adviser)		
	CIM (Canadian Investment Manager)		
	FCSI FICVM (in French-Fellow of the Canadian Securities Institute)		
Profession:	Investment Management		
Membership:	--		
Established:	1970		

Canadian Association of Logistics Management (CALM)

Designation:	NA	**Address:**	590 Alden Road, Suite 211,
Designatory Letters:	NA		Markham, Ontario L3R 9Z1,
Profession:	Logistics Management		Canada
Membership:	--	**Telephone:**	905-513-7300
Established:	1967	**Fax:**	905-513-0624
		E-mail:	--
		Web:	--

The Canadian Professional Logistics Institute CPLI)

Designation:	--	**Address:**	160 John Street, Suite 200,
Designatory Letters:	P.Log (Professional Logistician)		Toronto, Ontario M5V 2E5, Canada
Profession:	Logistics Management	**Telephone:**	416-363-3005
Membership:	1,700	**Fax:**	416-363-5598
Established:	1990	**E-mail:**	loginfo@loginstitute.ca
		Web:	www.loginstitute.ca

The Canadian Institute of Certified Administrative Managers (CICAM)

Designation:	--	**Address:**	Suite 800, 2 St. Clair Ave., E.,
Designatory Letters:	Ch.E (Chartered Executive)		Toronto, Ontario M4T 2TS, Canada
	CAM (Certified Administrative Manager)	**Telephone:**	416-921-7962
		Fax:	416-921-3959
	CHA (Certified Housing Administrator)	**E-mail:**	mailbox@cicam.org
		Web:	www.cicam.org
	CEA (Certified Environmental Administrator)		
	ACAM (Associate Member of the Institute of Certified Administrative Managers)		
	FCAM (Fellow Member of the Canadian Institute of Certified Administrative Managers)		
Profession:	Management		
Membership:	--		
Established:	1979		

Canadian Institute of Management

Designation:	--	**Address:**	15 Collier Street, Lower Level,
Designatory Letters:	P. Mgr Professional Manager)		Barrie, Ontario L4M 1G5, Canada
	CIM (Certificate in Management)	**Telephone:**	800-387-5774, 416-493-0155
		Fax:	905-894-1475
	FCIM (Fellow Canadian Institute of Management)	**E-mail:**	office@cim.ca
		Web:	www.cim.ca
Profession:	Management		
Membership:	--		
Established:	1942		

Financial Executives Institute (FEI) Canada

Designation:	NA	**Address:**	20 Adelaide St.E., Ste. 200,
Designatory Letters:	NA		Toronto, Ontario M5C 2T6,
Profession:	Management		Canada
Membership:	18,000	**Telephone:**	416-366-3007
Established:	1950	**Fax:**	416-366-3008
		E-mail:	imeharry@feicanada.org
		Web:	www.feicanada.org

Canadian Association of Management Consultants

Designation:	Certified Management Consultant	**Address:**	4 King Street W., Ste 815, Toronto, Ontario M5H 1B6, Canada
Designatory Letters:	CMC (Certified Management Consultant)	**Telephone:**	416-860-1515 or 800-268-1148
		Fax:	416-860-1535 or 800-662-2972
	FCMC (Fellow Certified Management Consultant)	**E-mail:**	consulting@camc.com
		Web:	www.camc.com
Profession:	Management Consulting		
Membership:	3,200		
Established:	1963		

Canadian Institute of Marketing (CIM)

Designation:	--	**Address:**	205 Miller Drive, Georgetown, Ontario, Canada.
Designatory Letters:	GCInst.M (Graduate Member of the Canadian Institute of Marketing)	**Telephone:**	905-877-5369
		Fax:	905-702-0819
	ACInst. M (Associate Member of the Canadian Institute of Marketing)	**E-mail:**	info@cinstmarketing.ca
		Web:	www.cinstmarketing.ca
	MCInst.M (Member of the Canadian Institute of Marketing)		
	FCInst.M (Fellow of the Canadian Institute of Marketing)		
Profession:	Marketing		
Membership:	--		
Established:	1988		

Canadian Institute of Mortgage Brokers and Lenders (CIMBL)

Designation:	Accredited Mortgage Professional	**Address:**	2255 Sheppard Avenue East, Atria 1, Suite 414, Toronto, Ontario M2J 4Y1, Canada
Designatory Letters:	AMP Accredited Mortgage Professional)	**Telephone:**	888-442-4625
Profession:	Mortgage Brokerage	**Fax:**	416-385-1177
Membership:	9,000	**E-mail:**	director@cimbl.ca
Established:	--	**Web:**	www.cimbl.ca

Association of Municipal Clerks and Treasurers of Ontario

Designation:	--	**Address:**	2680 Skymark Avenue, Suite 910, Mississauga, Ont. L4W 5L6, Canada
Designatory Letters:	AMCT A-(Associate Accredited Municipal Clerk-Treasurer)	**Telephone:**	905-602-4294
	AMCT (Accredited Municipal Clerk-Treasurer)	**Fax:**	905-602-4295
		E-mail:	amcto@amcto.com
	CMO (Certified Municipal Officer)	**Web:**	www.amcto.com
Profession:	Municipal Management		
Membership:	2,200		
Established:	--		

The Association of Administrative Assistants

Designation:	Qualified Administrative Assistant	**Address:**	72 Jerome Park Drive, Dundas, Ontario L9H 6H3, Canada
Designatory Letters:	Q.A.A - (Qualified Administrative Assistant	**Telephone:**	--
		Fax:	--
Profession:	Office Administration	**E-mail:**	registrar@aaa.ca
Membership:	--	**Web:**	www.aaa.ca
Established:	1951		

Canadian Payroll Association

Designation:	Certified Payroll Manager	**Address:**	250 Bloor St., E., Ste 1600, Toronto, Ontario M4W 1E6, Canada
Designatory Letters:	CPM (Certified Payroll Manager)	**Telephone:**	416-487-3380 or 800-387-4693
	PCP (Payroll Compliance Practitioner Certificate)	**Fax:**	416-487-3384
	PA (Payroll Administrator Certification)	**E-mail:**	infoline@payroll.ca
		Web:	www.payroll.ca
	PS (Payroll Supervisor Certification)		
	PM (Payroll Manager Certification)		
Profession:	Payroll Management		
Membership:	12,000		
Established:	--		

Institute of Public Administration of Canada

Designation:	NA	**Address:**	1075 Bay Stret, Ste 401, Toronto, Ontario M5S 2B1, Canada
Designatory Letters:	NA		
Profession:	Public Administration	**Telephone:**	416-924-8787
Membership:	--	**Fax:**	416-924-4992
Established:	1947	**E-mail:**	ntl@ipd.ca
		Web:	www.ipac.ca

Provincial Institutes of the Purchasing Management Association of Canada

Supported by a National Office located in Toronto, Ontario

Designation:	Certified Professional Purchaser	**Address:**	777 Bay Street, Suite 2701, Toronto, Ontario M5G 2CB, Canada
Designatory Letters:	CPP (Certified Professional Purchaser)	**Telephone:**	416-977-7111 888-799-0877
Profession:	Purchasing	**Fax:**	416-977-8886
Membership:	40,000	**E-mail:**	info@pmac.ca
Established:	1921	**Web:**	www.pmac.ca

Council of Quality and Leadership (CQL)

Designation:	Certified Quality Analyst	**Address:**	Accreditation Ontario, PO Box 60, 1114, Lau Camp Road, Algoma Mills, Ontario P0R 1A0, Canada.
Designatory Letters:	CQA (Certified Quality Analyst)		
Profession:			
Membership:	Quality Control	**Telephone:**	705-356-2782
Established:	--	**Fax:**	705-356-0080
	--	**E-mail:**	stacey@accreditationontario.com
		Web:	www.accreditationontario.com

National Quality Institute

Designation:	--	**Address:**	2275 Lakeshore Blvd., W., Ste 307,
Designatory Letters:	PEP (Professional		Etobicoke, Ontario M8V 3Y3,
Profession:	Excellence Program)		Canada
Membership:	Quality Management	**Telephone:**	416-251-7600 or 800-263-9648
Established:	--	**Fax:**	416-251-9131
	--	**E-mail:**	info@nqi.com
		Web:	www.nqi.com

Association of Professional Recruiters of Canada

Designation:	Registered Professional Recruiter	**Address:**	Suite 2210-1081 Ambleside Drive, Ottawa, Ontario K2B 8C8,
Designatory Letters:	RPR (Registered Professional Recruiter)	**Telephone:**	Canada 1-888-441-0000/613-721-5957
Profession:	Recruitment	**Fax:**	613-721-5850
Membership:	1,200	**E-mail:**	info@workplace.ca
Established:	1984	**Web:**	www.workplace.ca

Association of Professional Recruiters of Canada

Designation:	Registered Assessment Specialist	**Address:**	Suite 2210-1081 Ambleside Drive, Ottawa, Ontario K2B 8C8,
Designatory Letters:	RAS (Registered Assessment Specialist)	**Telephone:**	Canada 1-888-441-0000/613-721-5957
Profession:	Recruitment	**Fax:**	613-721-5850
Membership:	250	**E-mail:**	info@workplace.ca
Established:	2001	**Web:**	www.workplace.ca

Association of Professional Recruiters of Canada

Designation:	Registered Professional Trainer	**Address:**	Suite 2210-1081 Ambleside Drive, Ottawa, Ontario K2B 8C8,
Designatory Letters:	RPT (Registered Professional Trainer)	**Telephone:**	Canada 1-888-441-0000 613-721-5957
Profession:	Recruitment	**Fax:**	613-721-5850
Membership:	200	**E-mail:**	info@workplace.ca
Established:	2004	**Web:**	www.workplace.ca

Association of Professional Recruiters of Canada

Designation:	Canadian Management Professional	**Address:**	Suite 2210-1081 Ambleside Drive, Ottawa, Ontario K2B 8C8,
Designatory Letters:	CMP (Canadian Management Professional)	**Telephone:** **Fax:**	Canada 1-888-441-0000/613-721-5957 613-721-5850
Profession:	Recruitment	**E-mail:**	info@workplace.ca
Membership:	550	**Web:**	www.workplace.ca
Established:	1999		

Risk and Insurance Management Society Inc. (RIMS)

Designation:	--	**Address:**	42 Arlston, Toronto, Ontario M3H
Designatory Letters:	CRM (Canadian Risk Management)	**Telephone:**	4V9, Canada 416-638-1645
	FRM (Fellow in Risk Management)	**Fax:** **E-mail:**	-- bwasser@sympatico.ca
Profession:	Risk Management	**Web:**	www.rimscanada.rims.org
Membership:	--		
Established:	1950		

Canadian Professional Sales Association

Designation:	Certified Sales Professional	**Address:**	310 Front St., W, Ste 800, Toronto, Ontario M5V 3BJ, Canada
Designatory Letters:	CSP (Certified Sales Professional)	**Telephone:**	416-408-2685 or 800-267-2772
		Fax:	416-408-2684
Profession:	Sales Management	**E-mail:**	--
Membership:	30,000	**Web:**	www.cpsa.com
Established:	1994		

Canadian Institute of Traffic and Transportation (CITT)

Designation:	--	**Address:**	10 King Street East, Suite 400, Toronto, Ontario M5C 1C3, Canada
Designatory Letters:	CITT (Canadian Institute of Traffic and Transportation)		
		Telephone:	416-363-5696
	Supply Chain and	**Fax:**	416-363-5698
Profession:	Logistics	**E-mail:**	info@citt.ca
Membership:	2000	**Web:**	www.citt.ca
Established:	1958		

Treasury Management Association of Canada (TMAC)

Designation:	NA	**Address:**	8 King Street East, Suite 1010, Toronto, Ontario M5C 1B5, Canada
Designatory Letters:	NA		
Profession:	Treasury Management		
Membership:	--	**Telephone:**	416-367-8501
Established:	1982	**Fax:**	416-367-3240
		E-mail:	--
		Web:	www.tmac.ca

Canadian Institute of Chartered Business Valuators (CICBV)

Designation:	Chartered Business Valuator	**Address:**	277 Wellington Street West, Toronto, Ontario M5V 3H2, Canada
Designatory Letters:	CBV EEE (in French-Chartered Business Valuator)		
Profession:		**Telephone:**	416-204-3396
Membership:		**Fax:**	416-977-8585
Established:	FCBV (Fellow Chartered Business Valuator)	**E-mail:**	admin@cicbv.ca
	Valuation, Business	**Web:**	www.cicbv.ca
	1100		
	1970		

The Appraisal Institute of Canada

Designation:	--	**Address:**	203-150 Isabelle Street, Ottawa K1S 1V7, Ontario, Canada
Designatory Letters:	AACI (Accredited Appraiser Canadian Institute)	**Telephone:**	613-234-6533
		Fax:	613-234-7177
	CRA (Canadian Residential Appraiser)	**E-mail:**	info@aicanada.ca
		Web:	www.aicanada.ca
Profession:	Valuation, Residential		
Membership:	4,500		
Established:	1938		

CHILE

Colegio de Contadores de Chile A.G.

Designation:	--	**Address:**	Calle Dieciocho 121, Casilla
Designatory Letters:	--		10201, Santiago, Chile
Profession:	Accounting	**Telephone:**	56-2698-2361-231-8711-569-448-0347
Membership:	--		
Established:	--	**Fax:**	56-2-698-9930
		E-mail:	contach@netexpress.cl
		Web:	www.contach.cl

The Chilean Computer Society

Designation:	--	**Address:**	Departamento de Ingenieria
Designatory Letters:	--		Informatica, Usach, Av. Ecuador
Profession:	Information Technology		3659, Santiago, Chile
Membership:	--	**Telephone:**	56-2-6892-736
Established:	--	**Fax:**	56-2-6895-531
		E-mail:	sccc@dcc.uchile.cl
		Web:	www.sccc.cl

CHINA

Chinese Institute of Certified Public Accountants

Designation:	Certified Public Accountant	**Address:**	6th Floor, Guang Yuan Bldg., 5 Guang Yuan Zha, Haidian District, Beijing 100081, China
Designatory Letters:	CPA (Certified Public Accountant)	**Telephone:**	86-10-6872-1166
Profession:	Accounting	**Fax:**	86-10-6848-3041
Membership:	--	**E-mail:**	cicpai@cicpa.orgcn
Established:	1988	**Web:**	www.cicpaorg.cn

Chinese Institute of Electronics

Designation:	--	**Address:**	Puhuinanli Building No. 13, Room 308, Haidian District, PO Box 165, Beijing 100036, China
Designatory Letters:	--		
Profession:	Information Technology		
Membership:	--	**Telephone:**	86-10-6816-0825
Established:	--	**Fax:**	86-10-6823-9572
		E-mail:	zhoumg@public3.bta.net.cn
		Web:	www.cie-china.org

The Securities Association of China (SAC)-

Designation:	--	**Address:**	2/F Building B, Focus Plaza, 19 Jinrong Street, Xicheng District, Beijing, 100032, China
Designatory Letters:	--		
Profession:	Investment Management		
Membership:	--	**Telephone:**	8610-6657-5935
Established:	--	**Fax:**	8610-6657-5935
		E-mail:	ird@sac.net.cn
		Web:	www.sac.net

China Enterprise Confederation/China Enterprise Directors Association

Designation:	--	**Address:**	No. 17, Zizhuyan Nanlu, Haidian District, Beijing, China 100044
Designatory Letters:	--		
Profession:	Management Consulting	**Telephone:**	--
Membership:	--	**Fax:**	--
Established:	--	**E-mail:**	vipzet@cec-ceda.org.cn
		Web:	www.cec-ceda.org.cn

Institute of Management Consultants - China

Designation:	--	**Address:**	P 17# of Z. Zhu Yuan Nanlu of
Designatory Letters:	--		Haidian District, Beijing
Profession:	Management Consulting		100044, China
Membership:	--	**Telephone:**	86-10-6841-0048
Established:	--	**Fax:**	86-10-6870-3099
		E-mail:	sindyw56@yahoo.com.cn
		Web:	www.cec-ceda.org.cn

Project Management Research Committee

Designation:	--	**Address:**	PO Box 617, Northwestern
Designatory Letters:	--		Polytechnical University, Xi'an,
Profession:	Project Management		China 710072
Membership:	--	**Telephone:**	86-29-8492-484
Established:	1991	**Fax:**	86-29-8494-869
		E-mail:	pmrc@nwpu.edu.cn
		Web:	www.pm.org.cn

COLOMBIA

Confederacion de Asociación de Contadores Públicos de Colombia

Designation:	--	**Address:**	Carrera 13 No. 90-36, Oficina 703,
Designatory Letters:	--		Santafé de Bogota, Colombia.
Profession:	Accounting	**Telephone:**	5768-867-834/885-8590
Membership:	--	**Fax:**	5768-854-722
Established:	--	**E-mail:**	fedecop@fedecop.org
		Web:	--

Instituto Nacional de Contadores Públicos de Colombia

Designation:	Contador Público (Public Accountant)	**Address:**	Carrera 7, No. 27-52, Oficina 403, Apartado Aéreo 6275, Bogotá,
Designatory Letters:	CP (Contador Público Public Accountant))		Colombia
		Telephone:	571-342-720
Profession:	Accounting	**Fax:**	571-243-4319
Membership:	--	**E-mail:**	inccol@cable.net.co
Established:	--	**Web:**	www.incp.org.co

DEMOCRATIC REPUBLIC OF CONGO

Institute des Reviseurs-Comptables

Designation:	--	**Address:**	34C, Avenue du Commerce, PO
Designatory Letters:	--		Box 16713, Kin 1, Kinshasa –
Profession:	Accounting		D.R. Congo
Membership:	--	**Telephone:**	243-818-117-654
Established:	--	**Fax:**	--
		E-mail:	irc@reviseurs-comptables.org
		Web:	--

COSTA RICA

Colegio de Contadores Públicos de Costa Rica

Designation:	Contador Público Autorizado	**Address:**	San Vicente de Moravia 100m. del Colegio de Farmacéuticos de
Designatory Letters:	CPA (Contador Público Autorizado)		Costa Rica, Apartado 4368-1000, San José, Costa Rica
Profession:	Accounting	**Telephone:**	506/256-1529, 253-0233, 297-0045
Membership:	--	**Fax:**	506-240-2467
Established:	--	**E-mail:**	dzamora@ccpa.or.cr
		Web:	www.ccpa.or.cr

COTE D'IVOIRE

(See Ivory Coast)

CROATIA

Croatian Association of Accountants and Financial Experts

Designation:	--	**Address:**	J. Gotovca 1/11, P.P. 732, 1000
Designatory Letters:	--		Zagreb, Croatia
Profession:	Accounting	**Telephone:**	385-1-468-6505
Membership:	--	**Fax:**	385-1-468-6497
Established:	--	**E-mail:**	rif@rif.hr
		Web:	www.rif.hr

Hrvatsko Aktuarsko Drustvo

Designation:	--	**Address:**	Marticeva 73, Zagreb, Croatia
Designatory Letters:	--	**Telephone:**	--
Profession:	Actuarial Science	**Fax:**	--
Membership:	--	**E-mail:**	--
Established:	1996	**Web:**	www.aktuari.hr

Croatian InformationTechnology Society (CITS)

Designation:	--	**Address:**	Trg Mazuranica 8/111, 10000
Designatory Letters:	--		Zagreb, Croatia
Profession:	Information Technology	**Telephone:**	385-1-48-55-271
Membership:	--	**Fax:**	385-1-48-55-272
Established:	--	**E-mail:**	hiz@hiz.hr
		Web:	www.hiz.hr

UPS-AMC (Udruga Poslovnih Savjetnika-Association of Management Consultancies)

Designation:	--	**Address:**	Pavla Hatza 12, 10000 Zagreb,
Designatory Letters:	--		Croatia
Profession:	Management Consulting	**Telephone:**	385-1-4897-596
Membership:	--	**Fax:**	385-1-4897-587
Established:	--	**E-mail:**	ups@hup.hr
		Web:	www.ups-amc.org

CUBA

Asociación Nacional de Economistas y Contadores de Cuba

Designation:	--	**Address:**	Calle 22, No 901. esq 9°, Marimar
Designatory Letters:	--		Playa, Habana, CP 11300, Cuba
Profession:	Accounting	**Telephone:**	53-7-209-3303
Membership:	--	**Fax:**	53-7-202-3456
Established:	--	**E-mail:**	prendencia@anec.co.cu
		Web:	www.anec.cu

CYPRUS

Institute of Certified Public Accountants of Cyprus

Designation:	Certified Public Accountant	**Address:**	Hawaii Nicosia Tower, 5th Floor 503/504, 41 Them Dervis Street,
Designatory Letters:	CPA (Certified Public Accountant)	**Telephone:**	Nicosia CY-1066, Cyprus 357-2-2769-866
Profession:	Accounting	**Fax:**	357-2-766-360
Membership:	--	**E-mail:**	theodoros.phlippou@icpac.org.cy
Established:	--	**Web:**	www.icpac.org.cy

Cyprus Association of Actuaries

Designation:	--	**Address:**	PO Box 24894, 1305 Nicosia, Cyprus
Designatory Letters:	--		
Profession:	Actuarial Science	**Telephone:**	--
Membership:	--	**Fax:**	--
Established:	1993	**E-mail:**	george.psaras@actuaries-cy.org
		Web:	www.actuaries-cy.org

Cyprus Computer Society

Designation:	--	**Address:**	P.O. Box 27038, 1641 Nicosia, Cyprus
Designatory Letters:	--	**Telephone:**	357-22-754474
Profession:	Information Technology	**Fax:**	357-22-767-349
Membership:	786	**E-mail:**	ccs@spidernet.com.cy
Established:	--	**Web:**	www.ccs.org.cy

Cyprus Institute of Business Consultants

Designation:	--	**Address:**	Cyprus Technology Foundation, Ionion Nison No. 1, 1st Floor, Akropoli, PO Box 20783, 1663 Nicosia, Cyprus
Designatory Letters:	--	**Telephone:**	357-2-317288
Profession:	Management Consulting	**Fax:**	357-2-318087
Membership:	--	**E-mail:**	--
Established:	1999	**Web:**	--

Cyprus Institute of Marketing

Designation:	--	**Address:**	PO Box 5288, Nicosia, Cyprus
Designatory Letters:	--	**Telephone:**	357-2-448475
Profession:	Marketing	**Fax:**	357-2-459331
Membership:	--	**E-mail:**	ccma@spidernet.com.vy
Established:	1979	**Web:**	www.cima.com.cy

CZECH REPUBLIC

Chamber of Auditors of the Czech Republic

Designation:	--	**Address:**	Komora auditoru Ceske republiky, PO Box 772, Opletalova 55, 111 84 Prague 1, Czech Republic
Designatory Letters:	--		
Profession:	Accounting		
Membership:	--	**Telephone:**	420-2-2421-2670, 2160, 2121
Established:	--	**Fax:**	420-2-2421-1905
		E-mail:	kacr@kacr.cz
		Web:	www.kacr.cz

Union of Accountants of the Czech Republic

Designation:	--	**Address:**	Stepánská ulice c. 28, 110 00 Prague 1, Czech Republic
Designatory Letters:	--		
Profession:	Accounting	**Telephone:**	420-2-2404-1015
Membership:	--	**Fax:**	420-2-2404-2915
Established:	--	**E-mail:**	sekretariat@svaz-ucetnich.cz
		Web:	www.svaz-ucetnich.cz

Ceská Spolecnost Aktuárù (Czech Actuarial Society)

Designation:	--	**Address:**	Ministry of Labour and Social
Designatory Letters:	--		Affairs, Na poricnim pravu 1,
Profession:	Actuarial Science		128 00 Praha 2, Czech Republic
Membership:	--	**Telephone:**	420-2192-2593
Established:	1992	**Fax:**	420-2192-1277
		E-mail:	jaroslava.feistauerova@mpsv.cz
		Web:	www.actuaria.cz

Czech Society for Cybernetics and Informatics

Designation:	--	**Address:**	Pod vodarenskou vezi 2, CZ-182
Designatory Letters:	--		07 Prague 8, Liben, Czech
Profession:	Information Technology		Republic
Membership:	--	**Telephone:**	420-2-660-5-3901
Established:	--	**Fax:**	420-2-858-5789
		E-mail:	cski@utia.cas.cz
		Web:	www.cski.cz.hr

Association for Consulting to Business (APP)

Designation:	--	**Address:**	Veletrni 21, CZ -170 00, Prague 7,
Designatory Letters:	--		Czech Republic
Profession:	Management Consulting	**Telephone:**	420-2-20-8790-43
Membership:	194	**Fax:**	420-2-20-8790-43
Established:	--	**E-mail:**	asocpor@asocpor.cz
		Web:	www.asocpor.cz

Czech Institute of Marketing (CIMA)

Designation:	--	**Address:**	Geologická 2, 152 00 Prague 5,
Designatory Letters:	--		Czech Republic.
Profession:	Marketing	**Telephone:**	42-0-2965-554-1011
Membership:	--	**Fax:**	42-0-2516-81575
Established:	--	**E-mail:**	cima@cima.cz
		Web:	www.cima.cz

Ceska Asociace Treasury CAT (The Czech Association of Corporate Treasurers)

Designation:	--	**Address:**	Na Plzettce 2/1235, 150 00 Praha 5,
Designatory Letters:	--		Czech Republic
Profession:	Treasury Management	**Telephone:**	420-723-427-777
Membership:	--	**Fax:**	--
Established:	--	**E-mail:**	info@czechtreasury.cz
		Web:	www.czechtreasury.cz

D

DENMARK

Foreningen af Registrerede Revisorer

Designation:	Certified Accountant	**Address:**	1 Aaamarksvej, DK 2650,
Designatory Letters:	FRR		Hvidovre, Denmark
Profession:	Accounting	**Telephone:**	45-36-34 44 22
Membership:	--	**Fax:**	45-36-34 44 44
Established:	1970	**E-mail:**	jbr@frr.dk
		Web:	www.frr.dk

Foreningen af Statsautoriserede Revisorer

Designation:	--	**Address:**	Kronprinsessegade 8, 1306
Designatory Letters:	--		Copenhagen K, Denmark
Profession:	Accounting	**Telephone:**	45-33-939-191
Membership:	--	**Fax:**	45-33-110-913
Established:	--	**E-mail:**	fsr@fsr.dk
		Web:	--

Den Danske Aktuarforening

Designation:	--	**Address:**	Forsikring & Pension,
Designatory Letters:	--		Forsikringens Hus, Amaliegade
Profession:	Actuarial Science		10, 1256 Copenhagen, Denmark
Membership:	--	**Telephone:**	43-4355 -00
Established:	1901	**Fax:**	33-4355-01
		E-mail:	sk@forsikringenshus.dk
		Web:	www.aktuarforeningen.dk

Danish IT Society

Designation:	--	**Address:**	St. Kongensgade 59A, DK-1264,
Designatory Letters:	--		Copenhagen K, Denmark
Profession:	Information Technology	**Telephone:**	45-33-111-560
Membership:	--	**Fax:**	45-33-931580
Established:	--	**E-mail:**	dansk-it@dansk-it.dk
		Web:	www.dansk-it.dk

Danish Management Board

Designation:	Certified Management Consultant	**Address:**	HC Andersens Boulevard 18, DK-1787, Copenhagen, Denmark
Designatory Letters:	CMC (Certified Management Consultant)	**Telephone:**	45-7020-3375
		Fax:	45-7020-3376
		E-mail:	info@discmc.dk
Profession:	Management Consulting	**Web:**	www.dicmc.dk
Membership:	--		
Established:	1987		

Dansk Management Råd (DMR)

Designation:	--	**Address:**	D-K1787, Copenhagen V,
Designatory Letters:	--		Denmark
Profession:	Management Consulting	**Telephone:**	45-7020-3375
Membership:	--	**Fax:**	45-7020-3376
Established:	--	**E-mail:**	info@danskmanagementraad.dk
		Web:	www.dmr.nu

Dansk Marketing Forum (DMF)

Designation:	--	**Address:**	Ndr. Fasanvej 113-115, PO Box 40,
Designatory Letters:	--		2000 Frederiksberg, Denmark
Profession:	Marketing	**Telephone:**	45-3811-8787
Membership:	--	**Fax:**	45-3811-8747
Established:	--	**E-mail:**	dmf@d-m-f-dk
		Web:	www.d-m-f-dk

Foreningen Dansk Projektledelsa

Designation:	--	**Address:**	Saettedamnen, 4, 3400 Hillersd,
Designatory Letters:	--		Denmark
Profession:	Project Management	**Telephone:**	48-24-1488
Membership:	--	**Fax:**	48-24-1489
Established:	--	**E-mail:**	info@danskprojektledelse.dk
		Web:	www.projekforeningen.dk

Danish Association of Corporate Treasurers (DACT)

Designation:	--	**Address:**	c/o Superfos Frydenlundsvej, 30
Designatory Letters:	--		Dk 2950 Vedbaek, Denmark
Profession:	Treasury Management	**Telephone:**	45-456-70000
Membership:	--	**Fax:**	45-672-010
Established:	--	**E-mail:**	--
		Web:	--

DOMINICAN REPUBLIC

Instituto de Contadores Públicos Autorizados de la República Dominicana

Designation:	Contador Público Autorizado	**Address:**	Calle Caonabo No. 18 Esq. Pedro A. Lluberes, 3° Piso, Apartado
Designatory Letters:	CPA (Contador Público Autorizado)		Postal 1082, Santo Domingo, DN- Dominican Republic
Profession:	Accounting	**Telephone:**	809-566-2636/688-7080
Membership:	--	**Fax:**	809-562-4235
Established:	1944	**E-mail:**	icpard@codetel.net.do
		Web:	www.icpard.org

E

ECUADOR

Federación Nacional de Contadores del Ecuador

Designation:	--	**Address:**	Cristobal de Acuña, No. Oe3-135 y
Designatory Letters:	--		Av.América, Quito, Ecuador
Profession:	Accounting	**Telephone:**	5932-222-9500/222-8610
Membership:	--	**Fax:**	5932-252-3033
Established:	--	**E-mail:**	fnce@uio.satnet.net
		Web:	--

EGYPT

Arab Society of Certified Accountants

Designation:	Arab Certified Public Accountant	**Address:**	23 Wadi El Nil Mohandessen, PO Box 55, Mohamed Farid 11518,
Designatory Letters:	ACPA (Arab Certified Public Accountant)		Cairo, Egypt
		Telephone:	202-346-2951
Profession:	Accounting	**Fax:**	202-347-9952
Membership:	--	**E-mail:**	--
Established:	1984	**Web:**	--

Egyptian Society of Accountants & Auditors

Designation:	--	**Address:**	34 Abdel Khalak Sarwat Street, Mohamed Farid – 11518, Cairo,
Designatory Letters:	--		Egypt
Profession:	Accounting	**Telephone:**	202-395-4656
Membership:	--	**Fax:**	202-393-7407
Established:	--	**E-mail:**	egsocaa@yahoo.com
		Web:	--

Egyptian Society of Actuaries
(See International Actuarial Association in Appendix A)

Designation:	--	**Address:**	Cairo, Egypt
Designatory Letters:	--	**Telephone:**	--
Profession:	Actuarial Science	**Fax:**	--
Membership:	--	**E-mail:**	--
Established:	1999	**Web:**	--

Egyptian Computer Society

Designation:	--	**Address:**	PO Box 9009, Nasr City, Cairo,
Designatory Letters:	--		Egypt
Profession:	Information Technology	**Telephone:**	202-2608-182
Membership:	--	**Fax:**	202-2603-880
Established:	--	**E-mail:**	ecomps@ritsec3.com.eg
		Web:	www.ifip.org/members/egypt.htm

EL SALVADOR

Corporación de Contadores de El Salvador

Designation:	--	**Address:**	"Villa Fontana Rosa", Calle La
Designatory Letters:	--		Reforma No. 133, Colonia San
Profession:	Accounting		Benito, San Salvador-CA, El
Membership:	--		Salvador
Established:	--	**Telephone:**	503-298-1705-06, 276-5723
		Fax:	503-279-0233
		E-mail:	ipsa@mail.nttcb.net
		Web:	--

Instituto Salvadoreño de Contadores Públicos

Designation:	--	**Address:**	Av. Olimpica Pasaje La Union
Designatory Letters:	--		#112, Colonia Escalon,
Profession:	Accounting		San Salvador, El Salvador
Membership:	--	**Telephone:**	503-2245-5500
Established:	--	**Fax:**	503-2245-3070
		E-mail:	instituto.contadores@mail.nttcb.net
		Web:	--

ESTONIA

Audiitorkogn (Estonian Auditing Board)

Designation:	--	**Address:**	Ahtri 10A 1051 Tallinn, Estonia
Designatory Letters:	--	**Telephone:**	372-6684-216-7
Profession:	Accounting	**Fax:**	372-6684-218
Membership:	--	**E-mail:**	info@auditor-kogn.ee
Established:	--	**Web:**	www.auditorkogn.ee

Eesti Aktuaaride Liit (Estonian Actuarial Society)
(See International Actuarial Association in Designation in Appendix A)

Designation:	--	**Address:**	Estonia
Designatory Letters:	--	**Telephone:**	--
Profession:	Actuarial Science	**Fax:**	--
Membership:	--	**E-mail:**	--
Established:	1999	**Web:**	--

Estonian Management Institute

Designation:	--	**Address:**	Suitiste St 21, EE0034, Tallinn,
Designatory Letters:	--		Estonia
Profession:	Management	**Telephone:**	372-372-527359
Membership:	--	**Fax:**	372-372-521625
Established:	--	**E-mail:**	--
		Web:	--

ETHIOPIA

Ethiopian Information Technology Professionals Association (EITPA)

Designation:	--	**Address:**	PO Box 5164, Addis Ababa,
Designatory Letters:	--		Ethiopia
Profession:	Information Technology	**Telephone:**	251-11-550-9417
Membership:	--	**Fax:**	251-11-533-3368
Established:	--	**E-mail:**	eitpa_et@yahoo.com
		Web:	www.eitpa.org

Ethiopian Professional Association of Accountants and Auditors (EPAAA)

Designation:	--	**Address:**	PO Box 42875, Addis Ababa,
Designatory Letters:	--		Ethiopia
Profession:	Information Technology	**Telephone:**	251-9-215-779-536-073
Membership:	--	**Fax:**	251-1-523-834
Established:	--	**E-mail:**	epaaa@ethionet.et
		Web:	--

F

FIJI

Fiji Institute of Accountants

Designation:	Chartered Accountant	**Address:**	Fiji Teachers Union Building, 1-3
Designatory Letters:	CA (Chartered		Berry Road, Suva, Fiji
	Accountant)	**Telephone:**	679-305-807
Profession:	Accounting	**Fax:**	679-305-588
Membership:	540	**E-mail:**	fia@connect.com.fj
Established:	1972	**Web:**	www.fia.org.fj

FINLAND

HTM-tilintarkastajat ry

Designation:	Approved Auditor	**Address:**	Kastelholmantie 2, Helsinki 2,
Designatory Letters:	HTM - Auditor		Finland
Profession:	Accounting	**Telephone:**	358-9-4767-9304
Membership:	--	**Fax:**	358-9-4767-9306
Established:	--	**E-mail:**	--
		Web:	www.htm.fi

Finnish Institute of Authorized Public Accountants KHT-yhdistys-Föreningen CGR ry

Designation:	Auditor Authorised by	**Address:**	Fredrikinkatu 61 A, FIN-00100,
	the Central Chamber of		Helsinki, Finland
	Commerce	**Telephone:**	358-9-755-22010
Designatory Letters:	KHT-Auditor	**Fax:**	358-9-694-2250
Profession:	Accounting/Auditing	**E-mail:**	kht@kht.fi
Membership:	722	**Web:**	www.kht.fi
Established:	--		

Suomen Aktuaariyhdistys ry-Finlands Aktuarieföreng rf

Designation:	--	**Address:**	Sampo, PO Box 216, 20101 Turku,
Designatory Letters:	--		Finland
Profession:	Actuarial Science	**Telephone:**	358-2166-5302
Membership:	--	**Fax:**	358-2166-5300
Established:	1922	**E-mail:**	esko.kivisaari@varma-sampo.fi
		Web:	www.actuary.fi

Finnish Information Processing Association

Designation:	--	**Address:**	Lars Sonckin kaari 12, F1-02600
Designatory Letters:	--		Espoo, Finland
Profession:	Information Technology	**Telephone:**	358-20-741-9898
Membership:	--	**Fax:**	358-20-741-9889
Established:	--	**E-mail:**	natalia.ritonen@ttlry.fi
		Web:	www.ttlry.fi

Liikkeenjohdon Konsultit LJK ry (The Finnish Management Consultants)

Designation:	Certified Management Consultant	**Address:**	PO Box 122 FI-33210, Tampere, Finland
Designatory Letters:	CMC (Certified Management Consultant)	**Telephone:**	358-9-6220-4442
		Fax:	58-9-6220-1009
		E-mail:	ljk@ljk.fi
Profession:	Management Consulting	**Web:**	ww.ljk.fi
Membership:	--		
Established:	1961		

Finnish Marketing Association

Designation:	--	**Address:**	PO Box 199, Fabianinkatu 4B, SF-00131 Helsinki, Finland
Designatory Letters:	--		
Profession:	Marketing	**Telephone:**	35-89-687-7130
Membership:	--	**Fax:**	35-89-179-498
Established:	--	**E-mail:**	kari.hamalainen@mark.fi
		Web:	www.mark.fi

Institute of Marketing

Designation:	--	**Address:**	Töölöntullinkatu 6, SF-00250, Helsinki, Finland
Designatory Letters:	--		
Profession:	Marketing	**Telephone:**	358-0-47361
Membership:	--	**Fax:**	358-0-473-6400
Established:	--	**E-mail:**	--
		Web:	--

Project Management Association of Finland

Designation:	--	**Address:**	Elisantie 16, 02970 Espoo, Finland
Designatory Letters:	--	**Telephone:**	358-9-8542-373
Profession:	Project Management	**Fax:**	358-9-8542-373
Membership:	1,860	**E-mail:**	pry@pry.fi
Established:	1968	**Web:**	www.pry.fi

FRANCE

Compagnie Nationale des Commissaires aux Comptes (CNCC)

Designation:	--	**Address:**	8 Rue de lAmiral-de-Coligny, 75001 Paris, France
Designatory Letters:	--		
Profession:	Accounting	**Telephone:**	33-1-44-77-8282
Membership:	--	**Fax:**	33-1-4477-8228
Established:	1966	**E-mail:**	cncc.documentation@cncc.fr
		Web:	www.cncc.fr

Conseil Supérieur de l'Ordre des Experts-Comptables Francophones (OEC)

Designation:	--	**Address:**	153, Rue de Courcelles, 75817 Paris, Cedex France
Designatory Letters:	--		
Profession:	Accounting	**Telephone:**	33-1-44-15-6000
Membership:	--	**Fax:**	33-1-44-15-9005
Established:	--	**E-mail:**	rricol@experts-comptables.fr
		Web:	www.experts-comptables.org

Fédération Internationale des Experts-Comptables Francophones

Designation:	--	**Address:**	45, Rue des Petits Champs, 75001 Paris, France
Designatory Letters:	--		
Profession:	Accounting	**Telephone:**	33-1-55-04-3197
Membership:	--	**Fax:**	3-1-55-04-3149
Established:	1966	**E-mail:**	fidef@fidef.org
		Web:	www.fidef.org

Institut des Actuaires Francais

Designation:	--	**Address:**	243 rue Saint-Honoré, 75001 Paris, France
Designatory Letters:	--		
Profession:	Actuarial Science	**Telephone:**	426-01694
Membership:	--	**Fax:**	--
Established:	1890	**E-mail:**	--
		Web:	www.institutdesactuaires.org

Union Strasbourgeoise des Actuaires

Designation:	--	**Address:**	Maison des Actuaires-4 rue Chauveau Lagarde, 75008 Paris, France
Designatory Letters:	--		
Profession:	Actuarial Science		
Membership:	--	**Telephone:**	33-01-4151-7272
Established:	1988	**Fax:**	33-01-4151-7273
		E-mail:	--
		Web:	--

Institut de Science Financiére et d'Assurance

Designation:	--	**Address:**	43, Boulevard du 11-Novembre-1918, 69622 Villeurbanne Cedex, France
Designatory Letters:	--		
Profession:	Finance		
Membership:	--	**Telephone:**	724-31175
Established:	--	**Fax:**	724-21176
		E-mail:	--
		Web:	--

Societe des Electriciens et des electronics - SEe

Designation:	--	**Address:**	11-17 Rue Hamelin, F-75783 Paris, Cedex 16. France
Designatory Letters:	--		
Profession:	Information Technology	**Telephone:**	33-1-569-03700
Membership:	--	**Fax:**	33-1-569-03719
Established:	--	**E-mail:**	see@see.asso.fr
		Web:	www.see.asso.fr

Société Française des Analystes Financiers (SFAF)

Designation:	--	**Address:**	24 Rue de Penthièvre, F-75008 Paris, France
Designatory Letters:	--		
Profession:	Investment Management	**Telephone:**	33-1-56-434-310
Membership:	--	**Fax:**	33-1-45-630-058
Established:	--	**E-mail:**	sfaf@sfaf.com
		Web:	www.sfaf.com

Office Professionnel de Qualification des Conseils en Management

Designation:	--	**Address:**	73-77 rue de Sevres, 92514
Designatory Letters:	--		Boulogne Billancourt, Cedex,
Profession:	Management		Paris, France
Membership:	--	**Telephone:**	331-4699-1455
Established:	--	**Fax:**	331-4699-1456
		E-mail:	opqfc@opqfc.com
		Web:	www.opqcm.org

Syntec Conseil en Management (Chanbre Syndicale des Science Conseil)

Designation:	--	**Address:**	3 Rue Léon Bonnat, F-75016 Paris,
Designatory Letters:	--		France
Profession:	Management Consulting	**Telephone:**	33-144-3049-20
Membership:	--	**Fax:**	33-140-5073-57
Established:	1992	**E-mail:**	--
		Web:	www.syntec-management.com

DCF Les Dirigeants Commerciaux de France

Designation:	--	**Address:**	1 Villa Georges Sand, F-75016,
Designatory Letters:	--		Paris, France
Profession:	Marketing	**Telephone:**	33-1-4525-1144
Membership:	--	**Fax:**	33-1-4050-1556
Established:	--	**E-mail:**	idehouck.dcf@wanadoo.fr
		Web:	ww.dcf-france.com

l'Asociation Nationale du Marketing (ADETEM).

Designation:	--	**Address:**	92916 Paris, La Défense Cedex,
Designatory Letters:	--		France
Profession:	Marketing	**Telephone:**	33-1-4116-7650
Membership:	--	**Fax:**	33-1-4116-7658
Established:	--	**E-mail:**	adetem.asso@wanadoo.fr
		Web:	www.adetem.org

Association Francophone de Management de Projet

Designation:	Certification en Gestion de Projet	**Address:**	17 rue de Turbigo, 75002 Paris, France
	Certification en direction de Projet	**Telephone:**	33-1-55-80-70-60
		Fax:	33-1-55-80-70-69
Designatory Letters:	CGP (Certification en Gestion de Projet)	**E-mail:**	info@afitep.fr
	CDP (Certification en direction de Projet)	**Web:**	www.afitep.fr
Profession:	Project Management		
Membership:	1,000		
Established:	1982		

Association Francaise des Tresoriers d'Entreprise (French Association of Corporate Treasurers)

Designation:	--	**Address:**	20, rue d'Athenes, 75442 Paris,
Designatory Letters:	--		Cedex 09, France
Profession:	Treasury Management	**Telephone:**	33-13-462-6286
Membership:	--	**Fax:**	33-14-280-1890
Established:	--	**E-mail:**	--
		Web:	www.afte.com

G

Georgian Federation of Professional Accountants and Auditors

Designation:	--	**Address:**	61 Tsereteli Ave., Tbilisi 380064, Georgia
Designatory Letters:	--		
Profession:	Accounting	**Telephone:**	995-31-350-157
Membership:	--	**Fax:**	995-32-350-157
Established:	--	**E-mail:**	--
		Web:	www.gfpaa.ge

GERMANY

Institut der Wirtschaftsprüfer in Deuttschland e.V.

Designation:	--	**Address:**	Tersteegenstrasse 14, 40 474 Düsseldorf, Germany
Designatory Letters:	--		
Profession:	Accounting	**Telephone:**	49-211-45-6181
Membership:	--	**Fax:**	49-211-45-410-97
Established:	--	**E-mail:**	naumann@idw.de
		Web:	www.idw.de

Verband der Certified Public Accountant in Deutschland e.V. (GCPAS)

Designation:	Certified Public Accountant	**Address:**	--
		Telephone:	--
Designatory Letters:	CPA (Certified Public Accountant)	**Fax:**	--
		E-mail:	--
Profession:	Accounting	**Web:**	www.gcpas.de
Membership:	--		
Established:	--		

Deutsche Aktuarvereinigung e.V. (German Association of Actuaries)

Designation:	--	**Address:**	Hohenstaufenring 47-51, 50674 Cologne, Germany
Designatory Letters:	DAV		
Profession:	Actuarial Science	**Telephone:**	49-221-912554-0
Membership:	2,580	**Fax:**	49-221-912554-44
Established:	1993	**E-mail:**	info@aktuar.de
		Web:	www.aktuar.de

Deutsche Gesellschaft für Versicherungsund Finanzmathematik e.V.

Designation:	--	**Address:**	Hohenstaufenring 47-51, 50674 Cologne, Germany
Designatory Letters:	DGVM		
Profession:	Actuarial Science	**Telephone:**	49-221-912554-0
Membership:	2,607	**Fax:**	49-221-912554-44
Established:	1903	**E-mail:**	info@dgvfm.de
		Web:	www.dgvfm.de

Gesellschaft für Informatik e.V. (GI)

Designation:	--	**Address:**	Ahrstr. 45, D-53175, Bonn,
Designatory Letters:	--		Germany
Profession:	Information Technology	**Telephone:**	49-228-302-145
Membership:	--	**Fax:**	49-228-302-167
Established:	--	**E-mail:**	gs@gi-ev-de
		Web:	www.gi-ev.de

Deutsche Vereinigung für Finanzaanalyse und Asset Management (DVFA)

Designation:	--	**Address:**	Einsteinstrasse 5, D-63303,
Designatory Letters:	--		Dreieich, Germany
Profession:	Investment Management	**Telephone:**	495-6103-583320
Membership:	--	**Fax:**	49-6103-583333
Established:	--	**E-mail:**	ausbildung@dvfa.de
		Web:	www.dvfa.de

Bundesverband Deutscher Unternehmensberater (BDU) E.V.

Designation:	--	**Address:**	Zittelmannstrasse 22, D-53113
Designatory Letters:	--		Bonn, Germany.
Profession:	Management Consulting	**Telephone:**	49-228-9161-0
Membership:	--	**Fax:**	49-228-9161-26
Established:	--	**E-mail:**	info@bdu.de
		Web:	www.bdu.de

Deutscher Marketing – Verband e.V. (German Marketing Association)

Designation:	--	**Address:**	Benrather Str. 12, 40213
Designatory Letters:	--		Düsseldorf, Germany
Profession:	Marketing	**Telephone:**	49-211-86-40640
Membership:	--	**Fax:**	49-211-86-40640
Established:	--	**E-mail:**	info@marketingverband.de
		Web:	www.marketingverband.de

Deutsche Gesellschaft für Projektmanagement e.V (German Association of Project Management)

Designation:	Certified Project Management Practitioner	**Address:**	Berlin, Germany
		Telephone:	--
Designatory Letters:	CPMP (Certified Project Management Practitioner)	**Fax:**	--
		E-mail:	--
		Web:	www.gpm-ipmc.de
Profession:	Project Management		
Membership:	--		
Established:	1979		

Wirtschaftsprüferkammer

Designation:	Wirtschaftsprüfer Wirtschaftsprüfungsgesellschaft Vereidigter Buchprüfer Buchprüfungsgesellschaft	**Address:**	Rauchstrasse 26, D 10787, Berlin, Germany
		Telephone:	49-30-726-1610
		Fax:	49-30-726-161212
Designatory Letters:	WP (Wirtschaftsprüfer) WPG (Wirtschaftsprüfungsgesell-schaft) vBP (Vereidigter Buchprüfer) BPG (Buchprüfungsgesellschaft)	**E-mail:**	admin@wpk.de
		Web:	www.wpk.de
Profession:	Statutory Auditing		
Membership:	20,000		
Established:	1961		

Gesellschaft für Finanzwirtschaft in der Unternehmensfuehrung e.V. (GEFUI)

Designation:	--	**Address:**	Dahlienweg 11, 61381
Designatory Letters:	--		Friedrichsdorf, Germany
Profession:	Treasury Management	**Telephone:**	49-0-6172-598-709
Membership:	--	**Fax:**	49-0-6172-598-710
Established:	--	**E-mail:**	--
		Web:	www.gefiu.org

Veerband Deutscher Treasurer e.V. (VDT) (German Association of Corporate Treasurers)

Designation:	--	**Address:**	PO 500364, D-60393, Frankfurt,
Designatory Letters:	--		Germany
Profession:	Treasury Management	**Telephone:**	49-0-6438-923-929
Membership:	--	**Fax:**	49-0-66438-923930
Established:	--	**E-mail:**	info@vdtev.de
		Web:	www.vdtev.de

GHANA

Institute of Chartered Accountants (Ghana)

Designation:	Chartered Accountant Ghana Accounting Technician	**Address:**	PO Box 4268, Accra Central, Ghana
Designatory Letters:	CA (Chartered Accountant)	**Telephone**	666-954-5; 669 591-2
		Fax:	233-21-669.594
		E-mail:	info@icagh.com
	GAT (Ghana Accounting Technician)	**Web:**	www.icagh.com
Profession:	Accounting		
Membership:	--		
Established:	1963		

Chartered Institute of Marketing (CIM)

Designation:	--	**Address:**	PO Box T 102, Sports Stadium,
Designatory Letters:	--		Accra Central, Ghana
Profession:	Marketing	**Telephone:**	233-21-226-697
Membership:	--	**Fax:**	233-21-222-171
Established:	--	**E-mail:**	--
		Web:	--

GIBRALTAR

Gibraltar Society of Chartered and Certified Accountancy Bodies

Designation:	NA	**Address:**	--
Designatory Letters:	NA	**Telephone:**	--
Profession:	Accounting	**Fax:**	--
Membership:	--	**E-mail:**	--
Established:	1982	**Web:**	www.gibraltaraccountants.com

GREECE

Institute of Certified Public Accountants of Greece

Designation:	Certified Public Accountant	**Address:**	28 Kapodistriou Str, 106 82 Athens, Greece
Designatory Letters:	CPA (Certified Public Accountant)	**Telephone:**	30-210-389-1429
		Fax:	30-210-382-5159
Profession:	Accounting	**E-mail:**	iad@soel.gr
Membership:	--	**Web:**	www.soel.gr
Established:	--		

Association of Greek Actuaries

Designation:	Actuary License	**Address:**	c-o Ethniki Insurance Co., K.
Designatory Letters:	--		Servias 8, 10210 Athens, Greece
Profession:	Actuarial Science	**Telephone:**	01-3299-581
Membership:	--	**Fax:**	01-3236-101
Established:	1979	**E-mail:**	--
		Web:	--

Hellenic Actuarial Society

Designation:	--	**Address:**	--
Designatory Letters:	--	**Telephone:**	--
Profession:	Actuarial Science	**Fax:**	--
Membership:	--	**E-mail:**	--
Established:	1979	**Web:**	--

Greek Computer Society (GCS)

Designation:	--	**Address:**	Thessaloniki & Chandri 1,
Designatory Letters:	--		Moshato, GR-18346, Athens,
Profession:	Information Technology		Greece
Membership:	--	**Telephone:**	30-1-480-2886
Established:	--	**Fax:**	30-1-480-2889
		E-mail:	--
		Web:	www.epy.gr

Hellenic Association of Certified Stockmarket Analysts

Designation:	--	**Address:**	10 Sofokleous St., Athens, Greece
Designatory Letters:	--	**Telephone:**	21-033-66-778-9
Profession:	Investment Management	**Fax:**	--
Membership:	--	**E-mail:**	hacsagr@yahoo.gr
Established:	--	**Web:**	www.hacsa.gr

Hellenic Management Association (HMA)

Designation:	--	**Address:**	EEDE – Athens Office, 200 Ionias
Designatory Letters:	--		Ave., and Lakovaton Street, 111
Profession:	Management		44 Athens, Greece
Membership:	--	**Telephone:**	30-210-211-2000
Established:	1962	**Fax:**	30-210-211-20201
		E-mail:	eede@eede.gr
		Web:	www.eede.gr

Hellenic Association of Management Consulting Firms

Designation:	--	**Address:**	101 Vas, Sophias Avenue, Mavili
Designatory Letters:	--		Square, GR-115 21 Athens,
Profession:	Management Consulting		Greece
Membership:	--	**Telephone:**	301-6470-660
Established:	--	**Fax:**	301-6470-661
		E-mail:	sesma@hol.gr
		Web:	www.sesma.gr

H.I.M Hellenic Institute of Marketing

Designation:	--	**Address:**	200 Ionas Avenue & Iakovaton 61,
Designatory Letters:	--		11144, Kato Patissia, Athens, Greece
Profession:	Marketing	**Telephone:**	30-210-211-2000
Membership:	--	**Fax:**	30-210-211-2020
Established:	--	**E-mail:**	eim@eede.gr
		Web:	www.eede.gr

Hellenic Project Management Association

Designation:	--	**Address:**	4 Kassou Street, 11364 Athens, Greece
Designatory Letters:	--		
Profession:	Project Management	**Telephone:**	30-1-86-29660
Membership:	--	**Fax:**	30-1-8617-681
Established:	--	**E-mail:**	--
		Web:	--

GUATEMALA

Instituto Guatemalteco de Contadores Públicos y Auditores

Designation:	--	**Address:**	6ª Avenida 0-60, Zona 4, Torre Profesional 1, Oficina 603, 6° Nivel, Ciudad Guatemala-CA, Guatemala
Designatory Letters:	--		
Profession:	Accounting		
Membership:	--		
Established:	--	**Telephone:**	502-335-1972; 335.1885; 335-2197; 335-1880
		Fax:	502-335-1884
		E-mail:	igcpa@quetzal.net
		Web:	--

GUYANA

Institute of Chartered Accountants of Guyana

Designation:	Chartered Accountant	**Address:**	216 Almond Street, Queenstown, Georgetown, Guyana
Designatory Letters:	CA (Chartered Accountant)	**Telephone:**	592-2-65-2076
Profession:	Accounting	**Fax:**	592-265-3367
Membership:	--	**E-mail:**	colin@solutions2000.net
Established:	1966 (The Guyana Association of Accountants was established in 1966 and changed its name to the Institute of Chartered Accountants of Guyana in 1974)	**Web:**	--

H

HAITI

Ordre des Comptables Professionels Agrees d'Haiti

Designation:	--	**Address:**	17 rue baussan Turgeau,
Designatory Letters:	--		PO Box 19030,
Profession:	Accounting		Port-au-Prince, Haiti
Membership:	--	**Telephone:**	809-245-5944
Established:	--	**Fax:**	809-455-604
		E-mail:	--
		Web:	www.locapph.org

HONDURAS

Colegio de Hondureño de Profesionales Universitarios en Contaduría Pública

Designation:	--	**Address:**	Centro Comercial
Designatory Letters:	--		Centroamerica, Local 42C
Profession:	Accounting		por Emisoras Unidas
Membership:	--		Boulevard, Miraflores,
Established:	--		Apartado 3824,
			Tegucigalpa-DC, Honduras
		Telephone:	504-235-6947
		Fax:	504-235-9573
		E-mail:	--
		Web:	www.cohpucp.tripod.com

Colegio de Peritos Mercantiles y Contadores Públicos

Designation:	--	**Address:**	Edificio Colegio de Peritos
Designatory Letters:	--		Mercantiles y Contadores
Profession:	Accounting		Públicos, Boulevard
Membership:	--		Suyata, PO Box 588,
Established:	--		Tegucigalpa-HDC,
			Honduras
		Telephone:	504-232-4787-221-0232
		Fax:	504-232-9702
		E-mail:	colperitos@gbm.hn
		Web:	www.elcontador.org

HONG KONG

Hong Kong Institute of Accredited Accounting Technicians

Designation:	Accounting Technician	**Address:**	27/F Wu Chung House, 213
Designatory Letters:	CAC (Certified Accounts Clerk)		Queen's Road East,
	AAT (Associate Member of the		Wanchai, Hong Kong
	Hong Kong Institute of	**Telephone:**	852-2823-0600
	Accredited Accounting	**Fax:**	852-2823-0606
	Technicians)	**E-mail:**	hkiaat@hkiaat.org
	FAAT (Fellow Member of the	**Web:**	www.hkiaat.org.
	Hong Kong Institute of		
	Accredited Accounting		
	Technicians)		
Profession:	Accounting		
Membership:	--		
Established:	1988		

Hong Kong Institute of Certified Public Accountants

Designation:	Certified Public Accountant	**Address:**	37/F Wu Chung House, 213
Designatory Letters:	CPA (HK) (Certified Public Accountant Hong Kong)		Queen's Road East Wanchai, Hong Kong
Profession:	Accounting	**Telephone:**	852-2287-7228
Membership:	--	**Fax:**	852-2865-6603
Established:	1973	**E-mail:**	hkicpa@hkicpa.org.hk
		Web:	www.hkicpa.org.hk

Actuarial Society of Hong Kong

Designation:	--	**Address:**	2202 Tower Two, Lippo
Designatory Letters:	--		Centre, 89 Queensway,
Profession:	Actuarial Science		Hong Kong
Membership:	550	**Telephone:**	852-2147-9418
Established:	1994	**Fax:**	852-2147-2497
		E-mail:	info@actuaries.org.hk
		Web:	www.actuaries.org.hk

Hong Kong Institute of Company Secretaries
(Hong Kong arm of the international Institute of Chartered Secretaries and Administrators or ICSA)

Designation:	Chartered Secretary	**Address:**	3/F Hong Kong Diamond
Designatory Letters:	ACS (Associate Member of the Hong Kong Institute of Company Secretaries)		Exchange Building, 8 Duddell Street, Central, Hong Kong
	ACIS (Associate Member of the Institute of Chartered Secretaries and Administrators)	**Telephone:**	852-2881-6177
		Fax:	852-2881-5050
		E-mail:	ask@hkics.org.hk
		Web:	www.hkics.org.hk
	FCS (Fellow Member of the Hong Kong Institute of Company Secretaries)		
	FCIS (Fellow Member of the Institute of Chartered Secretaries and Administrators)		
Profession:	Corporate Secretary		
Membership:	--		
Established:	1949 (Hong Kong); 1891 (UK)		

Hong Kong Credit and Collection Management Association (HKCCMA)

Designation:	--	**Address:**	PO Box 2679, General Post
Designatory Letters:	MCCMA (Member of the Hong Kong Credit and Collections Management Association)		Office, Hong Kong
		Telephone:	852-8116-8816
		Fax:	852-8116-8826
	FCCMA (Fellow of the Hong Kong Credit and Collection Management Association)	**E-mail:**	--
		Web:	www.hkccma.org
Profession:	Credit Management		
Membership:	--		
Established:	1999		

Institute of Financial Planners of Hong Kong

Designation:	Associate Personal Financial Planner	**Address:**	Suites 802/803, the Hong Kong Club Building, Central Hong Kong
Designatory Letters:	APFP (Associate Personal Financial Planner)	**Telephone:**	852-2982-7888
Profession:	Financial Planning	**Fax:**	852-2982-7777
Membership:	3,300	**E-mail:**	info@ifphk.org
Established:	2000	**Web:**	www.ifphk.org.

Hong Kong Computer Society

Designation:	--	**Address:**	Unit 1801, 18/F Tai Tung Building, No. 8 Fleming Road, Wanchai, Hong Kong
Designatory Letters:	AHKCS (Associate Member of the Hong Kong Computer Society)		
	MHKCS (Member of the Hong Kong Computer Society)	**Telephone:**	852-2834-2228
	FHKCS (Fellow Member of the Hong Kong Computer Society)	**Fax:**	852-2834-3003
		E-mail:	hkcs@hkcs.org.hk
	Distinguished FHKCS (Distinguished Fellow Member of the Hong Kong Computer Society)	**Web:**	www.hkcs.org.hk
Profession:	Information Technology		
Membership:	--		
Established:	1970		

Hong Kong Securities Institute

Designation:	--	**Address:**	Room 2403-08 Wing On Centre, 111 Connaught Road, Sheung Wan, Hong Kong
Designatory Letters:	--		
Profession:	Investment Management		
Membership:	--		
Established:	--	**Telephone:**	852-3120-6100
		Fax:	852-2899-2611
		E-mail:	--
		Web:	www.hksi.org

Hong Kong Management Association

Designation:	--	**Address:**	Management House, 3rd Floor, 26 Canal Road, Hong Kong
Designatory Letters:	--		
Profession:	Management		
Membership:	--	**Telephone:**	--
Established:	--	**Fax:**	--
		E-mail:	hkma@hkma.org.hk
		Web:	www.hkma.org.hk

Hong Kong Management Consultancies Association (MCAHK)

Designation:	--	**Address:**	14th Floor, Room 1403B, 9 Queen's Road Central, Hong Kong
Designatory Letters:	--		
Profession:	Management Consulting	**Telephone:**	852-2856-3487
Membership:	--	**Fax:**	852-2565-6628
Established:	--	**E-mail:**	mcahk@mca.org.hk
		Web:	www.mca.org.hk

Hong Kong Institute of Marketing

Designation:	--	**Address:**	11 F Iuki Tower, 5 O'Brien Road, Hong Kong
Designatory Letters:	AHKIM (Associateof the Hong Kong Institute of Marketing)	**Telephone:**	852-2881-6682
	MHKIM (Member of the Hong Kong Institute of Marketing)	**Fax:**	852-2881-6057
	FHKIM (Graduate of the Hong Kong Institute of Marketing)	**E-mail:**	enquiry@hkim.org.hk
	HMKIM (Honourary Member of the Hong Kong Institute of Marketing)	**Web:**	www.hkim.org.hk
	EHMKIM (Executive Member of the Hong Kong Institute of Marketing)		
Profession:	Marketing		
Membership:	--		
Established:	1983		

Hong Kong Quality Management Association (HKQMA)

Designation:	--	**Address:**	Shop SHW3 Sheung Wan, MTR Station (Exit E7), PO Box 2867, General Post Office, Hong Kong
Designatory Letters:	AHKQMA (Associate of the Hong Kong Quality Management Association)		
	MHKQMA (Member of the Hong Kong Quality Management Association)	**Telephone:**	852-2581-2210
	FHKQMA (Fellow of the Hong Kong Quality Management Association)	**Fax:**	852-2581-2212
	Hon. FHQMA (Honourable Fellow of the Hong Kong Quality Management Association)	**E-mail:**	enquiry@hkqma.org
		Web:	www.hkqma.org
Profession:	Quality Management		
Membership:	--		
Established:	1983		

Association of Corporate Treasurers (Hong Kong)

Designation:	--	**Address:**	8th Floor, AIA Building, 1 Stubbs Road, Hong Kong
Designatory Letters:	--	**Telephone:**	852-259-12170
Profession:	Treasury Management	**Fax:**	--
Membership:	--	**E-mail:**	--
Established:	1997	**Web:**	--

HUNGARY

Chamber of Hungarian Auditors (CHA)

Designation:	Chartered Accountant	**Address:**	Szinyei Merse u. 8, PO Box 587, Budapest H-1063, Hungary
Designatory Letters:	CA (Chartered Accountant)		
Profession:	Accounting/Auditing		
Membership:	6,000	**Telephone:**	36-1-473-4500
Established:	1997	**Fax:**	36-1-473-4510
		E-mail:	mkvk@mkvk.hu
		Web:	www.mkvk.hu

Magyar Aktuárius Társaság (Hungarian Actuarial Society)

Designation:	--	**Address:**	H-1052 Budapest, Deak
Designatory Letters:	--		Ferenc utca 10, Hungary
Profession:	Actuarial Science	**Telephone:**	--
Membership:	--	**Fax:**	--
Established:	1991	**E-mail:**	postmaster@actuary.hu
		Web:	www.actuary.hu

John V. Neumann Society (NJSZT) for Computing Sciences

Designation:	--	**Address:**	PO Box 451, Bathouri u.16,
Designatory Letters:	--		H-1054, Budapest,
Profession:	Information Technology		Hungary
Membership:	--	**Telephone:**	36-1-332-9349
Established:	--	**Fax:**	36-1-331-8140
		E-mail:	titkarsag@njszt.hu
		Web:	www.njszt.hu

The Hungarian Capital Market Professionals' Society

Designation:	--	**Address:**	ITCB Csopaki u.6, Budapest,
Designatory Letters:	--		Hungary H-1022
Profession:	Investment Management	**Telephone:**	--
Membership:	--	**Fax:**	--
Established:	--	**E-mail:**	--
		Web:	www.capmarketprof.hu

Association of Management Consultants in Hungary—Vezetési Tan Magyarországi Szövetsége

Designation:	--	**Address:**	Szent István krt. 11, Budapest
Designatory Letters:	--		H-1055, Hungary
Profession:	Management Consulting	**Telephone:**	361-302-7681-3630-685-826
Membership:	--	**Fax:**	361-302-7681
Established:	--	**E-mail:**	office@vtmsz.hu
		Web:	www.vtmsz.hu

I

ICELAND

Félag löggiltra Endurskoðenda

Designation:	Löggiltra Endurskoðenda (State Authorized Public Accountant)	**Address:**	Sudurlandsbraut 6, 108 Reykjavik, Iceland
		Telephone:	354-568-8119
Designatory Letters:	--	**Fax:**	354-568-8139
Profession:	Accounting	**E-mail:**	gunnar@fle.is
Membership:	--	**Web:**	www.fle.is
Established:	1929		

Félag Islenskra Tryggingastærðfræðinga (Iceland Actuarial Society)

Designation:	--	**Address:**	Suðurlandsbraut 32, 108 Reykjavik, Iceland
Designatory Letters:	--		
Profession:	Actuarial Science	**Telephone:**	--
Membership:	--	**Fax:**	--
Established:	--	**E-mail:**	--
		Web:	www.actuaries.is

Project Management Association of Iceland (VSF)

Designation:	--	**Address:**	Postholf 8773, 128 Reykjavik, Iceland
Designatory Letters:	--		
Profession:	Project Management	**Telephone:**	--
Membership:	--	**Fax:**	--
Established:	--	**E-mail:**	vsf@skima.is
		Web:	www.vst.is

INDIA

Institute of Chartered Accountants of India

Designation:	Chartered Accountant	**Address:**	P.B. No. 7100, Indraprastha Marg, New Delhi, 110002, India
Designatory Letters:	ACA (Associate Member of the Institute of Chartered Accountants of India)		
		Telephone:	91-11-3011-0404; 3989-3989
	FCA (Fellow Member of the Institute of Chartered Accountants of India)	**Fax:**	91-11-3011-0581; 3011-0591
		E-mail:	president@icai.org
		Web:	www.icai.org
Profession:	Accounting		
Membership:	115,000		
Established:	1949		

Institute of Cost and Works Accountants of India

Designation:	Cost and Works Accountant	**Address:**	Cost Accountants' Hall, 12 Sudder Street, Calcutta – 700 016, India
Designatory Letters:	ACWA (Associate Member of the Institute of Cost and Works Accountants of India)		
		Telephone:	91-33-244-1031
	FCWA (Fellow Member of the Institute of Cost and Works Accountants of India)	**Fax:**	91-33-244-0993
		E-mail:	icwai@myicwai.com
		Web:	www.myicwai.com
Profession:	Accounting		
Membership:	20,000		
Established:	--		

Society of Certified Public Accountants of India

Designation:	Certified Public Accountant	**Address:**	23 Nagarjuna Hills, Punjagutta, Hyderabad 500 082, India
Designatory Letters:	CPA (Certified Public Accountant)		
Profession:	Accounting	**Telephone:**	91-0-2343-0431
Membership:	--	**Fax:**	91-040-5563-9711
Established:	1995	**E-mail:**	info@cpaindia.org
		Web:	www.cpaindia.org

Actuarial Society of India (ASI)

Designation:	Actuary	**Address:**	302 Indian Globe Chambers, 142 Fort Street, Off DN Road, Mumbai – 400 001, India
Designatory Letters:	AASI (Associate of the Actuarial Society of India) FASI (Fellow of the Actuarial Society of India)		
		Telephone:	9122-2269 1051-149
Profession:	Actuarial Science	**Fax:**	9122-2269-1052
Membership:	--	**E-mail:**	actsoc@actuariesindia.org
Established:	1944	**Web:**	www.actuariesindia.org

Society of Certified Investment Bankers

Designation:	Certified Investment Banker	**Address:**	52 Nagarjuna Hills, Punjagutta, Hyderabad 500 082, India
Designatory Letters:	CIB (Certified Investment Banker)		
Profession:	Banking	**Telephone:**	91-40-234-35368
Membership:	--	**Fax:**	91-40-2335-2521
Established:	1999	**E-mail:**	info@scibindia.org
		Web:	www.scibindia.org

International Institute of Islamic Business & Finance

Designation:	Certified Islamic Banker Certified Islamic Investment Analyst Certified Islamic Insurance Professional Postgraduate Diploma in Islamic Finance Postgraduate Diploma in Management	**Address:**	IBF Net (P) Ltd., 329 Shahid Nagar, Bhubaneswar, 751 007, India
		Telephone:	--
		Fax:	--
		E-mail:	info@netversity.org
		Web:	www.netversity.org
Designatory Letters:	CeIB (Certified Islamic Banker) CeIIA (Certified Islamic Investment Analyst) CeIIP (Certified Islamic Insurance Professional) PGDIF (Postgraduate Diploma in Islamic Finance) PGDM (Postgraduate Diploma in Management)		
Profession:	Banking/Finance, Islamic		
Membership:	--		
Established:	--		

The Institute of Company Secretaries

Designation:	Company Secretary	**Address:**	ICSI House, 22 Institutional area, Lodi Road, New Delhi 110003, India
Designatory Letters:	--		
Profession:	Corporate Secretary	**Telephone:**	011-415-04-444-246-17321-24
Membership:	--		
Established:	--	**Fax:**	011-246-262727
		E-mail:	info@icsi.edu
		Web:	www.icsi.edu

Institute for Customer Relationship Management (iCRMA)

Designation:	--	**Address:**	A-402 Ashiana Apartments, Vaishali, Ghaziabad, 201010, India
Designatory Letters:	--		
Profession:	Customer Relationship Management	**Telephone:**	91-120-477-8486
		Fax:	--
Membership:	--	**E-mail:**	--
Established:	--	**Web:**	--

Computer Society of India (CSI)

Designation:	--	**Address:**	122 T.V. Industrial Estate, S.K. Ahire Marg, Worli-Bombay 400 025, India
Designatory Letters:	--		
Profession:	Information Technology	**Telephone:**	91-22-2494-3422
Membership:	--	**Fax:**	91-22-2495-0543
Established:	1965	**E-mail:**	
		Web:	www.csi-india.org

Institute of Certified Risk and Insurance Managers (ICRIM)

Designation:	Certified Risk and Insurance Manager	**Address:**	52 Nagarjuna Hills, Punjagutta, Hyderabad 500 082, India
Designatory Letters:	C-RIM (Certified Risk and Insurance Manager)	**Telephone:**	91-40-335-7071
Profession:	Insurance	**Fax:**	91-40-335-2521
Membership:	--	**E-mail:**	info@icrimindia.org
Established:	2000	**Web:**	www.igie.org

Insurance Institute of India

Designation:	--	**Address:**	Universal Insurance Building, 6th Floor, Sir Pherozshah Mehta Road, Mumbai 400 001, India
Designatory Letters:	AIII (Associate Member of the Insurance Institute of India) FIII (Fellow Member of the Insurance Institute of India)	**Telephone:**	91-022-2287-2923
Profession:	Insurance	**Fax:**	91-022-2287-3491
Membership:	--	**E-mail:**	info@vsnl.in
Established:	1955	**Web:**	www.insuranceinstituteof india.com

Institute of Chartered Financial Analysts of India

Designation:	Chartered Financial Analyst	**Address:**	52 Nagarjuna Hills, Punjagutta, Hyderabad 500 082, Andhra Pradesh, India
Designatory Letters:	CFA (Chartered Financial Analyst)	**Telephone:**	91-40-2343-5368
Profession:	Investment Management	**Fax:**	91-40-2335-2521
Membership:	14,400	**E-mail:**	info@icfai.org
Established:	1984	**Web:**	www.icfai.org

Asia Pacific Institute of Management

Designation:	Post-Graduate Diploma in Business Management	**Address:**	3-4 Institutional Area, Jasola, New Delhi 110025, India
Designatory Letters:	PGDBM (Post-Graduate Diploma in Business Management)	**Telephone:**	91-11-558-05532-800-11-3334
Profession:	Management	**Fax:**	91-11-269-51541
Membership:	--	**E-mail:**	mailtous@pacific.edu
Established:	1996	**Web:**	www.asiapacific.edu

Institute of Management Consultants in India

Designation:	Certified Management Consultant	**Address:**	Centre No. 1, 11th Floor, Unit 2, World Trade Centre, Cuffe Parade, Mumbai 400 005, India
Designatory Letters:	CMC (Certified Management Consultant)		
Profession:	Management Consulting	**Telephone:**	91-22218-5319
Membership:	--	**Fax:**	91-22218-5319
Established:	1963	**E-mail:**	--
		Web:	www.imcindia.com

Indian Institute of Marketing & Management

Designation:	--	**Address:**	Marketing Tower, B-11, Qutab Institutional Area, New Delhi 110016, India
Designatory Letters:	--		
Profession:	Marketing		
Membership:	--	**Telephone:**	11-265-20892
Established:	1979	**Fax:**	11-265-20897
		E-mail:	info@immindia.com
		Web:	www.immindia.com

Project Management Associates

Designation:	--	**Address:**	A-48, Sector 5, Noida 201301, UP, India
Designatory Letters:	--		
Profession:	Project Management	**Telephone:**	91-120-242-0444-0463
Membership:	--	**Fax:**	91-120-242-1484-1482
Established:	1993	**E-mail:**	pma1@vsnl.com
		Web:	www.pma-india.org

Indian Institute of Quality Management

Designation:	Certified Internal Quality Auditor	**Address:**	STQC Directorate, Dept. of Information Technology, Ministry of Communications and Information Technology, Electronics Niketan, 3rd Floor, CGO Complex, Lodi Road, New Delhi 110 003, India
Designatory Letters:	CIQA (Certified Internal Quality Auditor)		
Profession:	Quality Management		
Membership:	--		
Established:	--		
		Telephone:	--
		Fax:	--
		E-mail:	dkgl@inet.gov.in
		Web:	http://stqc.nic.in/stqcnetwork/iiqms.htm

The Association of Certified Treasury Managers (ACTM)

Designation:	--	**Address:**	44 Nagarjuna Hills,
Designatory Letters:	--		Nyderabad, 500 082, India
Profession:	Treasury Management	**Telephone:**	040-335-3748
Membership:	--	**Fax:**	040-335-0193
Established:	--	**E-mail:**	--
		Web:	--

INDONESIA

Indonesian Institute of Accountants

Designation:	--	**Address:**	Graha Akuntan, Jalan
Designatory Letters:	--		Sindanglaya No. 1
Profession:	Accounting		Menteng, Jakarta 10310,
Membership:	--		Indonesia
Established:	--	**Telephone:**	61-021-3190-4232
		Fax:	61-021-724-5078
		E-mail:	iai-info@iaiglobal.or.id
		Web:	--

Persatuan Aktuaris Indonesia

Designation:	--	**Address:**	JL, Kali Besar Timur No.
Designatory Letters:	--		24-25, Jakarta 111110,
Profession:	Actuarial Science		Indonesia
Membership:	--	**Telephone:**	021-6910-438
Established:	1964	**Fax:**	021-6907-610
		E-mail:	--
		Web:	www.aktuaris.org

Yayasan Pendidikan Internal Audit (YPIA)

Designation:	Qualified Internal Auditor	**Address:**	Indonesia
Designatory Letters:	QIA (Qualified Internal Auditor)	**Telephone:**	--
Profession:	Internal Auditing	**Fax:**	--
Membership:	--	**E-mail:**	webmaster@internalauditing.or.id
Established:	--	**Web:**	www.internalauditing.or.id

Indonesian Association of Investment Managers

Designation:	--	**Address:**	Sentra Radio Dalam, Jl
Designatory Letters:	--		Antenna I No. 3,
Profession:	Investment Management		Kabayoran Baru, Jakarta
Membership:	--		Selatan 12140, Indonesia
Established:	--	**Telephone:**	62-21-722-8003
		Fax:	62-21-722-8003
		E-mail:	--
		Web:	www.asaf.org.au/members/

Indonesian Society of Security Analysts

Designation:	--	**Address:**	PT. Bank Dagang Negara
Designatory Letters:	--		(Persaro), BDN Bldg, 3rd
Profession:	Investment Management		Floor, Jl M.H. Thamrin 5,
Membership:	--		Jakarta 10340, Indonesia
Established:	--	**Telephone:**	62-21-230-0350
		Fax:	62-21-230-0826
		E-mail:	--
		Web:	--

Ikatan Nasional Konsultan Indonesia (National Association of Indonesian Consultants)

Designation:	NA	Address:	JL, Bendungan Hilir Raya
Designatory Letters:	NA		No. 29, Jakarta 10210,
Profession:	Management Consulting		Indonesia
Membership:	--	Telephone:	62-21-573-8577
Established:	--	Fax:	62-21-573-3474-5058
		E-mail:	inkindo@inkindo.org
		Web:	www.inkindo.org

Indonesian Marketing Association

Designation:	--	Address:	Wisma Dharmala Sakti, 5th
Designatory Letters:	--		Floor, Jl.Jenderal Sudirman
Profession:	Marketing		Kav.32, Jakarta 10220,
Membership:	--	Telephone:	Indonesia
Established:	1987	Fax:	62-21-251-2238
		E-mail:	62-21-251.2248
		Web:	--

IRAN

Iranian Association of Certified Public Accountants

Designation:	--	Address:	No. 4, 16th Alley, B. Hesary
Designatory Letters:	--		(South Razan) St.,
Profession:	Accounting		Mirdamad Avenue,
Membership:	--		Tehran, Iran.
Established:	--	Telephone:	98-21-226-8935
		Fax:	98-21-227-8878
		E-mail:	info@iacpa.ir
		Web:	www.iacpa.ir

Iranian Institute of Certified Accountants

Designation:	Certified Accountant	Address:	152 Nejatollahi Street,
Designatory Letters:	CA (Certified Accountant)		PO Box 15815-3691,
Profession:	Accounting		Tehran, Iran
Membership:	--	Telephone:	98-21-890-2926
Established:	1972	Fax:	98-21-889-9722
		E-mail:	--
		Web:	www.iranianica.com

Investment Industry Development Association of Iran

Designation:	NA	Address:	Unit 9, No. 36 East Garmsar
Designatory Letters:	NA		Street, South Shiraz Ave.,
Profession:	Investment Management		Molla Sadra Ave.,
Membership:	--		Tehran, Iran
Established:	--	Telephone:	9821-8050-8356
		Fax:	9821-8215-800
		E-mail:	Info@Iran-Invest.org
		Web:	www.Iran-Invest.org

Iranian Institute of Project and Process Management

Designation:	--	Address:	Industrial Engineering Dept.,
Designatory Letters:	--		Sharit University of
Profession:	Project Management		Tehran, Azadi Ave.,
Membership:	--		Tehran, Iran.
Established:	2005	Telephone:	--
		Fax:	--
		E-mail:	--
		Web:	www.ippma.ir

IRAQ

Iraqi Union of Accountants and Auditors

Designation:	--	**Address:**	Union of Accountants and Auditors Bldg., Union Street, Mansoor District, Baghdad, Iraq
Designatory Letters:	--		
Profession:	Accounting		
Membership:	--		
Established:	--	**Telephone:**	964-1-537-5500
		Fax:	964-1-887-3403
		E-mail:	--
		Web:	--

IRELAND

Institute of Accounting Technicians in Ireland (IATI)

Designation:	Accounting Technician	**Address:**	87-89 Pembroke Road, Dublin 4, Ireland
Designatory Letters:	MIATI (Member of the Institute of Accounting Technicians in Ireland)	**Telephone:**	353-1-637-7200
		Fax:	353-1-668-0842
Profession:	Accounting	**E-mail:**	gay.sheehan@iati.ie
Membership:	4,600	**Web:**	www.iati.ie/
Established:	1983		

Institute of Certified Public Accountants in Ireland

Designation:	Certified Public Accountant	**Address:**	9 Ely Place, Dublin 2, Ireland
Designatory Letters:	CPA (Associate Member of the Institute of Certified Public Accountants in Ireland)	**Telephone:**	353-1-676-7353
		Fax:	353-1-661-2367
		E-mail:	cpa@cpaireland.ie
	FCPA (Fellow Member of the Institute of Certified Public Accountants in Ireland)	**Web:**	www.cpaireland.ie
Profession:	Accounting		
Membership:	5,000		
Established:	1943		

Institute of Chartered Accountants in Ireland

Designation:	Chartered Accountant	**Address:**	Chartered Accountants' House, 87-89 Pembroke Road, Dublin 4, Ireland
Designatory Letters:	ACA (Associate Member of the Institute of Chartered Accountants in Ireland)		
		Telephone:	353-1-637-7200
	FCA (Fellow Member of the Institute of Chartered Accountants in Ireland)	**Fax:**	353-1-668-0842
		E-mail:	ca@icai.ie
		Web:	www.icai.ie
Profession:	Accounting		
Membership:	15,000		
Established:	1888		

Institute of Incorporated Public Accountants

Designation:	State Authorized Public Accountant	**Address:**	Abbey Moat House, Abbey St., Naas, Co. Kildare, Ireland
Designatory Letters:	AIPA (Associate Member of the Institute of Incorporated Public Accountants)	**Telephone:**	045-895-936
		Fax:	045-895-830
	FIPA (Fellow Member of the Institute of Incorporated Public Accountants)	**E-mail:**	info@iipa.ie
		Web:	www.iipa.ie
Profession:	Accounting		
Membership:	--		
Established:	1981		

Society of Actuaries in Ireland

Designation:	--	**Address:**	102 Pembroke Road,
Designatory Letters:	--		Dublin 4, Ireland
Profession:	Actuarial Science	**Telephone:**	353-1-660-3064
Membership:	750	**Fax:**	353-1-660-3074
Established:	1972	**E-mail:**	--
		Web:	www.actuaries.ie

The Institute of Bankers in Ireland

Designation:	Certified Banker	**Address:**	1 North Wall Quay, Dublin 1,
	Qualified Financial Adviser		Ireland
Designatory Letters:	CeB (Certified Banker)	**Telephone:**	353-1-611-6500
	QFA (Qualified Financial	**Fax:**	353-1-611-6565
	Adviser)	**E-mail:**	info@bankers.ie
Profession:	Banking	**Web:**	www.bankers.ie
Membership:	22,000		
Established:	1898		

Irish Institute of Credit Management (IICM)

Designation:	--	**Address:**	121 Loer Baggit Street,
Designatory Letters:	--		Dublin 2, Ireland
Profession:	Credit Management	**Telephone:**	353-1-659-9466
Membership:	--	**Fax:**	353-1-659-9401
Established:	--	**E-mail:**	info@iicm.ie
		Web:	www.iicm.ie

Institute of Management Consultants and Advisers (IMCA)

Designation:	Certified Management	**Address:**	329 Gardner House, Walton
	Consultant		Place, Dublin 2, Ireland
Designatory Letters:	CMC (Certified Management	**Telephone:**	01-353-661-6577
	Consultant)	**Fax:**	01-353-704-8598
Profession:	Management Consulting	**E-mail:**	info@imca.ie
Membership:	--	**Web:**	www.imca.ie
Established:	2006 (Merger of the Institute of		
	Management Consultants		
	established in 1980 and the		
	Republic of Ireland Branch of		
	the Institute of Business		
	Advisers)		

Irish Computer Society

Designation:	--	**Address:**	Crescent Hall, Mount Street
Designatory Letters:	--		Crescent, Dublin 2, Ireland
Profession:	Information Technology	**Telephone:**	353-1-644-7840
Membership:	--	**Fax:**	353-1-662-0224
Established:	--	**E-mail:**	info@ics.ie
		Web:	www.ics.ie

The Marketing Institute of Ireland

Designation:	--	**Address:**	South County Business Park, Leopardstown, Dublin 18, Ireland
Designatory Letters:	MMII (Member of the Marketing Institute of Ireland)		
	MMII Grad (Graduate Member of the Marketing Institute of Ireland)	**Telephone:**	353-1-295-2355
		Fax:	353-1-295-2453
		E-mail:	info@mii.ie
Profession:	Marketing	**Web:**	www.mii.ie
Membership:	3,500		
Established:	--		

Institute of Project Management of Ireland

Designation:	Certified Project Management Associate	**Address:**	23 Upper Mont Street, Dublin 2, Ireland
	Certified Project Manager	**Telephone:**	01-661-4677
	Certified Senior Project Manager	**Fax:**	01-661-3588
	Certified Project Director	**E-mail:**	info@projectmanagement.ie
Designatory Letters:	CPMA (Certified Project Management Associate)	**Web:**	www.projectmanagement.ie
	CPM (Certified Project Manager)		
	CSPM (Certified Senior Project Manager)		
	CPD (Certified Project Director)		
Profession:	Project Management		
Membership:	--		
Established:	1989		

Irish Association of Corporate Treasurers

Designation:	--	**Address:**	19 Fitzwilliam Place, Dublin 2, Ireland
Designatory Letters:	--		
Profession:	Treasury Management	**Telephone:**	353-676-9411
Membership:	300	**Fax:**	353-676-9415
Established:	1986	**E-mail:**	info@treasurers.ie
		Web:	www.treasurers.ie

ISRAEL

Institute of Certified Public Accountants in Israel

Designation:	Certified Public Accountant	**Address:**	20 Shefer Street, Tel Aviv 65166, Israel
Designatory Letters:	CPA (Certified Public Accountant)	**Telephone:**	972-3-516-1114
Profession:	Accounting	**Fax:**	972-3-510-3105
Membership:	--	**E-mail:**	iris-o@icpas.org.il
Established:	--	**Web:**	www.icpa.org.il

Israel Association of Actuaries (IAA)

Designation:	Actuary	**Address:**	1 Goldberg Street, Tel Aviv 65784, Israel
Designatory Letters:	FILAA (Fellow of the Israel Association of Actuaries)	**Telephone:**	972-3-5661155
Profession:	Actuarial Science	**Fax:**	972-3-5661177
Membership:	--	**E-mail:**	--
Established:	1946	**Web:**	www.actuaries.org.il

IPA - Information Technology Association of Israel

Designation:	--	**Address:**	PO Box 50006, Tel Aviv
Designatory Letters:	--		61500, Israel
Profession:	Information Technology	**Telephone:**	972-3-514-0503
Membership:	--	**Fax:**	972-3-514-0077
Established:	--	**E-mail:**	moshe.gottlieb@mail.biu.ac.il
		Web:	www.ifip.or.at/members/israel

ITALY

Consiglio Nazionale Dei Dottori Commercialisti

Designation:	Dott. - Dottore Commercialista [Used before an individual's name]	**Address:**	Piazza della Repubblica 59, 00185 Roma, Italy
Designatory Letters:	--	**Telephone:**	39-06-47-86-3310
Profession:	Accounting	**Fax:**	39-06-47-86-3349
Membership:	--	**E-mail:**	morano@consiglio.cndc.it
Established:	1952	**Web:**	www1.cndc.it

Consiglio Nazionale dei Ragionieri e Periti Commerciali

Designation:	--	**Address:**	Via Paisiello 24, 00198
Designatory Letters:	--		Roma, Italy
Profession:	Accounting	**Telephone:**	39-06-8523.6341-2
Membership:	--	**Fax:**	39-06-841-7829
Established:	--	**E-mail:**	estero@consrag.it
		Web:	www.consrag.it

Organismo Italiano di Contabilità (OIC)

Designation:	--	**Address:**	Via Poli, 29 00187 Roma,
Designatory Letters:	--		Italy
Profession:	Accounting	**Telephone:**	39-06-697-6681
Membership:	--	**Fax:**	39-06-697-683
Established:	--	**E-mail:**	--
		Web:	www.fondazioncoic.it

Instituto Italiano degli Attuari (Italian Institute of Actuaries)

Designation:	--	**Address:**	Milano, Italy
Designatory Letters:	--	**Telephone:**	--
Profession:	Actuarial Science	**Fax:**	--
Membership:	--	**E-mail:**	--
Established:	1897	**Web:**	www.italian-actuaries.org

Associazione Italiana per l'Informatica ed il Calcolo Automatico (A.I.C.A.)

Designation:	--	**Address:**	Piazzale R. Morandi, 2,
Designatory Letters:	--		1-20121 Milan, Italy
Profession:	Information Technology	**Telephone:**	39-02-760-14082
Membership:	--	**Fax:**	39-02-760-15717
Established:	--	**E-mail:**	aica@aicanet.it
		Web:	www.aicanet.it

Associazione Italiana degli Analisti Finanziari (AIAF)

Designation:	--	**Address:**	Via Dante 9, I-20123,
Designatory Letters:	--		Milan 6, Italy
Profession:	Investment Management	**Telephone:**	39-2-7202-3500
Membership:	--	**Fax:**	39-2-7202-3652
Established:	--	**E-mail:**	info@aiaf.it
		Web:	www.aiaf.it

Associazione Fra Società e Studi di Consulenza di Direzione e Organizzazione Aziendale (ASSCO)

Designation:	--	**Address:**	Piazza Velasca 6, I-20122
Designatory Letters:	--		Milan Italy
Profession:	Management Consulting	**Telephone:**	39-02-866-686
Membership:	--	**Fax:**	39-02-890-12750
Established:	--	**E-mail:**	assoconsult@fastwebnet.it
		Web:	www.assoconsult.org

Associazione Professionale dei Consultenti di Direzione e Organizzazione Aziendale (APCO)

Designation:	--	**Address:**	Corso Venezia, 49, 20121
Designatory Letters:	--		Milano, Italy
Profession:	Management Consulting	**Telephone:**	392-775-0449
Membership:	--	**Fax:**	392-775-0480
Established:	1968	**E-mail:**	info@apcoitalia.it
		Web:	www.apcoitalia.it

Associazione Nazionale di Impiantistica Industride

Designation:	--	**Address:**	Corso Venezia 18, Milano
Designatory Letters:	--		20121, Italy
Profession:	Project Management	**Telephone:**	39-2-76-008755
Membership:	--	**Fax:**	39-2-78-4374
Established:	--	**E-mail:**	--
		Web:	--

Associazione Italiana Tesrieri d'Impresa-AITI (Italian Association of Corporate Treasurers)

Designation:	--	**Address:**	c/o Cino Ricci, Via Lanzone
Designatory Letters:	--		36, 20123 Milano, Italy
Profession:	Treasury Management	**Telephone:**	39-335-207-468
Membership:	--	**Fax:**	--
Established:	--	**E-mail:**	aiti@aiti.it
		Web:	www.aiti.it

IVORY COAST

Ordre des Experts Comptables et Comptables Agréés de Côte d'Ivoire

Designation:	--	**Address:**	7, Rue des Avodirés, 01 BP
Designatory Letters:	--		8671, Abidjan 01, Ivory
Profession:	Accounting		Coast
Membership:	--	**Telephone:**	225-21 14 59
Established:	--	**Fax:**	225-22 55 49
		E-mail:	--
		Web:	--

Institute des Actuaires de Côte d'Ivoire (Institute of Actuaries of Côte d'Ivoire)
(See International Actuarial Association in Appendix A)

Designation:	--	**Address:**	--
Designatory Letters:	--	**Telephone:**	--
Profession:	Actuarial Science	**Fax:**	--
Membership:	--	**E-mail:**	--
Established:	1999	**Web:**	--

J

JAMAICA

Institute of Chartered Accountants of Jamaica

Designation:	Chartered Accountant	**Address:**	8 Ruthven Road, Kingston 10, Jamaica
Designatory Letters:	ACA (Associate Member of the Institute of Chartered Accountants of Jamaica)	**Telephone:**	876-929-5869
		Fax:	876-929-6082
		E-mail:	icaj@cwjamaica.com
	FCA (Fellow Member of the Institute of Chartered Accountants of Jamaica)	**Web:**	www.icaj.org
Profession:	Accounting		
Membership:	880		
Established:	1965		

Caribbean Actuarial Association (CAA)

Designation:	NA	**Address:**	39A Gordon St., Port of Spain, Trinidad & Tobago
Designatory Letters:	NA		
Profession:	Actuarial Science	**Telephone:**	868-623-5000
Membership:	--	**Fax:**	868-625-8108
Established:	1991	**E-mail:**	president@caa.com
		Web:	www.caa.com.bb

JAPAN

Financial Accounting Standards Foundation (FASF)

Designation:	NA	**Address:**	--
Designatory Letters:	NA Accounting Standards Board of Japan	**Telephone:**	--
		Fax:	--
		E-mail:	--
Profession:	Accounting	**Web:**	www.asb.or.jp
Membership:	--		
Established:	--		

Japan Federation of Certified Public Tax Accountants' Association (JFCPTA)

Designation:	Certified Public Tax Accountant	**Address:**	4F Toshiba Building, 1-1-1 Sibaura, Minato-ku, Tokyo 105, Japan
Designatory Letters:	CPTA (Certified Public Tax Accountant)	**Telephone:**	81-3-3798-0031
Profession:	Accounting	**Fax:**	81-3-3798-0037
Membership:	--	**E-mail:**	--
Established:	--	**Web:**	--

The Japanese Institute of Certified Public Accountants

Designation:	Certified Public Accountant	**Address:**	4-4-1,Kudan-Minami, Chiyoda-ku,
Designatory Letters:	CPA (Certified Public Accountant)	**Telephone:**	Tokyo 102-8264, Japan
		Fax:	81-3-3515-1130
Profession:	Accounting	**E-mail:**	81-3-5226-3356
Membership:	22,700	**Web:**	international@jicpa.or.jp
Established:	1948		www.jicpa.or.jp

The Institute of Actuaries of Japan (IAJ)

Designation:	--	**Address:**	Daiya Shinbashi, Building 8F,
Designatory Letters:	--		1-10-7 Shinbashi, Minato--ku,
Profession:	Actuarial Science		Tokyo 105-0004, Japan
Membership:	--	**Telephone:**	813-3571-0887
Established:	1899	**Fax:**	813-3571-0892
		E-mail:	iaj96@bekkoame.ne.jp
		Web:	www.actuaries.jp

Japanese Society of Certified Pension Actuaries (JSCPA)

Designation:	Certified Pension Actuary	**Address:**	Tokyo, Japan
Designatory Letters:	CPA (Certified Pension Actuary)	**Telephone:**	--
		Fax:	--
Profession:	Actuarial Science	**E-mail:**	secretary@jscpa.or.jp
Membership:	--	**Web:**	www.jscpa.or.jp
Established:	1989		

Information Processing Society of Japan (IPSJ)

Designation:	--	**Address:**	4F Kagaku-Kaikan (Chemistry
Designatory Letters:	--		Hall), 1-5 Kanda-Surugadai,
Profession:	Information Technology		Chiyoda-ku, Tokyo 101-8307,
Membership:	21,000		Japan
Established:	--	**Telephone:**	81-3-3518-8374
		Fax:	81-3-3518-8375
		E-mail:	ayukawa@ipsj.or.jp
		Web:	www.ipsj.or.jp

The Institute of Internal Auditors—Japan

Designation:	Qualified Internal Auditor	**Address:**	3F Sankyo Bldg. 2-7-12 Tsukiji
Designatory Letters:	QIA (Qualified Internal Auditor)		Cho-Ku, Tokyo 104-0045, Japan
		Telephone:	81-3-3542-7571
Profession:	Internal Auditing	**Fax:**	81-3-3542-7584
Membership:	--	**E-mail:**	info@iiajapan.com
Established:	1957	**Web:**	www.iiajapan.com

The Security Analysts Association of Japan (SAAJ)

Designation:	Member of the The Security Analysts Association of Japan	Address:	5F Tokyo Stock Exchange Building, 2-1 Nihonbashi Kabutocho, Chuo-Ku, Tokyo 103-0026, Japan
Designatory Letters:	SAAJ (Member of the Security Analysts Association of Japan)	Telephone:	81-3-3666-7866
		Fax:	81-3-3666-5845
Profession:	Investment Management	E-mail:	asaf-manager@saa.or.jp
Membership:	--	Web:	www.asaf.org.au
Established:	--		

Zen-Noh-Ren (All Japan Federation of Management Organisations)

Designation:	NA	Address:	Kindai Building 6F 12-5, Kohimachi, 3Chome, Chiyoda-Ku, Tokyo 102-0083, Japan
Designatory Letters:	NA		
Profession:	Management		
Membership:	--	Telephone:	81-3-3221-5051
Established:	1949	Fax:	81-3-3221-5054
		E-mail:	imcj@zen-noh-ren.or.jp
		Web:	www.zen-noh-ren.or.jp

Japan Marketing Association

Designation:	NA	Address:	9th Floor, Yamada Building, 3-5-27 Roppongi, Tokyo 106, Japan
Designatory Letters:	NA		
Profession:	Marketing	Telephone:	81-03-5875-2101
Membership:	--	Fax:	81-03-5575-0626
Established:	1957	E-mail:	jma02@jma-jp.org
		Web:	www.jma-jp.org

Japan Project Management Forum

Designation:	--	Address:	CYD Bldg., 4-5, Nishi-Shimbahi, I-Chrome, Minato-ku, Tokyo, 105-0003, Japan
Designatory Letters:	--		
Profession:	Project Management		
Membership:	--	Telephone:	81-3-3502-4441
Established:	--	Fax:	81-3-3502-5500
		E-mail:	--
		Web:	--

Japan Association for CFO (JACFO)

Designation:	--	Address:	102-0093 Shiozaki Building 2-7-1, Hirakawacho, Choyoda-ku, Tokyo, Japan
Designatory Letters:	--		
Profession:	Treasury Management		
Membership:	--	Telephone:	813-3556-2334
Established:	--	Fax:	--
		E-mail:	info@cfo.co.jp
		Web:	www.cfo.jp

JORDAN

Arab Society of Certified Accountants

Designation:	Arab Certified Professional Accountant	**Address:**	German-Jordanian University, Talal Abu Ghazaleh College of Business, Mecca Street, Amman or PO Box 922104, Amman1192, Jordan
Designatory Letters:	ASPA (Associate of the Arab Society of Certified Professional Accountants) FSPA (Fellow of the Arab Society of Certified Professional Accountants)	**Telephone:** **Fax:** **E-mail:** **Web:**	962-6-550-9101 62-6-550-9100 info@ascasociety.org www.ascasociety.org
Profession:	Accounting		
Membership:	1,256		
Established:	1983		

Jordanian Association of Certified Public Accountants

Designation:	Jordanian Certified Public Accountant	**Address:** **Telephone:**	Shmeisani, PO Box 927267, Amman 11110, Jordan
Designatory Letters:	JCPA (Jordanian Certified Public Accountant)	**Fax:** **E-mail:** **Web:**	962-6-566-9916-8 962-6-5687-610 jacapa@go.com.jo
Profession:	Accounting		--
Membership:	--		
Established:	--		

Institute of Management Consultants of Jordan

Designation:	Certified Management Consultant	**Address:**	PO Box 926550, Amman 1111, Jordan
Designatory Letters:	CMC (Certified Management Consultant)	**Telephone:** **Fax:** **E-mail:**	962-6-553-0856/7 62-6-553-0858 imc@go.com.jo
Profession:	Management Consulting	**Web:**	ww.imc.com.jo
Membership:	--		
Established:	1995		

K

KAMPUCHEA

Institute of Certified Public Accountants and Auditors of Kampuchea (KICPAA)

Designation:	--	**Address:**	273 Preah Ang Duong (crossing of Streets 67 and 110), Sangkat Wat, Phnom, Khan Daun Penh, Phnom Penh, Kampuchea
Designatory Letters:	--		
Profession:	Accounting		
Membership:	--		
Established:	2002	**Telephone:**	855-23-990-664
		Fax:	855-23-991-037
		E-mail:	kicpaa@kicpaa.org
		Web:	www.kicpaa.org

KAZAKHSTAN

Chamber of Auditors of the Republic of Kazakhstan

Designation:	--	**Address:**	Microregion 6, Building 56a, Almaty 480036, Kazakhstan
Designatory Letters:	--		
Profession:	Accounting	**Telephone:**	7-3272-285-744
Membership:	--	**Fax:**	7-3272-285-744
Established:	--	**E-mail:**	--
		Web:	www.audit.kz

Kazakhstan Project Management Institute

Designation:	--	**Address:**	Auezova Street 82, Office 510, Kazakhstan 050008
Designatory Letters:	--		
Profession:	Project Management	**Telephone:**	7-3272-423-877
Membership:	--	**Fax:**	7-3272-423-877
Established:	--	**E-mail:**	prom@intelsoft.kz
		Web:	www.kpma.kz

KENYA

Institute of Certified Public Accountants of Kenya

Designation:	Certified Public Accountant	**Address:**	CPA Centre, Ruaraka Thika Road, PO Box 59963, Nairobi, Kenya
Designatory Letters:	CPA (Kenya) (Member of the Institute of Certified Public Accountants of Kenya)	**Telephone:**	254-2-802635, 802636,860930,862768
	FCPA (Kenya) (Fellow of the Institute of Certified Public Accountants of Kenya)	**Fax:**	254-2-862-206
		E-mail:	icpak@icpak.com
		Web:	www.icpak.com
Profession:	Accounting		
Membership:	--		
Established:	1978		

Association of Project Management Kenya

Designation:	--	**Address:**	Professional Centre, St. John's Gate, Parliament Road, PO Box 72643-00200, Nairobi, Kenya
Designatory Letters:	--		
Profession:	Project Management		
Membership:	--	**Telephone:**	254-2-222-119
Established:	--	**Fax:**	254-2-341-883
		E-mail:	--
		Web:	www.apmapseac.org

KOREA (NORTH)

Pyongyang Office of Auditors of the Democratic Peoples Republic of Korea

Designation:	NA	**Address:**	Saemaul 1-dong, Pyongchon District, Pyongyang, DPR of Korea
Designatory Letters:	NA		
Profession:	Accounting		
Membership:	--	**Telephone:**	850-218-117 ext 8568
Established:	1976	**Fax:**	850-238-4410
		E-mail:	defmof@co.chesin.com
		Web:	--

KOREA (SOUTH)

Korean Institute of Certified Public Accountants

Designation:	Certified Public Accountant	**Address:**	KICPA Building, 185-10 Chungjongno 2Ga, Seodaemun-Ku, 120-012, Seoul, Korea
Designatory Letters:	CPA (Certified Public Accountant)	**Telephone:**	82-2-3149-0100
Profession:	Accounting	**Fax:**	82-2-3149-0340
Membership:	--	**E-mail:**	global@kicpa.or.kr
Established:	--	**Web:**	www.kicpa.or.kr

The Korean Actuarial Association (KAA)

Designation:	--	**Address:**	c/o the Insurance Supervisory Board, 35-53 Tongeui-Dong, Chongro-ku, Seoul, Korea
Designatory Letters:	--		
Profession:	Actuarial Science		
Membership:	--	**Telephone:**	02-782-7440
Established:	1963	**Fax:**	--
		E-mail:	actuary@actuary.or.kr
		Web:	www.actuary.or.kr

Korea Information Science Society (KISS)

Designation:	--	**Address:**	Room 401, Meorijae Bldg., 984-1, Bangbae-3 dong, Seocho-gu, Seoul 137 849, Korea
Designatory Letters:	--		
Profession:	Information Technology		
Membership:	--	**Telephone:**	82-2-588-9246
Established:	--	**Fax:**	82-2-521-1352
		E-mail:	kiss@kiss.or.kr
		Web:	--

The Korea Certified Investment Analysts Association

Designation:	--	**Address:**	45-2 Youido-dong, Youngdungpo-gu, Seoul 15-0974, Korea
Designatory Letters:	--		
Profession:	Investment Management	**Telephone:**	82-2-784-1865
Membership:	--	**Fax:**	82-2-782-3314
Established:	--	**E-mail:**	ksaacho@hanmail.net
		Web:	kciaa.or.kr

Korea Marketing Association

Designation:	--	**Address:**	45 4-GA, Namdaemoon-Ro, Chung-
Designatory Letters:	--		ku, Seoul 100-743, Korea
Profession:	Marketing	**Telephone:**	82-2-779-3581-753-5011
Membership:	--	**Fax:**	82-2-752-8074
Established:	1965	**E-mail:**	--
		Web:	--

Korean Institute of Project Management & Technology

Designation:	--	**Address:**	Korean Power Engineering Co., Inc.,
Designatory Letters:	--		87 Samson-Dong, Kangnam –GU,
Profession:	Project Management		Seoul, Korea 135-090
Membership:	--	**Telephone:**	--
Established:	--	**Fax:**	--
		E-mail:	promat@promat.org
		Web:	www.promat.org

KOSOVO

Society of Certified Acountants and Auditors of Kosovo (SCAAK)

Designation:	--	**Address:**	65 Sylejman Vokshi No. 14,
Designatory Letters:	--		Pristina, Kosovo
Profession:	Accounting	**Telephone:**	381-38-249-043
Membership:	--	**Fax:**	381-38-249-043
Established:	--	**E-mail:**	ardiana@scaak-ks.org
		Web:	www.scaak-ks.org

KYRGYSTAN

Union of Accountants and Auditors of Kyrgyzstan

Designation:	--	**Address:**	69 Kievskaya St., Room #6,
Designatory Letters:	--		Bishkeke 720001, Kyrgyzstan
Profession:	Accounting	**Telephone:**	996-312-664-844, 661-085,
Membership:	--		780-583
Established:	--	**Fax:**	996-312-664-844
		E-mail:	oba99@oba.kg
		Web:	www.oba.kg

KUWAIT

Kuwait Association of Accountants and Auditors

Designation:	--	**Address:**	PO Box 22472, Safat-Code No.
Designatory Letters:	--		13085, Kuwait
Profession:	Accounting	**Telephone:**	965-484-1662
Membership:	--	**Fax:**	965-483-6012
Established:	--	**E-mail:**	--
		Web:	www.kse.org.kw

Kuwait Project Management Certification Body

Designation:	--	**Address:**	--
Designatory Letters:	--	**Telephone:**	--
Profession:	Project Management	**Fax:**	--
Membership:	--	**E-mail:**	--
Established:	--	**Web:**	www.kse.org.kw

L

LAOS

Laos Institute of Certified Public Accountants (LICPA)

Designation:	Certified Public Accountant	**Address:**	--
Designatory Letters:	CPA (Certified Public Accountant)		
Profession:	Accounting	**Telephone:**	--
Membership:	--	**Fax:**	--
Established:	--	**E-mail:**	--
		Web:	--

LATVIA

Latvijas Aktuaru Asociacija

Designation:	--	**Address:**	Riga, Latvia
Designatory Letters:	--	**Telephone:**	--
Profession:	Actuarial Science	**Fax:**	--
Membership:	--	**E-mail:**	--
Established:	1997	**Web:**	--

Latvian Association of Certified Auditors

Designation:	--	**Address:**	Dzirnavu eila 147/2, Riga, LV-1050, Latvia
Designatory Letters:	LZRA		
Profession:	Auditing	**Telephone:**	371-722-3338
Membership:	280	**Fax:**	371-722-3339
Established:	1994	**E-mail:**	ksl@lzra.lv
		Web:	www.lzra.lv/en

Latvia Association of Business Consultants (LABC)

Designation:	--	**Address:**	Riga, Latvia
Designatory Letters:	--	**Telephone:**	--
Profession:	Management Consulting	**Fax:**	3717-279-808
Membership:	--	**E-mail:**	lbka@lbka.lv
Established:	--	**Web:**	www.lbka.lv

Latvian National Project Management Association

Designation:	--	**Address:**	Riga, Latvia
Designatory Letters:	--	**Telephone:**	--
Profession:	Project Management	**Fax:**	--
Membership:	--	**E-mail:**	--
Established:	--	**Web:**	--

LEBANON

Lebanese Association of Certified Public Accountants (LACPA)

Designation:	Certified Public Accountant	**Address:**	Museum Region, Hotel Dieu Street, Mathaf Commercial Center, LACPA Building, 1st Floor, PO Box 11-5821, Beirut, Lebanon
Designatory Letters:	CPA (Certified Public Accountant)		
Profession:	Accounting	**Telephone:**	961-1-366-161, 961-1-616-013
Membership:	1,591	**Fax:**	961-1-616-013
Established:	1994	**E-mail:**	lacpa@sodetel.net.lb
		Web:	www.lacpa.org.lb

Middle East Society of Associated Accountants

Designation:	--	**Address:**	Hamra Street-Ras Beirut, Strand Building, 2nd Floor, Beirut, Lebanon
Designatory Letters:	--		
Profession:	Accounting		
Membership:	--	**Telephone:**	961-1-344-437
Established:	--	**Fax:**	961-1-349-060
		E-mail:	gsa@gsaweida.com
		Web:	--

Lebanese Association of Actuaries

Designation:	--	**Address:**	Beirut, Lebanon
Designatory Letters:	--	**Telephone:**	--
Profession:	Actuarial Science	**Fax:**	--
Membership:	--	**E-mail:**	--
Established:	2001	**Web:**	--

The Muhanna Foundation

Designation:	--	**Address:**	1501 Gefinor Center, Beirut, Lebanon
Designatory Letters:	--		
Profession:	Actuarial Science	**Telephone:**	9611-751-290
Membership:	--	**Fax:**	9611-751-292
Established:	--	**E-mail:**	--
		Web:	www.muhanna.org/

LESOTHO

Lesotho Institute of Accountants

Designation:	--	**Address:**	5 Orden Road, Canada House, Old Europa, Maseru 100, Lesotho
Designatory Letters:	TA (L) (Technician Accountant of Lesotho)		
	GA (L) (General Accountant of Lesotho)	**Telephone:**	266-312-115
		Fax:	266-320-022
	CA (L) (Chartered Accountant of Lesotho)	**E-mail:**	lia@lia.org.ls
		Web:	www.lia.org.ls
Profession:	Accounting		
Membership:	230		
Established:	1978		

LIBERIA

The Liberian Institute of Certified Public Accountants

Designation:	Certified Public Accountant	**Address:**	Kings Building – 2nd Floor, Broad Street, Monrovia, Liberia
Designatory Letters:	CPA (Certified Public Accountant)		
Profession:	Accounting	**Telephone:**	231-227-617
Membership:	--	**Fax:**	231-227-617
Established:	--	**E-mail:**	--
		Web:	--

LIBYA

Libyan Certified and Public Accountants Union

Designation:	--	**Address:**	PO Box No. 1633, Benghazi, Libya
Designatory Letters:	--		
Profession:	Accounting	**Telephone:**	218-61-222-8219-222-1453
Membership:	--	**Fax:**	218-61-223-9365
Established:	--	**E-mail:**	--
		Web:	--

LITHUANIA

Lithuanian Chamber of Auditors

Designation:	Atestuotas Auditorius or Certified Auditor	**Address:**	J. Galvydzio St. 5-104, Vilnius, LT-08236, Lithuania
Designatory Letters:	VAA (Auditoriaus pažymejimas or Auditor's Certificate)	**Telephone:**	370-5-274-5424
		Fax:	370-5-274-5423
		E-mail:	lar@lar.lt
Profession:	Auditing	**Web:**	www.lar.lt
Membership:	402		
Established:	2000		

Lithuanian Computer Society

Designation:	--	**Address:**	A. Gostauto 12-211, LT-2600, Vilnius, Lithuania
Designatory Letters:	--		
Profession:	Information Technology	**Telephone:**	370-5-262-0536
Membership:	--	**Fax:**	370-5-261-9905
Established:	--	**E-mail:**	liks@liks.lt
		Web:	www.liks.lt

LUXEMBOURG

Institut des Réviseurs d'Entreprises

Designation:	--	**Address:**	68 Avenue de la Liberté, B.P. 2056, L-1020, Luxembourg
Designatory Letters:	--		
Profession:	Accounting	**Telephone:**	352-29.11.39
Membership:	--	**Fax:**	352-29.13.34
Established:	--	**E-mail:**	--
		Web:	www.ire.lu

Ordre des Experts Comptables Luxembourgeois

Designation:	--	**Address:**	L-1615 7 Street Alcide de Gasperi, Luxembourg
Designatory Letters:	--		
Profession:	Accounting	**Telephone:**	352-29-1333
Membership:	--	**Fax:**	352-29-1334
Established:	1951	**E-mail:**	--
		Web:	www.oec.lu

The Luxembourg Society of Portfolio Managers and Financial Analysts

Designation:	--	**Address:**	c/o Foyer Patrimonium & Associates S.A., 46 rue Léon Laval, L-3372 Leudelange, Luxembourg
Designatory Letters:	--		
Profession:	Investment Management		
Membership:	--		
Established:	--	**Telephone:**	352-437-43-6012
		Fax:	352-2644-0307
		E-mail:	dub@fpa.lu
		Web:	www.algafi.lu

Association des Trésoriers d'Entreprises à Luxembourg (ATEL) (Luxembourg Association of Corporate Treasurers)

Designation:	--	**Address:**	c/o CLT-UFA, 45, Boulevard Pierre Fieden, L-1543 Luxembourg
Designatory Letters:	--		
Profession:	Treasury Management		
Membership:	--	**Telephone:**	352-4388-1602
Established:	--	**Fax:**	352-42-9382
		E-mail:	--
		Web:	--

M

MACEDONIA

Association of Accountants, Financial Experts and Auditors of the Republic of Macedonia

Designation:	--	**Address:**	ul. Crvena opstina, bb, Skopje
Designatory Letters:	--		91000, Macedonia
Profession:	Accounting	**Telephone:**	99-389-2311-4791
Membership:	--	**Fax:**	99-389-2321-4791
Established:	--	**E-mail:**	--
		Web:	--

MADAGASCAR

Ordre des Experts Comptables et Financiers et des Comptables Agréés de Madagascar

Designation:	--	**Address:**	10, Rue Patrice Lumumba, B.P.
Designatory Letters:	--		8737, Antananarivo 101,
Profession:	Accounting		Madagascar
Membership:	--	**Telephone:**	261-20-22-222-4485
Established:	--	**Fax:**	261-20-22-66343
		E-mail:	oeccam@dts.mg
		Web:	--

MALAWI

Public Accountants Examination Council of Malawi

Designation:	NA	**Address:**	PO Box 2271, Blantyre, Malawi
Designatory Letters:	NA	**Telephone:**	--
Profession:	Accounting	**Fax:**	--
Membership:	--	**E-mail:**	--
Established:	--	**Web:**	--

The Society of Accountants in Malawi

Designation:	Certified Public Accountant of Malawi	**Address:**	Stansfield House, Haile Selassie Road, Blantyre, Malawi
Designatory Letters:	CPA(M) (Certified Public Accountant of Malawi)	**Telephone:**	265-620-301
		Fax:	265-624-312
Profession:	Accounting	**E-mail:**	--
Membership:	--	**Web:**	--
Established:	1969		

MALAYSIA

Institute of Commercial and Industrial Accountants

Designation:	Certified Commercial and Industrial Accountant	**Address:**	Kompleks Mutiara (Level 8), 3½ mileJalan Ipoh, 51200 Kuala Lumpur, Malaysia
Designatory Letters:	ACIA (Associate Member of the Institute of Commercial and Industrial Accountants)	**Telephone:** **Fax:** **E-mail:** **Web:**	60-3-6257-2930 603-6257-3935 secretariat@icia.org.my www.icia.org.my
	FCIA (Fellow Member of the Institute of Commercial and Industrial Accountants)		
Profession:	Accounting		
Membership:	--		
Established:	--		

Malaysian Accounting Standards Board

Designation:	NA	**Address:**	Suites 501-503, 5th Floor, 338 Jalan Tuanku, Abdul Rahman, 50100 Kuala Lumpur, Malaysia
Designatory Letters:	NA		
Profession:	Accounting		
Established:	1997	**Telephone:**	603-2715-9199
		Fax:	603-2715-9212
		E-mail:	masb@masb.org.my
		Web:	www.masb.org.my

Malaysian Institute of Accountants

Designation:	--	**Address:**	Dewan Akauntan, No. 2 Jalan tun Sambanthan 3, Brickfields, 50470 Kuala Lumpur, Malaysia
Designatory Letters:	C.A. (M) (Chartered Accountant of Malaysia)		
	L.A. (M) (Licensed Accountant of Malaysia)	**Telephone:**	60-3-2279-9200
	R.A. (M) (Registered Accountant of Malaysia)	**Fax:** **E-mail:** **Web:**	60-3-2274-1783 mia@mia.org.my www.mia.org.my
	P.A. (M) (Public Accountant of Malaysia)		
Profession:	Accounting		
Membership:	--		
Established:	1967		

Malaysian Institute of Certified Public Accountants

Designation:	Certified Public Accountant	**Address:**	No. 15 Jalan Medan Tuanku, 50300 Kuala Lumpur, Malaysia
Designatory Letters:	CPA (Certified Public Accountant)	**Telephone:** **Fax:**	60-3-269-89622 60-3-269-89403
Profession:	Accounting	**E-mail:**	--
Membership:	--	**Web:**	www.micpa.com.my
Established:	1958		

Actuarial Society of Malaysia (ASM) Persatuan Aktuari Malaysia

Designation:	--	**Address:**	c/o Actuarial Department, ING Insurance Berhad, Menara ING, 84 Jalan Raja Chulan, 50200 Kuala Lumpur, Malaysia
Designatory Letters:	--		
Profession:	Actuarial Science	**Telephone:**	603-2056-2757
Membership:	225	**Fax:**	603-2056-2791
Established:	1978	**E-mail:**	secretary@actuaries.org.my
		Web:	www.actuaries.org.my

Malaysian Association of The Institute of Chartered Secretaries and Administrators (MAICSA)

Designation:	Chartered Secretary	**Address:**	No. 57 The Boulevard, Mid Valley City, Lingkaran Syed Putra, Malaysia
Designatory Letters:	ACIS (Associate Member of the Institute of Chartered Secretaries and Administrators)	**Telephone:**	603-2282-9276
		Fax:	603-2282-9281
		E-mail:	maicsa@maicsa.org.my
	FCIS (Fellow Member of the Institute of Chartered Secretaries and Administrators)	**Web:**	www.maicsa.org.my
Profession:	Corporate Governance		
Membership:	--		
Established:	--		

Institute for Customer Relationship Management (iCRM)

Designation:	--	**Address:**	Sdn.Bhd., Ste 3A-3, Level 3, Block 3A, Plaza Sentral, Jalan StesenSentral 5, 50470 Kuala Lumpur, Malaysia
Designatory Letters:	--		
Profession:	Customer Relationship Management		
Membership:			
Established:	--	**Telephone:**	603-2267-3399
	--	**Fax:**	603-2272-1830
		E-mail:	--
		Web:	www.institutecrm.com

Malaysian National Computer Confederation

Designation:	NA	**Address:**	Unit 916, 9th Floor, Block A, Damansara Intan No. 1, Jalan SS20/27, 47400 Petaling Jaya, Malaysia
Designatory Letters:	NA		
Profession:	Information Technology	**Telephone:**	603-7118-3040
Membership:	--	**Fax:**	603-7118-2930
Established:	--	**E-mail:**	admin@mncc.po.my
		Web:	www.mncc.com.my

Institute of Internal Auditors–Malaysia (IIA--Malaysia)

Designation:	--	**Address:**	160-3-3 Komplexs Maluri, Jalan Jejaka, Taman Maluri, Charas, 55100 Kuala Lumpur, Malaysia.
Designatory Letters:	AIIA (Associate Member of the Institute of Internal Auditors--Malaysia)		
		Telephone:	603-9282-1148-7750, 9200-8897
		Fax:	603-9282-8897
	CMIIA (Chartered Member of the Institute of Internal Auditors--Malaysia)	**E-mail:**	ijdm@po.jaring.my
		Web:	www.iiam.com.my
	CFIIA (Chartered Fellow of the Institute of Internal Auditors--Malaysia)		
Profession:	Internal Auditing		
Membership:	--		
Established:	1977		

Research Institute of Investment Analysts

Designation:	--	**Address:**	Ground Floor, Exchange Square, off Jalan Samantan, Damansara Height, 50490 Kuala Lumpur, Malaysia
Designatory Letters:	--		
Profession:	Investment Management		
Membership:	--		
Established:	1985	**Telephone:**	60-3-254-6433/6662-6815-6376
		Fax:	60-3-254-7631
		E-mail:	FAUZI@klse.com.my
		Web:	www.bursamalaysia.com

Yayasan Pengurusan Malaysia (Malaysian Institute of Management)

Designation:	--	**Address:**	Management House, 227 Jalan Ampang, 50450 Kuala Lumpur, Malaysia
Designatory Letters:	AMIM (Associate Member of the Malaysian Institute of Management)		
		Telephone:	603-2164-5255
		Fax:	603-2164-3171
	FMIM (Fellow Member of the Malaysian Institute of Management)	**E-mail:**	--
		Web:	www.mim.edu
Profession:	Management		
Membership:	--		
Established:	--		

Institute of Certified e-Commerce Consultants (Malaysian Regional Office)

Designation:	--	**Address:**	49 A First Floor, Jalan SS, 15/4E, 47500 Subang Jaya, Selangor Darul Ehsan, Malaysia
Designatory Letters:	--		
Profession:	Management Consulting		
Membership:	--	**Telephone:**	--
Established:	--	**Fax:**	--
		E-mail:	--
		Web:	www.institutecec.org/my/

Institute of Management Consultants, Malaysia

Designation:	--	**Address:**	c/o Asian Strategy & Leadership Institute, Level 1, Menara Sungei Way, Jalan Lagun Timur, Bandar Sunway, Petaling Jaya 46150, Malaysia
Designatory Letters:	--		
Profession:	Management Consulting		
Membership:	--		
Established:	1976		
		Telephone:	603-735-2811
		Fax:	603-736-4048
		E-mail:	musghaz@tm.net.my
		Web:	--

Malaysian Institute of Taxation

Designation:	--	**Address:**	Unit B-13-2, Block B, 13th Floor, Megan Avenue 11, No. 12, Jalan Yap Kwan Seng, 50450 Kuala Lumpur, Malaysia
Designatory Letters:	ATII (Associate Member of the Malaysian Institute of Taxation)		
	FTII (Fellow Member of the Malaysian Institute of Taxation)	**Telephone:**	603-2162-8989
		Fax:	603-2162-8990
		E-mail:	secretariat@mit.org.my
Profession:	Taxation	**Web:**	www.mit.org.my
Membership:	--		
Established:	1991		

Malaysian Association of Corporate Treasurers (MACT)

Designation:	--	**Address:**	9th Floor, Balai Felda, Jalan Gurney Satu, 54000 Kuala Lumpur, Malaysia
Designatory Letters:	--		
Profession:	Treasury Management		
Membership:	--	**Telephone:**	60-3-240-5201
Established:	--	**Fax:**	60-3-298-2677
		E-mail:	anne.r@felda.net.my
		Web:	--

MALTA

Malta Institute of Accountants

Designation:	--	**Address:**	Accountancy House, 14 Princess Elizabeth Street, Ta Xbiex MSD 11, Malta
Designatory Letters:	--		
Profession:	Accounting		
Membership:	--	**Telephone:**	356-323-991-2
Established:	--	**Fax:**	356-323-990
		E-mail:	nzerafa@miamalta.org
		Web:	www.miamalta.org

MAURITIUS

The Society of Chartered Accountants—Mauritius

Designation:	Certified Public Accountant	**Address:**	c/o Mr G. Poujnet, Deshazel Du Mee, PO Box 799, Port Louis, Mauritius
Designatory Letters:	CPA (Certified Public Accountant)		
		Telephone:	92-30-208-7923
Profession:	Accounting	**Fax:**	92-30-208-0086
Membership:	--	**E-mail:**	--
Established:	1990	**Web:**	--

ICT and Knowledge Management Association (ICTKMA)

Designation:	--	**Address:**	c/o VCILT, University of
Designatory Letters:	--		Mauritius, Reduit, Republic of
Profession:	Information Technology		Mauritius
Membership:	--	**Telephone:**	--
Established:	--	**Fax:**	--
		E-mail:	--
		Web:	--

MEXICO

Instituto Mexicano de Contadores Públicos, A.C.

Designation:	Contador Público Autorizado	**Address:**	Tabachines 44, Fracc. Bosques de las Lomas, Mexico 11700, D.F.,
Designatory Letters:	CPA (Contador Público Autorizado)		Mexico
		Telephone:	525-267-6415
Profession:	Accounting	**Fax:**	525-596-6950
Established:	--	**E-mail:**	asist.presidencia@imcp.org.mx
		Web:	www.imcp.org.mx

Asociación Mexicana de Actuarios, A.C.

Designation:	--	**Address:**	Miguel Serrano, No. 21 Int. 901,
Designatory Letters:	--		Col. Del Valle, 01460 México,
Profession:	Actuarial Science		D.F.
Membership:	--	**Telephone:**	55-59-0514
Established:	1983	**Fax:**	--
		E-mail:	--
		Web:	www.amac.org.mx/

Colegio Nacional de Actuarios A.C.

Designation:	--	**Address:**	Av. Patriotismo 711-4, torre A,
Designatory Letters:	--		03910 México, D.F.
Profession:	Actuarial Science	**Telephone:**	598-7690
Membership:	--	**Fax:**	598-7690
Established:	1967	**E-mail:**	--
		Web:	www.conac.org.mx

MOLDOVA

Association of Professional Accountants and Auditors of the Republic of Moldova

Designation:	--	**Address:**	65 M. Varlaam Str. Of 411,
Designatory Letters:	--		Chisinau, MD-2012, Moldova
Profession:	Accounting	**Telephone:**	373-221-3592
Membership:	--	**Fax:**	373-222-1825
Established:	--	**E-mail:**	info@acap.md
		Web:	www.acap.ngo.moldnet.md

MONGOLIA

Mongolian Institute of Certified Public Accountants (MonICPA)

Designation:	Certified Public Accountant	**Address:**	Chingeltei District, 3rd Khoroo, Ulaanbaatar-44, Mongolia
Designatory Letters:	CPA (Mon) (Certified Public Accountant of Mongolia)	**Telephone:**	976-11-317-444
		Fax:	976-11-317-444
		E-mail:	badmaa@monicpa.mn
Profession:	Accounting	**Web:**	www.monicpa.mn
Membership:	--		
Established:	--		

Mongolian Marketing Association

Designation:	--	**Address:**	Ministry of Trade and Industry Building, 211238 Ulaanbaatar-38, Mongolia
Designatory Letters:	--		
Profession:	Marketing		
Membership:	--	**Telephone:**	976-13-27472
Established:	--	**Fax:**	976-13-26325
		E-mail:	--
		Web:	--

MONTENEGRO

Institute of Accountants and Auditors of Montenegro

Designation:	--	**Address:**	Malo brdo, Momisici A N/3 i N/4 Podgorica 81000, Serbia & Montenegro
Designatory Letters:	--		
Profession:	Accounting		
Membership:	--	**Telephone:**	381-81-227-754
Established:	--	**Fax:**	381-81-227-708
		E-mail:	zorant@irrcg.cg.yu
		Web:	www.irrcg.cg.yu

MOROCCO

Ordre des Experts Compatbles du Royaume du Maroc (Morocco) – Certified Public Accountants Association

Designation:	--	**Address:**	24 France Avenue de Rabat, Morocco
Designatory Letters:	--		
Profession:	Accounting	**Telephone:**	212-3777-9924
Membership:	--	**Fax:**	212-37-77-9939
Established:	--	**E-mail:**	oeccrc@wanadoopro.ma
		Web:	--

Société Marocaine des Analystes Financiers (SMAF)

Designation:	--	**Address:**	c/o Polyfinance, 309 Boulevard Ziraoui, 20100 Casablanca, Morocco
Designatory Letters:	--		
Profession:	Investment Management		
Membership:	--	**Telephone:**	212-3777-9924
Established:	--	**Fax:**	212-37-77-9939
		E-mail:	--
		Web:	--

AMTE

Designation:	--	**Address:**	c/o AKCE Finance, 213 Rond-Point d'Europe, Mers Sultan, Casablanca, Morocco
Designatory Letters:	--		
Profession:	Treasury Management		
Membership:	--	**Telephone:**	212-248-4550
Established:	--	**Fax:**	--
		E-mail:	--
		Web:	--

MOZAMBIQUE

Mozambique Association of Accountants

Designation:	--	**Address:**	Av. Marginal, Pavilhao No. 32-Facim, Caixa Postal 1892, Maputo, Mozambique
Designatory Letters:	--		
Profession:	Accounting		
Membership:	--	**Telephone:**	217-818-869
Established:	--	**Fax:**	212-37-77-9939
		E-mail:	nhampossa2002@yahoo.com.br
		Web:	--

MYANMAR (BURMA)

Myanmar Accounting Council

Designation:	--	**Address:**	Rangoon, Myanmar
Designatory Letters:	--		
Profession:	Accounting	**Telephone:**	--
Membership:	--	**Fax:**	--
Established:	--	**E-mail:**	--
		Web:	--

N

NAMIBIA

Institute of Chartered Accountants of Namibia

Designation:	Chartered Accountant of Namibia	**Address:**	342 San Nujoula Avenue, Paramount House, Klein Windhoek, Windhoek, Namibia
Designatory Letters:	CA (N) (Chartered Accountant of Namibia)	**Telephone:**	264-61-220-218
		Fax:	264-61-230-014
Profession:	Accounting	**E-mail:**	secretariat@icanpaab.com
Membership:	--	**Web:**	--
Established:	1990		

NEPAL

Institute of Chartered Accountants of Nepal

Designation:	Chartered Accountant Registered Auditor Class "B"	**Address:**	Ramshah Path, Putali Sadak, Box 5289, Kathmandu, Nepal
	Registered Auditor Class "C"	**Telephone:**	977-1-258-569
		Fax:	977-1-258-568
	Registered Auditor Class "D"	**E-mail:**	ican@ntc.net.np
		Web:	www.ican.org.np
Designatory Letters:	CA (N) (Chartered Accountant of Nepal)		
	RA (Class B) (Registered Auditor Class "B")		
	RA (Class C) (Registered Auditor Class "C")		
	RA (Class D) (Registered Auditor Class "D")		
Profession:	Accounting		
Membership:	300		
Established:	--		

THE NETHERLANDS

Koninklijk Nederlands Instituut van Registeraccountants (Royal NIVRA)

Designation:	Registeraccountant	**Address:**	A.J. Ernstraat 55, 1083 GR Amsterdam, Netherlands
Designatory Letters:	RA (Registeraccountant)		
Profession:	Accounting	**Telephone:**	31-20-301-0304
Membership:	--	**Fax:**	31-20-301-0309
Established:	--	**E-mail:**	g.smit@nivra.nl
		Web:	www.nivra.nl

Het Actuarieel Genootschap (Netherlands Institute of Actuaries)

Designation:	--	**Address:**	PO Box 540, 3440 Am Woerden, The Netherlands
Designatory Letters:	--		
Profession:	Actuarial Science	**Telephone:**	31-348-439-640
Membership:	--	**Fax:**	31-348-430-555
Established:	1946	**E-mail:**	info@ag-ni.nl
		Web:	www.ag-ai.nl/

Nederlands Instituut voor Financicel-economische Administratieve.opleidingen (NIFA)

Designation:	Accountant-Administratieconsulent	**Address:**	Morsweg 234 a 2332 EV Leiden, Nederlands
Designatory Letters:	AA (Accountant-Administratieconsulent)	**Telephone:**	--
		Fax:	--
Profession:	Administration/Accounting	**E-mail:**	bosnifa@xs4all.nl
Membership:	--	**Web:**	www.nifa-balans.nl
Established:	--		

Nederlandse Vereniging van Banken

Designation:	--	**Address:**	Postbus 3543, 1001 AH Amsterdam, Netherlands
Designatory Letters:	--		
Profession:	Banking	**Telephone:**	31-205-50-2888
Membership:	--	**Fax:**	31-206-23-9748
Established:	--	**E-mail:**	--
		Web:	www.nvb.nl

Nederlands Genootschap voor Informatica (NGI)

Designation:	--	**Address:**	PO Box 548, NL-5140 AM Waalwijk, The Netherlands
Designatory Letters:	--		
Profession:	Information Technology	**Telephone:**	31-416-565025
Membership:	--	**Fax:**	31-416-565030
Established:	--	**E-mail:**	--
		Web:	www.ngi.nl

Netherlands Order of Registered EDP Auditors (NOREA), Association of Registered Controllers (VRC), Association for Environmental Accounting (VMA)

Designation:	Register EDP Auditor	**Address:**	Royal NVRA, Postbus 7984, 1008 AD Amsterdam, The Netherlands
Designatory Letters:	RE (Register EDP Auditor)	**Telephone:**	020-3010-301
Profession:	Information Technology Auditing/Audit	**Fax:**	020-3010-302
		E-mail:	--
Membership:	--	**Web:**	--
Established:	--		

Vereniging Register Operational Auditors (VRO)

Designation:	Register Operational Auditor	**Address:**	Postbus 505, 9200 AM Drachten, The Netherlands
Designatory Letters:	RO (Register Operational Auditor)	**Telephone:**	06-132-17-442
		Fax:	0512-53-7565
Profession:	Internal Auditing	**E-mail:**	secretariaat@vronet.nl
Membership:	--	**Web:**	www.vronet.nl
Established:	--		

The Dutch Analysts Association – Vereniging van Beleggingsanalisten

Designation:	--	**Address:**	Herengracht 479, 1017 BS Amsterdam, The Netherlands
Designatory Letters:	--		
Profession:	Investment Management	**Telephone:**	31-020-618-2812
Membership:	900	**Fax:**	31-020-618-2542
Established:	--	**E-mail:**	secretariaat@nvba.nl
		Web:	www.nvba.nl

Ordre Van Organisatiekundigen en-Adviseurs

Designation:	--	**Address:**	Postbus 1058, NL 3860,
Designatory Letters:	--		BBNijkerk, The Netherlands
Profession:	Management Consulting	**Telephone:**	31-33-247-3442
Membership:	--	**Fax:**	31-33-246-0470
Established:	1940	**E-mail:**	--
		Web:	www.ooa.nl

Raad Van Organisatie-Adviesbureaus (ROA)

Designation:	--	**Address:**	PO Box 310, 4200 AH Gorwatem,
Designatory Letters:	--		The Hague, The Netherlands
Profession:	Management Consulting	**Telephone:**	0183-62-1153
Membership:	--	**Fax:**	0183-62-1601
Established:	1970	**E-mail:**	roa@cantrijn.nl
		Web:	www.roa-advies.nl

Netherlands Institute of Marketing (NIMA)

Designation:	--	**Address:**	PO Box 7352, NL-1007 JJ,
Designatory Letters:	--		Amsterdam, Netherlands
Profession:	Marketing	**Telephone:**	31-20-5039-345
Membership:	--	**Fax:**	31-20-5039-390
Established:	--	**E-mail:**	info@nima.nl
		Web:	ww.nima.nl

Project Management Instiuut Nederlands

Designation:	IPMA Certificering	**Address:**	Buitenpleats 135, 8212 AE
	International Competence Baseline		Lelystad, The Nederlands
	Nederlandse Competence	**Telephone:**	31-0-320-222-464
	Baseline	**Fax:**	31-0-320-280434
Designatory Letters:	CITO (IPMA Certificering)	**E-mail:**	ipma@cito.nl
	ICB (International Competence Baseline)	**Web:**	www.pmi-nl.org
	NCB (Nederlandse Competence Baseline)		
Profession:	Project Management		
Membership:	1,400		
Established:	1979		

Dutch Association of Corporate Treasurers (DACT)

Designation:	--	**Address:**	PO Box 1483, 5602 BL Eindhoven,
Designatory Letters:	--		The Netherlands
Profession:	Treasury Management	**Telephone:**	3-140-242-1744
Membership:	--	**Fax:**	3-140-242-9425
Established:	1996	**E-mail:**	--
		Web:	www.dact.nl

NEW ZEALAND

Institute of Chartered Accountants of New Zealand

Designation:	Chartered Accountant	**Address:**	Level 2, CIGNA House, 40 Mercer Street, Wellington, New Zealand
Designatory Letters:	ACA (Associate of the Institute of Chartered Accountants of New Zealand) FCA (Fellow of the Institute of Chartered Accountants of New Zealand)	**Telephone:** **Fax:** **E-mail:** **Web:**	64-4-474-7848 64-4-460-0394 garry_muriwai@nzica.com www.nzica.com
Profession:	Accounting		
Membership:	28,000		
Established:	--		

The New Zealand Society of Actuaries, Inc. (NZSA)

Designation:	--	**Address:**	PO Box 1965, Wellington, New Zealand
Designatory Letters:	--		
Profession:	Actuarial Science	**Telephone:**	04-473-6661
Membership:	265	**Fax:**	04-473-6661
Established:	1957	**E-mail:**	--
		Web:	www.actuaries.org.nz

Chartered Institute of Corporate Management (New Zealand) Inc.(CICM) representing the Institute of Chartered Secretaries and Administrators (ICSA)

Designation:	Chartered Secretary	**Address:**	Administrator House, 44 Anzac Avenue, Auckland, New Zealand
Designatory Letters:	ACIS (Associate Member of the Institute of Chartered Secretaries and Administrators) ACCM (Associate of the Chartered Institute of Corporate Management [New Zealand] Inc.) FCIS (Fellow Member of the Institute of Chartered Secretaries and Administrators) FCCM (Fellow of the Chartered Institute of Corporate Management [New Zealand] Inc.)	**Telephone:** **Fax:** **E-mail:** **Web:**	64-9-377-0130 64-9-366-3979 info@csnz.org www.csnz.org
Profession:	Corporate Governance		
Membership:	1,600		
Established:	1937 (NZ); 1891 (UK)		

Institute of Management Consultants New Zealand Incorporated

Designation:	Certified Management Consultant	**Address:**	PO Box 273, Auckland, New Zealand
Designatory Letters:	CMC (Certified Management Consultant)	**Telephone:**	64-9-0274-457-190
		Fax:	64-9-427-4400
	MIMC (Member of the Institute of Management Consultants)	**E-mail:**	IMCNZ@barley.co.nz
		Web:	www.imcnz.org
	FIMC (Fellow of the Institute of Management Consultants)		
Profession:	Management Consulting		
Membership:	--		
Established:	1970		

Project Management Institute of New Zealand Inc

Designation:	--	**Address:**	PO Box 26-103, Newlands, Wellington, New Zealand
Designatory Letters:	--		
Profession:	Project Management	**Telephone:**	--
Membership:	1,200	**Fax:**	--
Established:	--	**E-mail:**	president@pmi.org.nz
		Web:	www.pmi.org.nz

Institute of Finance Professionals New Zealand Inc. (INFINZ)

Designation:	Certified Securities Analyst Professional	**Address:**	PO Box 10350, Wellington 6036, New Zealand
	Certified Treasury Professional	**Telephone:**	64-4-499-1870
		Fax:	64-4-499-1840
	Certified Finance and Investment Professional (CFIP)	**E-mail:**	mail@infinz.com
		Web:	www.infinz.com
Designatory Letters:	CSAP (Certified Securities Analyst Professional)		
	CTP (Certified Treasury Professional)		
	CFIP (Certified Finance and Investment Professional)		
Profession:	Treasury Management		
Membership:	--		
Established:	2002 (INFINZ inherited the memberships of the New Zealand Society of Corporate Treasurers and the New Zealand Society of Investment Analysts Inc.)		

NICARAGUA

Colegio de Contadores Públicos de Nicaragua

Designation:	--	**Address:**	De la Gasolinera Bello Horizonte,
Designatory Letters:	--		200 Cuadras hacia lago, PO Box
Profession:	Accounting		1172, Managua, Nicaragua
Membership:	--	**Telephone:**	505-249-5570
Established:	--	**Fax:**	505-249-9995
		E-mail:	--
		Web:	www.ccpn.org.ni

NIGERIA

Institute of Chartered Accountants of Nigeria

Designation:	Chartered Accountant	**Address:**	Plot No. 16, IDOWU Taylor Street,
Designatory Letters:	ACA (Associate of the Institute of Chartered Accountants of Nigeria) FCA (Fellow of the Institute of Chartered Accountants of Nigeria)		Victoria Island, PO Box 1580, Lagos, Nigeria
Profession:	Accounting	**Telephone:**	234-1-261-2152, 262-2394,
Membership:	17,000		261-4239
Established:	--	**Fax:**	234-1-261-0304
		E-mail:	info.ican@ican.org.ng
		Web:	www.ican.org.ng

Institute of Cost and Management Accountants of Nigeria

Designation:	Cost and Management Accountant	**Address:**	No.7A Junction Road, PO Box 508, Kaduna, Nigeria
Designatory Letters:	ACMA (Associate Member of the Institute of Cost and Management Accountants of Nigeria) FCMA (Fellow Member of the Institute of Cost and Management Accountants of Nigeria)	**Telephone:** **Fax:** **E-mail:** **Web:**	234-62-245-172 234-62-210-822 info@icma-ng.org www.icma-ng.org
Profession:	Accounting		
Membership:	--		
Established:	--		

Institute of Chartered Secretaries and Administrators of Nigeria (ICSAN)

Designation:	Chartered Secretary	**Address:**	Elephant Cement Way, Alausa,
Designatory Letters:	ACIS (Associate Member of the Institute of Chartered Secretaries and Administrators of Nigeria) FCIS (Fellow Member of the Institute of Chartered Secretaries and Administrators)		PO Box 15705, Ikeja, Lagos, Nigeria
		Telephone:	234-1-496-7070/794-0632/471-12396
		Fax:	--
		E-mail:	--
		Web:	--
Profession:	Corporate Governance		
Membership:	--		
Established:	--		

Nigeria Computer Society (NCS)

Designation:	--	**Address:**	190 Ikorodu Road, Palmgrove,
Designatory Letters:	--		P.M.B. 4800, Surulere, Lagos,
Profession:	Information Technology		Nigeria
Membership:	--	**Telephone:**	234-1774-4600
Established:	--	**Fax:**	--
		E-mail:	execsec@ncs-nig.org
		Web:	www.ncs-nig.org

Chartered Insurance Institute of Nigeria

Designation:	--	**Address:**	27 Lagos Street, P.M.B. 1053,
Designatory Letters:	ACIIN (Associate Member of the Chartered Insurance Institute of Nigeria)		Ebute Metta, Lagos, Nigeria
		Telephone:	234-470-5512/812-8748/812-8749
		Fax:	--
		E-mail:	--
	FCIIN (Fellow Member of the Chartered Insurance Institute of Nigeria)	**Web:**	www.ciinigeria.com
Profession:	Insurance		
Membership:	--		
Established:	1959		

The Nigerian Institute of Management (NIM)

Designation:	--	**Address:**	Management House, Plot 22,
Designatory Letters:	AMNIM (Associate Member of the Nigerian Institute of Management)		Idowu Taylor Street or PO Box 2557, Victoria Island, Lagos, Nigeria
	MNIM (Member of the Nigerian Institute of Management)	**Telephone:**	234-1-4617-148-616-203-614-116-615-105
		Fax:	--
	FNIM (Fellow of the Nigerian Institute of Management)	**E-mail:**	info@managementnigeria.org
		Web:	www.managementnigeria.org
Profession:	Management		
Membership:	--		
Established:	1961		

Institute of Management Consultants

Designation:	--	**Address:**	PO Box 9194, Kaduna, Nigeria
Designatory Letters:	AMIMC (Associate Member of the Institute of Management Consultants)	**Telephone:**	062-214073
		Fax:	234-62-241048
		E-mail:	nimc@inet-global.com
	MIMC (Member of the Institute of Management Consultants)	**Web:**	www.inet-global.com
	FIMC (Fellow of the Institute of Management Consultants)		
	PGDMS (Postgraduate Diploma in Management Studies)		
Profession:	Management Consulting		
Membership:	--		
Established:	1983		

Chartered Institute of Marketing of Nigeria

Designation:	--	**Address:**	Lagos, Nigeria
Designatory Letters:	AMNIM (Associate Member of the Chartered Institute of Marketing of Nigeria) FCNIM (Fellow Member of the Chartered Institute of Marketing of Nigeria)	**Telephone:** **Fax:** **E-mail:** **Web:**	-- -- -- www.cimn.8m.com
Profession:	Marketing		
Membership:	--		
Established:	--		

Chartered Institute of Taxation Nigeria

Designation:	--	**Address:**	37rd and 4th Floors, Don De Dieu Plaza, Maryland, Lagos, Nigeria
Designatory Letters:	ACTI (Associate Member of the Chartered Institute of Taxation of Nigeria) FCTI (Fellow Member of the Chartered Institute of Taxation of Nigeria)	**Telephone:** **Fax:** **E-mail:** **Web:**	234-1-774-1273 234-1-493-5059 -- www.citn.org
Profession:	Marketing		
Membership:	--		
Established:	1982		

NORWAY

Norges Interne Revisorers Forening (IIA-Norway)

Designation:	Diplomet Intern Revisor	**Address:**	Pilestredet 75D, PO Box 5864, Majorstua, N-0308, Oslo, Norway
Designatory Letters:	Dipl.I.R. (Diplomet Intern Revisor)		
Profession:	Accounting	**Telephone:**	47-2-336-5200
Membership:	--	**Fax:**	47-2-269-0555
Established:	--	**E-mail:**	phanstad@revisornett.no
		Web:	www.revisornett.no

Norges Registrerte Revisorers Forening (The Norwegian Institute of Registered Auditors)

Designation:	Registrert Revisor (Registered Public Accountant-Auditor)	**Address:**	Gyldenloves gate 44, 0260 Oslo 2, Norway
		Telephone:	22-335400
Designatory Letters:	RR (Registrert Revisor)	**Fax:**	22-335410
Profession:	Accounting	**E-mail:**	--
Membership:	--	**Web:**	--
Established:	--		

Norges Statsautoriserte Revisorers Forening

Designation:	Statsautorisert Revisor (State Authorized Public Accountant-Auditor)	**Address:**	Revisorenes Hus, Uranienborg, Terrasse 9, Oslo 0351, Norway
Designatory Letters:	SR (Statsautorisert Revisor)		
Profession:	Accounting	**Telephone:**	47-22-695910
Membership:	--	**Fax:**	47-22-690555
Established:	--	**E-mail:**	--
		Web:	--

Den Norske Aktuarforening

Designation:	--	**Address:**	Postboks 3132, Elisenberg, Oslo
Designatory Letters:	--		0208, Norway
Profession:	Actuarial Science	**Telephone:**	011-4722-968156
Membership:	--	**Fax:**	011-4722-969480
Established:	1904	**E-mail:**	--
		Web:	www.aktfor.no/

Norwegian Computer Society

Designation:	--	**Address:**	Youngstorget, N-0028, Oslo,
Designatory Letters:	--		Norway
Profession:	Information Technology	**Telephone:**	47-22-36-4880
Membership:	--	**Fax:**	47-22-36-3701
Established:	--	**E-mail:**	dnd@dnd.no
		Web:	www.dnd.no

Abelia Bedriftsrådgiverforening (Norwegian Association of Management Consultants – NAMC)

Designation:	--	**Address:**	Middelthunsgate 27, PB 5490
Designatory Letters:	--		Majorstua, N-0305 Oslo, Norway
Profession:	Management Consulting	**Telephone:**	47-23-08-80-70
Membership:	--	**Fax:**	47-23-08-80-71
Established:	--	**E-mail:**	--
		Web:	www.abelia.no

Norsk Forening for Projektleddse (NFP)

Designation:	--	**Address:**	PO Box 2312, Solli, 0201 Oslo,
Designatory Letters:	--		Norway
Profession:	Project Management	**Telephone:**	47-229-47-520
Membership:	--	**Fax:**	47-229-47-502
Established:	--	**E-mail:**	else.dahl@tekna.no
		Web:	www.prosjektledelse.com

O

OMAN

College of Engineering, Information Engineering Department

Designation:	--	**Address:**	Sultan Qaboos University,
Designatory Letters:	--		PO Box 50, Muscat 123,
Profession:	Information Technology		Sultanate of Oman
Membership:	--	**Telephone:**	968-513-333
Established:	--	**Fax:**	968-514-455
		E-mail:	naamany@squ.edu.om
		Web:	www.squ.edu.om

P

PAKISTAN

Association of Accounting Technicians of Pakistan

Designation:	--	**Address:**	Bungalow No. A-8, Defence View, Shaheed-e-Millat Express Way, Near Hino Chowrangi off Korangi Road, Karachi 75500, Pakistan
Designatory Letters:	--		
Profession:	Accounting		
Membership:	--		
Established:	--		
		Telephone:	92-21-580-0412
		Fax:	92-21-580-0412
		E-mail:	--
		Web:	--

Institute of Chartered Accountants of Pakistan

Designation:	Chartered Accountant	**Address:**	Chartered Accountants Avenue, Clifton, Karachi-75600-11, Pakistan
Designatory Letters:	ACA (P) (Associate of the Institute of Chartered Accountants of Pakistan)		
		Telephone:	92-21-111-000-422
		Fax:	92-21-924-3342
	FCA (P) (Fellow of the Institute of Chartered Accountants of Pakistan)	**E-mail:**	icap@icap.org.pk
		Web:	www.icap.org.pk
Profession:	Accounting		
Membership:	4,000		
Established:	1961		

Institute of Cost and Management Accountants of Pakistan

Designation:	Cost and Management Accountant	**Address:**	St-18-C, Block-6, PO Box No. 17642, Gulshan-e-Iqbal, Karachi 75300, Pakistan
Designatory Letters:	ACMA (P) (Associate of the Institute of Cost and Management Accountants of Pakistan)		
		Telephone:	92-21-924-3900
		Fax:	92-21-924-3342
		E-mail:	ed@icmap.com.pk
	FCMA (P) (Fellow of the Institute of Cost and Management Accountants of Pakistan)	**Web:**	www.icmap.com.pk
Profession:	Accounting		
Membership:	--		
Established:	1951		

Pakistan Institute of Public Finance Accountants

Designation:	--	**Address:**	1005 Park Avenue, 10th Floor, 24-A
Designatory Letters:	--	**Telephone:**	Block 6, P.E.C.H.S., Shara-e-
Profession:	Accounting	**Fax:**	Faisal, Near Hino Chowrangi,
Membership:	--	**E-mail:**	Off Korangi Road, Karachi
Established:	--	**Web:**	75400, Pakistan

92-042-5879-64
92-21-452-4871
pipfa@cyber.net.pk
www.pipfa.org.pk

The Pakistan Society of Actuaries (PSA)

Designation:	--	**Address:**	c/o Akhtar & Hasan (Pvt) Ltd., 2nd
Designatory Letters:	--		Floor (Annexe), State Life No.1
Profession:	Actuarial Science		Building, Chundrigar Road,
Membership:	--		Karachi 74000, Pakistan
Established:	--	**Telephone:**	021-241-1084, 242-0154, 242-5714
		Fax:	021- 241- 7810
		E-mail:	--
		Web:	--

Institute of Chartered Secretaries and Managers

Designation:	--	**Address:**	68-B, Block-2, P.E.C.H.S., Karachi
Designatory Letters:	--		75400, Pakistan
Profession:	Management	**Telephone:**	92-21-455-6253-455-3890-455-
Membership:	--		8365
Established:	--	**Fax:**	92-21-453-9146
		E-mail:	--
		Web:	--

Institute of Corporate Secretaries of Pakistan

Designation:	Corporate Secretary	**Address:**	ICSP House, ST-8-D, Block 1,
Designatory Letters:	ACIS (Associate Member of the Institute of Corporate Secretaries of Pakistan)		Scha 5, Clifton, Karachi, Pakistan
		Telephone:	92-21-583-7650-587-7582
		Fax:	92-21-587-7583
	FCIS (Fellow Member of the Institute of Corporate Secretaries of Pakistan)	**E-mail:**	info@icsp.org.pk
		Web:	www.icsp.org.pk
Profession:	Management		
Membership:	--		
Established:	1974		

Institute of Marketing Management

Designation:	--	**Address:**	68-B, Block-2, P.E.C.H.S., Karachi
Designatory Letters:	--		75400, Pakistan
Profession:	Marketing	**Telephone:**	92-21-55-6253-455-3890-455-8365
Membership:	--	**Fax:**	92-21-453-9146
Established:	--	**E-mail:**	--
		Web:	--

Marketing Association of Pakistan

Designation:	--	**Address:**	403 Burhani Chambers, Abdullah
Designatory Letters:	--		Haroon Road, Karachi, Pakistan
Profession:	Marketing	**Telephone:**	922-1772-9952
Membership:	--	**Fax:**	922-1455-0187
Established:	--	**E-mail:**	--
		Web:	--

Project Management Association of Pakistan

Designation:	--	**Address:**	--
Designatory Letters:	--	**Telephone:**	--
Profession:	Project Management	**Fax:**	--
Membership:	--	**E-mail:**	--
Established:	2004	**Web:**	--

Pakistan Institute of Quality Control

Designation:	--	**Address:**	15-A-1 Peco Road, Township,
Designatory Letters:	--		Lahore, Pakistan
Profession:	Quality Management	**Telephone:**	92-42-514-0001-02
Membership:	--	**Fax:**	92-42-514-0003
Established:	--	**E-mail:**	piqc@brain.net.pk
		Web:	www.piqc.com.pk

Institute of Taxation Management

Designation:	--	**Address:**	68-B, Block-2, P.E.C.H.S., Karachi
Designatory Letters:	--		75400, Pakistan
Profession:	Taxation	**Telephone:**	92-21-455-6253-455-3890-455-
Membership:	--		8365
Established:	--	**Fax:**	92-21-453-9146
		E-mail:	--
		Web:	--

PANAMA

Asociación de Contadores Publicos Autorizados de Panamá

Designation:	--	**Address:**	Apartado Postal 6-4793,
Designatory Letters:	--		El Dorado, Panamá
Profession:	Accounting	**Telephone:**	507-227-0007
Membership:	--	**Fax:**	507-225-6651
Established:	--	**E-mail:**	acontapanama@cableonda.net
		Web:	--

Asociación de Mujeres Contadoras Públicas Autorizadas de Panamá

Designation:	--	**Address:**	Calle 51 Camp Alegre, Area
Designatory Letters:	--		Bancaria. Edif. Proconsa 2do
Profession:	Accounting		piso, Ofic. 2B, Apartado Postal
Membership:	--		4103, Panamá
Established:	--	**Telephone:**	597-269-5195
		Fax:	507-264-7981
		E-mail:	amucopa@cwpanama.net
		Web:	www.amucopa.com

Colegio de Contadores Públicos Autorizados de Panamá

Designation:	--	**Address:**	Urbanizacion Los Angelos, Calle G
Designatory Letters:	--		Casa, J-18, Panama
Profession:	Accounting	**Telephone:**	507-236-6571
Membership:	--	**Fax:**	507-236-6570
Established:	--	**E-mail:**	ccpap@sinfo.net
		Web:	--

PAPUA NEW GUINEA

Certified Practising Accountants of Papa New Guinea

Designation:	Certified Practising Accountant	**Address:**	PO Box 1937, Port Moresby, NCD 121, Papa New Guinea.
Designatory Letters:	CPA (Certified Practising Accountant)	**Telephone:**	675-321-3644
		Fax:	675-320-0469
Profession:	Accounting	**E-mail:**	pngia@pngia.org.pg
Membership:	--	**Web:**	www.pngia.org.pg
Established:	1996		

PARAGUAY

Colegio de Contadores de Paraguay

Designation:	--	**Address:**	Yegros # 860, c-o Manuel
Designatory Letters:	--		Domínguez, Casilla Correo
Profession:	Accounting		#2932, Asunción, Paraguay
Membership:	--	**Telephone:**	595-21-524-981-493-111-447-155
Established:	--	**Fax:**	595-21-524-981-440-362
		E-mail:	--
		Web:	www.ccpy.prg.py

Consejo de Contadores Públicos del Paraguay

Designation:	--	**Address:**	Independencia Nacional 821,
Designatory Letters:	--		Edifcio Lider VI, Piso 10,
Profession:	Accounting		Asunción, Paraguay
Membership:	--	**Telephone:**	595-21-491-571
Established:	--	**Fax:**	--
		E-mail:	devaca@cyce.com.py
		Web:	--

PERU

Junta de Decanos de Colegios de Contadores Públicos del Perú

Designation:	Contador Público Autorizado	**Address:**	Av. Arequipa 998 7mo Piso Urb. Sta. Santa Beatriz, Lima 1, Peru
Designatory Letters:	CPA (Contador Público Autorizado)	**Telephone:**	51-1433-5320-433-4862
		Fax:	51-1-433-3171-424-4913
Profession:	Accounting	**E-mail:**	--
Membership:	--	**Web:**	www.fccpp.org
Established:	--		

PHILIPPINES

Philippine Institute of Certified Public Accountants

Designation:	Certified Public Accountant	**Address:**	PICPA Building, 700 Shaw Boulevard, Mandaluyong, Metro
Designatory Letters:	CPA (P) (Certified Public Accountant of the Philippines)		Manila, Philippines
		Telephone:	63-2-723-0691-95
		Fax:	63-2-723-6305
Profession:	Accounting	**E-mail:**	picpamd@pldtdsl.net or
Membership:	19,000		picmaadm@pldtdsl.net
Established:	1973	**Web:**	www.picpa.com.ph

Actuarial Society of the Philippines (ASP)

Designation:	--	**Address:**	PO Box 413, Makati Central Post
Designatory Letters:	AASP (Associate		Office, Makati, Metro Manila,
	Member of the Actuarial		1200 Philippines
	Society of the	**Telephone:**	892-5274
	Philippines)	**Fax:**	892-5274
	FASP (Fellow Member	**E-mail:**	
	of the Actuarial Society	**Web:**	www.actuary.org.ph
	of the Philippines)		
Profession:	Actuarial Science		
Membership:	--		
Established:	1953		

Institute of Management Consultants of the Philippines

Designation:	--	**Address:**	7th Floor, RCI Building, 105 Rade
Designatory Letters:	--		St, Legaspi Village, Makati City
Profession:	Management Consulting		1229, Metro Manila, Philippines
Membership:	--	**Telephone:**	632-893-5005
Established:	1985	**Fax:**	632-892-1880
		E-mail:	--
		Web:	www.imphil.org

Philippine Marketing Practitioners Association, Inc.

Designation:	Certified Marketing	**Address:**	Cattleya Condominum Building,
	Practitioner		Unit 818, 8th Floor, Salcedo
Designatory Letters:	CMP (Certified		Village, Makati, Metro Manila,
	Marketing Practitioner)		Philippines
		Telephone:	632-02-491-0224
Profession:	Marketing	**Fax:**	632-833-9212
Membership:	--	**E-mail:**	--
Established:	1954	**Web:**	www.marketingpractitioners.org

POLAND

National Board of Chartered Accountants Association in Poland

Designation:	--	**Address:**	00-443-Warszawa, ul. Górnoslaska
Designatory Letters:	--		5, Poland
Profession:	Accounting	**Telephone:**	48-22-622-7739
Membership:	--	**Fax:**	48-22-622-7781
Established:	1907	**E-mail:**	skwp@skwp.org.pl
		Web:	www.skwp.org.pl

Polskie Stowarzyszenie Aktuariuszy (Polish Society of Actuaries)

Designation:	--	**Address:**	Siedziba, PZU Zycie S.A., 00-133
Designatory Letters:	--		Warszawa, al. Jana Pawla II 24,
Profession:	Actuarial Science		Poland
Membership:	--	**Telephone:**	48-22-582-3435
Established:	1991	**Fax:**	48-22-582-3436
		E-mail:	--
		Web:	www.actuary.org.pl

National Chamber of Statutory Auditors

Designation:	Biegly Rewident or Statutory Auditor	**Address:**	Al. Jana Pawla II nr 80, 00-175, Warszawa, Poland
Designatory Letters:	--	**Telephone:**	48-22-637-3081
Profession:	Auditing	**Fax:**	48-22-637-3084
Membership:	7,500	**E-mail:**	international@kibr.org.pl
Established:	1991	**Web:**	www.kibr.org.pl

Polish Academy of Sciences

Designation:	--	**Address:**	PO Box 24, Plac Defilad 1, PL-00, 901, Warsaw, Poland
Designatory Letters:	---		
Profession:	Information Technology	**Telephone:**	48-22-620-4970
Membership:	--	**Fax:**	48-22-620-4910
Established:	--	**E-mail:**	--
		Web:	www.pan.pl

Zwiazek Maklerów i Doradców (Polish Association of Brokers and Investment Advisors)

Designation:	--	**Address:**	ul. Marszalkowska 68-70 m.30, 00-676 Warsawa, Poland
Designatory Letters:	--		
Profession:	Investment Management	**Telephone:**	--
Membership:	--	**Fax:**	--
Established:	--	**E-mail:**	biuro@zmid.org.pl
		Web:	www.pabia.org.pl

Association of Economic Consultants

Designation:	--	**Address:**	Stowarzyszenie Doradcow Gospodarczych, Warszawa 02-532, ul. Rakowiecka 36, Poland
Designatory Letters:	--		
Profession:	Management Consulting	**Telephone:**	48-22-606-3972
Membership:	--	**Fax:**	48-22-606-3972
Established:	--	**E-mail:**	--
		Web:	--

Stowarzyszenie Doradcow Gospodarczych w Polsce (SDG)

Designation:	--	**Address:**	ul. Lokajskiego 30 m. 43, PL-07-793 Warsaw, Poland
Designatory Letters:	--		
Profession:	Management Consulting	**Telephone:**	48-22-446-3406
Membership:	--	**Fax:**	48-22-520-6200-05
Established:	--	**E-mail:**	--
		Web:	www.sdg.com.pl

Stowarzyszemie Project Management Poska (Polish Project Management Association)

Designation:	--	**Address:**	Al. Jerozolimske 29-12, 00-508 Warsaw, Poland
Designatory Letters:	--		
Profession:	Project Management	**Telephone:**	48-22-622-2112
Membership:	--	**Fax:**	48-22-622-2110
Established:	--	**E-mail:**	biuro@spmp.org.pl
		Web:	www.spmp.org.pl

PORTUGAL

Ordem dos Revisores Oficiais de Contas

Designation:	--	**Address:**	Rua do Salitre, 51-53, 1250-198
Designatory Letters:	--		Lisbon, Portugal
Profession:	Accounting	**Telephone:**	351-21-353-6158
Membership:	--	**Fax:**	351-21-353-6149
Established:	--	**E-mail:**	secgeral@oroc.pt
		Web:	www.oroc.pt

Portuguese Association of Accountants

Designation:	Accountant	**Address:**	R. Douradores, 20-1°, 1100-206
Designatory Letters:	APPC		Lisboa, Portugal
Profession:	Accounting	**Telephone:**	351-21-887-8509
Membership:	--	**Fax:**	351-21-887-8509
Established:	1975	**E-mail:**	lisboa@apc.pt
		Web:	www.apc.pt

Instituto dos Actuários Portugueses (Portuguese Institute of Actuaries)

Designation:	--	**Address:**	Alameda D. Afonso Henriques
Designatory Letters:	--		n°72 r-c, 1000 Lisboa, Portugal
Profession:	Actuarial Science	**Telephone:**	351-1-846-3882
Membership:	--	**Fax:**	351-1-846-3882
Established:	1945	**E-mail:**	--
		Web:	www.iap.com.pt

Associação Portuguesa para a Promoção e Desenvolvimento da Sociedad da Informação (APDSI)

Designation:	--	**Address:**	Madan Parque – PCTAS, Edifico
Designatory Letters:	--		VI, Campus da Caparica, Monte
Profession:	Information Technology		de Caparica, PT-2829-516,
Membership:	--		Caparica, Portugal
Established:	--	**Telephone:**	351-212-949-606
		Fax:	351-212-949-607
		E-mail:	secretariado@apdsi.pt
		Web:	www.apdsi.pt

Associação Portuguesa de Projectistas e Consultores (APPC)

Designation:	--	**Address:**	Av. António Augusto Aguiar 126-
Designatory Letters:	--		7°, P-1050-020 Lisbon, Portugal
Profession:	Management Consulting	**Telephone:**	351-21-358-0785-6
Membership:	--	**Fax:**	351-21-315-0413
Established:	--	**E-mail:**	info@appconsultores.org.pt
		Web:	www.appconsultores.org.pt

Instituto Portugues de Consultores de Gestão

Designatory Letters:	--	**Address:**	Largo Rafael Pinheiro, 16-1200-
Profession:	Management Consulting		369 Lisboa, Portugal
Membership:	--	**Telephone:**	351-21-325-4114
Established:	--	**Fax:**	351-21-325-4111
		E-mail:	--
		Web:	wwwipcg-pt.org

Associação Portuguesa dos Profissionais de Marketing (The Portuguese Marketing Association - APPM)

Designation:	--	**Address:**	Avenida elias Garcia, 172-2º e,
Designatory Letters:	--		1050-103 Lisboa, Portugal
Profession:	Marketing	**Telephone:**	351-21-780-3550
Membership:	--	**Fax:**	351-21-780-3559
Established:	--	**E-mail:**	info@appm.pt
		Web:	www.appm.pt

Associação Portuguesa de Gestão de Projectos (Portuguese Project Management Association)

Designation:	Certified Project Management Associate	**Address:**	Praca de Alvalade 9-4-4, 1700-037 Lisboa, Portugal
	Certified Project Manager	**Telephone:**	351-21-848-1440
	Certified Senior Project Manager	**Fax:**	--
		E-mail:	info@apogep.pt
	Certified Project Director	**Web:**	www.apogep.pt
Designatory Letters:	CPMA (Certified Project Management Associate)		
	CPM (Certified Project Manager)		
	CSPM (Certified Senior Project Manager)		
	CPD (Certified Project Director)		
Profession:	Project Management		
Membership:	--		
Established:	--		

PUERTO RICO

Colegio de Contadores Públicos Autorizados de Puerto Rico

Designation:	Contador Público Autorizado	**Address:**	Edif. Capital Center 1, 239 Av. Arterial Hostos, Suite 1402,
Designatory Letters:	CPA (Contador Público Autorizado)		San Juan, PR 00918-1477, Puerto Rico
Profession:	Accounting	**Telephone:**	787-641-5063-754-1950
Membership:	--	**Fax:**	787-753-0212
Established:	1973	**E-mail:**	colegiocpa@colegiocpa.com
		Web:	www.colegiocpa.com

Academia de Actuarios de Puerto Rico

Designation:	--	**Address:**	--
Designatory Letters:	--	**Telephone:**	--
Profession:	Actuarial Science	**Fax:**	--
Membership:	--	**E-mail:**	--
Established:	--	**Web:**	--

R

Corpul Expertilor Contabili si Contabililor Autorizati din Romania – The Body of Experts and Licensed Accountants of Romania (CECCAR)

Designation:	--	Address:	Bd. Mircea Voda nr. 35 bl. M27,
Designatory Letters:	--		sc.1, et. 1, Sect. 3, 74214
Profession:	Accounting		Bucharest, Romania
Membership:	--	Telephone:	40-21-327-6380
Established:	--	Fax:	40-21-326-7173
		E-mail:	ceccar@ceccaro.ro
		Web:	www.ceccaro.ro

The Chamber of Financial Auditors of Romania

Designation:	--	Address:	12, Bd. Libertăþii, 5th Floor, Room
Designatory Letters:	--		458, Sector 5, Bucharest, OP 5
Profession:	Auditing		CP 83, Romania
Membership:	--	Telephone:	40-21-337-4925
Established:	--	Fax:	40-21-335-2604
		E-mail:	cornelia.stanes.cu@cafr.ro
		Web:	www.cafr.ro

Asociatia Consultantilor in Management din Romania

Designation:	--	Address:	Str. Economu Cezarescu 47-59,
Designatory Letters:	--		sector 6 Bucharest, parter, c05.
Profession:	Management Consulting		Romania
Membership:	--	Telephone:	40723-330713
Established:	--	Fax:	40212-11-5175
		E-mail:	office@amcor.ro
		Web:	www.amcor.ro

Romanian Management Consultants Association (AMCOR)

Designation:	--	Address:	47-49 Ion Brezoianu St., Entr. B,
Designatory Letters:	--		Level 2, Apt. 166, 1st District,
Profession:	Management Consulting		Bucharest, Romania
Membership:	61	Telephone:	40-723-330713
Established:	--	Fax:	40-212-11-5175
		E-mail:	office@amcor.ro
		Web:	www.amcor.ro

Project Management Association of Romania

Designation:	--	Address:	Romania
Designatory Letters:	--	Telephone:	--
Profession:	Project Management	Fax:	--
Membership:	--	E-mail:	--
Established:	--	Web:	--

RUSSIA

Association of Accountants and Auditors of the Commonwealth

Designation:	--	**Address:**	ul. Bolshaya Pokrovskya 15 Office
Designatory Letters:	--		10, 603005 Nizhny, Novgordk,
Profession:	Accounting		Russia
Membership:	--	**Telephone:**	8312-330027
Established:	1993	**Fax:**	8312-330136
		E-mail:	--
		Web:	innuv.ru

Institute of Professional Accountants of Russia (IPAR)

Designation:	--	**Address:**	3 Nastasyinsky pereulok, Building
Designatory Letters:	--		3/2, Office 305, 127006
Profession:	Accounting		Moscow, Russia
Membership:	46,440	**Telephone:**	495-975-7200
Established:	1997	**Fax:**	495-975-7200
		E-mail:	oom@ipbr.ru
		Web:	www.ipbr.ru

Russian Collegium of Auditors

Designation:	--	**Address:**	2/6 Kolokolnikov Lane, Moscow
Designatory Letters:	--		103045, Russia
Profession:	Accounting	**Telephone:**	7-095-208-4615
Membership:	--	**Fax:**	7-095-97-8775
Established:	--	**E-mail:**	isp.dir@rka.org.ru
		Web:	www.rka.org.ru

Institute of Russian Professional Auditors

Designation:	--	**Address:**	Moscow, Russia
Designatory Letters:	--	**Telephone:**	--
Profession:	Auditing	**Fax:**	--
Membership:	--	**E-mail:**	--
Established:	1997	**Web:**	--

Russian Academy of Sciences

Designation:	--	**Address:**	Leninski prospect 14 119991
Designatory Letters:	--		GSP-1, Moscow V-71, Russia.
Profession:	Information Technology	**Telephone:**	7-095-938-0309
Membership:	--	**Fax:**	7-095-954-3320
Established:	--	**E-mail:**	--
		Web:	www.ras.ru

Guild of Investment and Financial Analysts (GIFA)

Designation:	--	**Address:**	103055 Novoslobodskaya Str., 36/1
Designatory Letters:	--		Moscow, Russia
Profession:	Investment Management	**Telephone:**	7-095-956-2276
Membership:	--	**Fax:**	7-095-216-7290
Established:	--	**E-mail:**	info@gifa.ru
		Web:	www.gifa.ru

National Institute of Certified Management Consultants (NICMC)

Designation:	--	**Address:**	r 320 82 Vernadsky Avenue,
Designatory Letters:	--		Moscow 119571, Russia
Profession:	Management Consulting	**Telephone:**	7-095-433-2526
Membership:	--	**Fax:**	7-095-433-2526
Established:	2004	**E-mail:**	--
		Web:	--

Russian Marketing Association

Designation:	--	**Address:**	2, B. Trekhsvyatitelsky per.,
Designatory Letters:	--		Moscow 109028, Russia.
Profession:	Marketing	**Telephone:**	7-095-231-7068
Membership:	--	**Fax:**	7-095-231-7066
Established:	--	**E-mail:**	--
		Web:	www.ram.ru

Russian Project Management Association (SOVNET)

Designation:	--	**Address:**	Suite 504, 7, Kibalchicha St.,
Designatory Letters:	--		Moscow 129366.
Profession:	Project Management	**Telephone:**	7-095-913-7162
Membership:	--	**Fax:**	7-095-913-9128
Established:	1990	**E-mail:**	--
		Web:	www.sovnet.ru

S

SAMOA

Samoa Society of Accountants

Designation:	--	**Address:**	PO Box 3687, Apia, Samoa, Pacific
Designatory Letters:	--		
Profession:	Accounting	**Telephone:**	--
Membership:	--	**Fax:**	685-23-888
Established:	1984	**E-mail:**	fmulitalo@samoa-ws
		Web:	--

SAUDI ARABIA

Saudi Organization for Certified Public Accountants

Designation:	Certified Public Accountant	**Address:**	PO Box 22646, Riyadh 11416, Saudi Arabia
Designatory Letters:	CPA (Certified Public Accountant)	**Telephone:**	966-1-402-8555
Profession:	Accounting	**Fax:**	966-1-402-5616
Membership:	--	**E-mail:**	socpa@anet.net.sa
Established:	1992	**Web:**	--

SERBIA

The Association of Accountants and Auditors of the FR of Yugoslavia

Designation:	--	**Address:**	Njegoseva 19, POB 403, 11000 Belgrade, Serbia & Montenegro
Designatory Letters:	--		
Profession:	Accounting		
Membership:	--	**Telephone:**	381-11-323-94444, 323-4719
Established:	--	**Fax:**	381-11-331-220, 632-569
		E-mail:	info@srrs.co.yu
		Web:	www.srrs.org.yu

Serbian Association of Accountants and Auditors

Designation:	--	**Address:**	Njegoseia 19, PO Box 403, 11000 Belgrade
Designatory Letters:	--		
Profession:	Accounting	**Telephone:**	381-11-323-9444
Membership:	--	**Fax:**	381-11-323-1220
Established:	--	**E-mail:**	skobicz@SITS.org.yu
		Web:	www.SITS.org.yu

Project Management Institute of Yugoslavia

Designation:	--	**Address:**	Vdruženje za upravljanje projektine Sribije I Crne Gore-YUMA, Jove Ilica 154 Belgrade, Serbia and Montenegro
Designatory Letters:	--		
Profession:	Project Management		
Membership:	--		
Established:	--		
		Telephone:	011-3950-870
		Fax:	011-3950-870
		E-mail:	yupma@fon.bg.ac.yu
		Web:	www.yupma.org.yu

SIERRA LEONE

The Institute of Chartered Accountants of Sierra Leone (ICASL)

Designation:	Chartered Accountant	**Address:**	65 Siaka Stevens Street,
Designatory Letters:	CA (Chartered Accountant)		Freetown, Sierra Leone
Profession:	Accounting	**Telephone:**	232-22-228-176
Membership:	--	**Fax:**	232-22-228-149
Established:	--	**E-mail:**	icasl@securicom.sl.com
		Web:	--

SINGAPORE

Institute of Certified Public Accountants of Singapore

Designation:	Certified Public Accountant	**Address:**	#06-02 CPA House, 20
Designatory Letters:	CPA (Certified Public Accountant)		Aljunied Road, Singapore 389805
Profession:	Accounting	**Telephone:**	65-749-8060
Membership:	--	**Fax:**	65-749-8061
Established:	1963	**E-mail:**	cpasingapore@icpas.org.sg
		Web:	www.accountants.org.sg

The Singapore Actuarial Society (SAS)

Designation:	--	**Address:**	c/o Monetary Authority of
Designatory Letters:	--		Singapore, Insurance
Profession:	Actuarial Science		Commissioner's
Membership:	--		Department, 10 Shenton
Established:	1976		Way, MAS Building,
			Singapore 0207
		Telephone:	--
		Fax:	532-2214
		E-mail:	--
		Web:	www.actuaries.org.sg

Institute of Banking and Finance

Designation:	--	**Address:**	138 Cecil Street, #4-01 Cecil
Designatory Letters:	FICS (Financial Industry Competency Standards)		Court, Singapore 069538, Republic of Singapore
Profession:	Banking	**Telephone:**	65-220-8566
Membership:	--	**Fax:**	65-224-4947
Established:	1974	**E-mail:**	ibf@ibf.org.sg
		Web:	www.ibf.org.sg

The Singapore Association of the Institute of Chartered Secretaries and Administrators

Designation:	Chartered Secretary	**Address:**	149 Rochor Road, 04-07 Fu
Designatory Letters:	ACIS (Associate Member of the Institute of Chartered Secretaries and Administrators)		La Shou Complex, Singapore 188425, Republic of Singapore
	FCIS (Fellow Member of the Institute of Chartered Secretaries and Administrators)	**Telephone:**	334-4302
		Fax:	334-4669
		E-mail:	enquiry@saicsa.org.sg
		Web:	www.saicsa.com
Profession:	Corporate Governance		
Membership:	--		
Established:	--		

Singapore Computer Society

Designation:	--	**Address:**	53-53A Neil Road, Singapore 088891, Republic of Singapore
Designatory Letters:	--		
Profession:	Information Technology	**Telephone:**	65-226-2567
Membership:	--	**Fax:**	65-226-2569
Established:	--	**E-mail:**	jennifer.ong@scs.org.sg
		Web:	www.scs.org.sg

Singapore Society of Financial Analysts (SSFA)

Designation:	--	**Address:**	SSFA Secretariat, 10 Anson Road, #26-01 International Plaza, Singapore 079903, Republic of Singapore
Designatory Letters:	CGIPS (Certificate in Global Investment Performance Standards)		
Profession:	Investment Management	**Telephone:**	65-6323-6679
Membership:	--	**Fax:**	65-6323-7657
Established:	1987	**E-mail:**	info@ssfa.org.sg
		Web:	www.ssfa.org.sg

Institute of Management Consultants—Singapore

Designation:	Certified Management Consultant	**Address:**	20 Maxwell Road, 04-2H Maxwell House, Singapore 069113
Designatory Letters:	CMC (Certified Management Consultant)	**Telephone:**	65-372-1728
Profession:	Management Consulting	**Fax:**	65-372-1727
Membership:	--	**E-mail:**	secretariat@imcsingapore.com
Established:	1986		www.imcsingapore.com
		Web:	

Marketing Institute of Singapore

Designation:	--	**Address:**	30 Prinsep Street, #01-02 Prinsep House, Singapore 188647
Designatory Letters:	AMIS (Associate of the Marketing Institute of Singapore)		
	MMIS (Member of the Marketing Institute of Singapore)	**Telephone:**	65-6221-7788
		Fax:	65-6223-8785
		E-mail:	admin@mis.org.sg
	FMIS (Fellow of the Marketing Institute of Singapore)	**Web:**	www.mis.org.sg
Profession:	Marketing		
Membership:	--		
Established:	1973		

Association of Corporate Treasurers (Singapore)

Designation:	--	**Address:**	35 Bangkit Road, #17-03 Chestervale, Singapore 679975, Republic of Singapore
Designatory Letters:	--		
Profession:	Treasury Management		
Membership:	--		
Established:	--	**Telephone:**	65-9822-4345
		Fax:	65-6764-6577
		E-mail:	admin@act.org.sg
		Web:	www.act.org.sg

SLOVAKIA

Slovenska Spolocnost Aktuarov (Slovakian Actuarial Society)

Designation:	--	**Address:**	--
Designatory Letters:	--	**Telephone:**	--
Profession:	Actuarial Science	**Fax:**	--
Membership:	--	**E-mail:**	--
Established:	1995	**Web:**	--

Slovenska Komora Auditorov

Designation:	--	**Address:**	Mliekarenska 10, 824 92
Designatory Letters:	--		Bratislava, Slovakia
Profession:	Auditing	**Telephone:**	421-7-5341-2860
Membership:	--	**Fax:**	421-7-5341-2860
Established:	--	**E-mail:**	--
		Web:	--

Slovak Society for Computer Science (SSCS)

Designation:	--	**Address:**	MFF UK, Mlynska dolina,
Designatory Letters:	--		SK-842, 48 Bratislava,
Profession:	Information Technology		Slovak Republic
Membership:	--	**Telephone:**	421-2-6542-6635
Established:	--	**Fax:**	421-2-6542-7041
		E-mail:	SSCS@alpha.dcs.fmph.uniba.sk
		Web:	informatika.sk

Spolocnest Pre Projektove Riadenie (SPPR)—Project Management Association of Slovakia

Designation:	--	**Address:**	PO Box 211, Potsal 1, 91701
Designatory Letters:	--		Trnava, Slovakia
Profession:	Project Management	**Telephone:**	421-805-559-1806
Membership:	--	**Fax:**	421-805-599-1818
Established:	1994	**E-mail:**	sppr@excite.com
		Web:	www.sppr.sk

Slovak Association of Finance and Treasury (SAF)

Designation:	--	**Address:**	Radnicne namastie 4,
Designatory Letters:	--		82105 Bratislava, Slovakia
Profession:	Treasury Management	**Telephone:**	4212-4363-5667
Membership:	--	**Fax:**	--
Established:	1996	**E-mail:**	kancelaria@asicfin.sk
		Web:	www.asoc.fin.sk

SLOVENIA

The Slovenian Institute of Auditors

Designation:	--	**Address:**	Dunajska cesta 106, 1000
Designatory Letters:	--		Ljubljana, Slovenia
Profession:	Accounting	**Telephone:**	386-1-568-5554
Membership:	--	**Fax:**	386-1-568-6332
Established:	1993	**E-mail:**	barbara@rfr.si
		Web:	www.si-reviizija.si

Slovensko Aktuarsko Drustvo (Slovenian Actuarial Society)

Designation:	--	**Address:**	Železna cesta 14, 1000
Designatory Letters:	--		Ljubljana, Slovenia
Profession:	Actuarial Science	**Telephone:**	--
Membership:	--	**Fax:**	--
Established:	1997	**E-mail:**	info@aktuarji.com
		Web:	www.aktuarji.com

Slovenian Society INFORMATIKA

Designation:	--	**Address:**	Vozarski pot 12, SLO-1000,
Designatory Letters:	--		Ljubjana, Slovenia
Profession:	Information Technology	**Telephone:**	386-123-40836
Membership:	--	**Fax:**	386-123-40860
Established:	--	**E-mail:**	info@drustvo-informatika.si
		Web:	www.drustvo-informatika.si

Association of Management Consultants of Slovenia

Designation:	--	**Address:**	Dimiceva 13, 1504 Ljubljana,
Designatory Letters:	--		Slovenia
Profession:	Management Consulting	**Telephone:**	386-1-589-8252
Membership:	--	**Fax:**	386-1-589-8200
Established:	--	**E-mail:**	majda.dobravc@gzs.si
		Web:	www.gzs.si

Slovesko Szdruźenje za Projektne Management (Slovenian Project Management Association)

Designation:	--	**Address:**	Prešernova 10, 1000
Designatory Letters:	--		Ljubljana, Slovenia
Profession:	Project Management	**Telephone:**	--
Membership:	--	**Fax:**	--
Established:	--	**E-mail:**	zpm-educ@zpm-si.com
		Web:	www.sl.zpm-si.com

Slovenia Corporate Treasurers Association

Designation:	--	**Address:**	Ljubljana, Slovenia
Designatory Letters:	--	**Telephone:**	--
Profession:	Treasury Management	**Fax:**	--
Membership:	--	**E-mail:**	--
Established:	--	**Web:**	www.zpts.org

SOLOMON ISLANDS

Solomon Islands Institute of Accountants

Designation:	--	**Address:**	PO Box 70, Honiara,
Designatory Letters:	--		Solomon Islands
Profession:	Accounting	**Telephone:**	577-22509
Membership:	--	**Fax:**	--
Established:	--	**E-mail:**	ddenis@qbe.com.au
		Web:	--

SOUTH AFRICA

South African Institute of Chartered Accountants (SAICA)

Designation:	Chartered Accountant	**Address:**	Integritas, 7 Zulberg Close, Bruma Lake 2198, Johannesburg, South Africa
Designatory Letters:	CA (SA) (Chartered Accountant [SA])		
	AGA (SA) (Associate General Accountant [SA])	**Telephone:**	27-11-621-6000
		Fax:	27-11-621-6775
	AAT (SA) (Associate Accounting Technician [SA])	**E-mail:**	saica@saica.co.za
		Web:	www.saica.co.za
	CTA (Certificate in the Theory of Accountancy)		
Profession:	Accounting		
Membership:	25,500		
Established:	The SAICA was established in 1980 as an amalgamation of four Provincial Societies of Chartered Accountants (all established between 1904-1909).		

South African Institute of Professional Accountants

[Formerly the Institute of Commercial and Financial Accountants of Southern Africa]

Designation:	Commercial and Financial Accountant	**Address:**	Block 3, Riviera Office Park, 66 Oxford Road, Riviera 2193, Johannesburg, South Africa
Designatory Letters:	CFA (SA) (Commercial and Financial Accountant of South Africa)		
		Telephone:	27-11-486-0283
Profession:	Accounting	**Fax:**	27-11-486-0632
Membership:	--	**E-mail:**	ceo@cfasa.co.za
Established:	1982	**Web:**	www.cfa-sa.co.za

The Actuarial Society of South Africa (ASSA)

Designation:	--	**Address:**	PO Box 4464, Cape Town 8000, South Africa
Designatory Letters:	FASSA (Fellow of the Actuarial Society of South Africa)		
		Telephone:	021-509-5242
Profession:	Actuarial Science	**Fax:**	021-509-0160
Membership:	--	**E-mail:**	assa@assa.org.za
Established:	1948	**Web:**	www.assa.org.za/

Independent Regulatory Board for Auditors (IRBA)

Designation:	NA	**Address:**	Maneo, 7 Ernest Oppenheimer Ave., Bruma, South Africa
Designatory Letters:	NA		
Profession:	Auditing/Accounting		
Established:	2006	**Telephone:**	011-622-8533
		Fax:	011-622-4029
		E-mail:	--
		Web:	www.paab.co.za

Institute of Bankers in South Africa (IBSA)

Designation:	--	**Address:**	PO Box 61420, Marshalltown 2107, or 1st Floor, Sunnyside Ridge Building, Sunnyside Office Park, 32 Princess of Wales Terrace, Parktown, South Africa
Designatory Letters:	CAIB (SA) (Certified Associate of the Institute of Bankers in South Africa)		
	FIBSA (Fellow of the Institute of Bankers in South Africa)		
Profession:	Banking	**Telephone:**	11-481-7000
Membership:	--	**Fax:**	11-481-8716
Established:	1904	**E-mail:**	iobinfo@iob.co.za
		Web:	www.iob.co.za

Institute of Certified Book-keepers of South Africa

Designation:	--	**Address:**	PO Box 2237,
Designatory Letters:	A*f*ICB (SA) (Affiliate of the Institute of Certified Book-keepers of South Africa)		Cape Town, South Africa
		Telephone:	021-421-1110
	AICB (SA) (Associate of the Institute of Certified Book-keepers of South Africa)	**Fax:**	021-421-1136
		E-mail:	admin@icb.org.za
		Web:	www.icb.org.za
	CICB (SA) (Certificate of the Institute of Certified Book-Keepers of South Africa)		
	MICB (SA) (Member of the Institute of Certified Book-keepers of South Africa)		
	FICB (SA) (Fellow of the Institute of Certified Book-keepers of South Africa)		
Profession:	Bookkeeping		
Membership:	4,000		
Established:	1931		

Institute of Administration and Commerce

Designation:	--	**Address:**	PO Box 36477, Glossderry,
Designatory Letters:	AIAC (Associate of the Institute of Administration and Commerce)		Cape Town 7702, South Africa
		Telephone:	021-761-6211
	MIAC (Member of the Institute of Administration and Commerce)	**Fax:**	021-761-6739
		E-mail:	pedro@iacsa.co.za
		Web:	www.iacsa.co.za
	FIAC (Fellow of the Institute of Administration and Commerce)		
Profession:	Commerce		
Membership:	--		
Established:	1927		

Institute of Chartered Secretaries and Administrators (ICSA)

Designation:	Chartered Secretary	**Address:**	PO Box 331, WITS, 2050,
Designatory Letters:	ACIS (Associate Member of the Institute of Chartered Secretaries and Administrators)		South Africa
		Telephone:	011-403-2900
		Fax:	011-403-1522
		E-mail:	icsa@icsa.co.za
	FCIS (Fellow Member of the Institute of Chartered Secretaries and Administrators)	**Web:**	www.icsa.co.za
	Grad ICSA (Graduate of the Institute of Chartered Secretaries and Administrators)		
Profession:	Corporate Governance		
Membership:	--		
Established:	1891		

Institute of Credit Management of South Africa

Designation:	--	**Address:**	PO Box 73752, Fairland 2030, South Africa
Designatory Letters:	MICM (Member of the Institute of Credit Management)	**Telephone:**	011-478-3830
	AICM (Associate Member of the Institute of Credit Management)	**Fax:**	011-478-3841
		E-mail:	icm@icmorg.co.za
		Web:	www.icmorg.co.za
	FICM (Fellow Member of the Institute of Credit Management)		
Profession:	Credit Management		
Membership:	6,500		
Established:	1953		

The Computer Society of South Africa (CS)

Designation:	--	**Address:**	PO Box 1714, Halfway House, 1685 Gauteng, South Africa
Designatory Letters:	AMCSSA (Associate of the Computer Society of South Africa)	**Telephone:**	27-11-315-1319
	MCSSA (Member of the Computer Society of South Africa)	**Fax:**	27-11-3150-2276
		E-mail:	info@cssa.org.za
		Web:	www.cssa.org.za
	FCSSA (Fellow of the Computer Society of South Africa)		
	PCSSA (Professional of the Computer Society of South Africa)		
Profession:	Information Technology		
Membership:	--		
Established:	--		

The Insurance Institute of South Africa (IISA)

Designation:	--	**Address:**	PO Box 61837, Marshalltown 2107, South Africa or 2nd Floor, Nedbank Park, 13 Girton Road, Parktown, Johannesburg 2193, South Africa
Designatory Letters:	AIISA (Associate of the Insurance Institute of South Africa)		
	FIISA (Fellow of the Insurance Institute of South Africa)		
Profession:	Insurance	**Telephone:**	27-11-274-8400
Membership:	--	**Fax:**	27-11-484-1703
Established:	1966	**E-mail:**	--
		Web:	--

Life Underwriters Association of South Africa (LUASA)

Designation:	--	**Address:**	51 Empire Road, Parktown, Johannesburg/ Private Bag 44, Auckland Park, Johannesburg, South Africa
Designatory Letters:	ALSA (Accredited Lifewriter of South Africa)		
Profession:	Insurance		
Membership:	--	**Telephone:**	011-694-3100-03
Established:	--	**Fax:**	011-726-7508
		E-mail:	luasa@luasa.co.za
		Web:	www.luasa.co.za

Institute of Internal Auditors—South Africa (IIA-SA)

Designation:	--	**Address:**	Unit 2, Bedfordview Office Park, Bedfordview 2008, South Africa
Designatory Letters:	IAT (SA) (Internal Audit Technician [South Africa]) GIA (SA) (General Internal Auditor [South Africa])	**Telephone:** **Fax:**	011-450-1040 011-450-1070
Profession:	Internal Auditing	**E-mail:**	--
Membership:	--	**Web:**	www.iiasa.org.za
Established:	--		

Design, Technology and Management Society International—South Africa

Designation:	--	**Address:**	PO Box 306, Ladismith, Western Cape, South Africa
Designatory Letters:	AMDTMS (Associate Member of the Design, Technology and Management Society International – South Africa)	**Telephone:** **Fax:**	27-0-28-551-2098 27-0-28-551-1305
	MDTMS (Member of the Design, Technology and Management Society International – South Africa) [The CEO of the Society advised that this is an MBA degree level equivalent]	**E-mail:** **Web:**	info@dtmsi.co.za or johanp@telkomsa.net www.dtmsi.co.za
	FDTMS (Fellow Member of the Design, Technology and Management Society International – South Africa) [The CEO of the Society advised that this is a doctorate degree]		
	Pr Admin (Professional Administrator)		
	Pr LodgeM (Professional Lodge Manager)		
	Pr PM (Professional Project Manager)		
	Pr MktM (Professional Marketing Manager)		
	Pr ConstrM (Professional Construction Manager)		
	Pr FinM (Professional Financial Manager)		
	Pr BusC (Professional Business Consultant)		
	RPM (Registered Project Manager)		
	R MktM (Registered Marketing Manager)		
	R ConstrM (Registered Construction Manager)		
	R BusM (Registered Business Manager)		
Profession:	Management		
Membership:	--		
Established:	1995		

Institute of Management Consultants of Southern Africa

Designation:	--	**Address:**	PO Box 787, Hurlingham Manor 2070, South Africa
Designatory Letters:	AFIMC (Affiliate of the Institute of Management Consultants of Southern Africa)	**Telephone:**	27-11-789-9996
	AIMC (Associate of the Institute of Management Consultants of Southern Africa)	**Fax:**	27-11-886-0072
		E-mail:	info@global.co.za
	MIMC (Member of the Institute of Management Consultants of Southern Africa)	**Web:**	www.imcsa.org.za
	FIMC (Fellow of the Institute of Management Consultants of Southern Africa)		
Profession:	Management Consulting		
Membership:	--		
Established:	1972		

Institute of Marketing Management (IMM)

Designation:	--	**Address:**	PO Box 1714, Halfway House, 1685 Gauteng, South Africa
Designatory Letters:	--		
Profession:	Marketing	**Telephone:**	27-11-628-2000
Membership:	--	**Fax:**	27-11-726-4505-726-6540
Established:	1949	**E-mail:**	imm@imm.co.za
		Web:	www.imm.co.za

Institute of People Management

Designation:	--	**Address:**	PO Box 5911, Rivonia 2128, South Africa
Designatory Letters:	--		
Profession:	Personnel Management	**Telephone:**	27-11-785-6800
Membership:	--	**Fax:**	27-11-803-5316-17
Established:	--	**E-mail:**	info@ipm.co.za
		Web:	www.ipm.co.za

Project Management Institute of South Africa (PMSA)

Designation:	--	**Address:**	PO Box 68913, Bryanston 2021, South Africa
Designatory Letters:	M.PMSA (Member of the Project Management Institute of South Africa)	**Telephone:**	--
	PM.PMSA (Professional Member of the Project Management Institute of South Africa)	**Fax:**	27-11-706-6813
		E-mail:	info@pmisa.org.za
		Web:	www.pmisa.co.za
	F.PMSA (Fellow Member of the Project Management Institute of South Africa)		
Profession:	Project Management		
Membership:	1,200		
Established:	1997		

Institute of Risk Management of South Africa (IRMSA)

Designation:	--	**Address:**	PO Box 781437, Sandtown
Designatory Letters:	AIRMSA (Associate Member of		2146, South Africa
	the Institute of Risk	**Telephone:**	27-11-235-4128
	Management of South Africa)	**Fax:**	27-11-235-4006
	FIRMSA (Fellow Member of the	**E-mail:**	adminy@irmsaorg.za
	Institute of Risk Management	**Web:**	www.irmsaorg.za
	of South Africa)		
Profession:	Risk Management		
Membership:	--		
Established:	--		

Association of Corporate Treasurers of South Africa (ACT SA)

Designation:	Corporate Treasurer	**Address:**	PO Box 5853, Cresta 2118,
Designatory Letters:	ACTSA (Associate Member of		South Africa
	the Association of Corporate	**Telephone:**	27-11-482-1512
	Treasurers of Southern	**Fax:**	27-11-806-5558
	Africa)	**E-mail:**	actsa@altavista.net
Profession:	Treasury Management	**Web:**	www.actsa.org.za
Membership:	--		
Established:	--		

SPAIN

Asociación Española de Contabilidad y Administración (Spanish Association of Accountants and Business Administrators – AEIA)

Designation:	--	**Address:**	C/Rafael, bergamin, 16-B,
Designatory Letters:	--		28043 Madrid, Spain
Profession:	Accounting	**Telephone:**	91-547-3756-4465
Membership:	--	**Fax:**	91-541-3484
Established:	1979	**E-mail:**	info@aeca.es
		Web:	www.aeca.es

Instituto de Auditores-Censores Jurados de Cuentas de España (IACJCE)

Designation:	Auditor de Cuentas (Certified	**Address:**	C/Sor Eulalia d'Anzizu, 41,
	Public Accountant)		C/General Arrando, 9,
Designatory Letters:	--		Barcelona 08034, Spain
Profession:	Accounting	**Telephone:**	34-93-280-3100
Membership:	--	**Fax:**	34-93-252-1501
Established:	--	**E-mail:**	internacional@icjce.es
		Web:	www.icjce.es

Instituto de Contabilidad y Auditoria de Cuentas (ICAC)

Designation:	--	**Address:**	C/Huertas 26, 28014
Designatory Letters:	--		Madrid, Spain
Profession:	Accounting	**Telephone:**	--
Membership:	--	**Fax:**	91-429-9486
Established:	--	**E-mail:**	contabilidad@icac.meh.es
		Web:	www.icac.meh.es

Col.Legi D'Actuaris de Catalunya

Designation:	--	**Address:**	Via Laietana, 32 4a planta
Designatory Letters:	--		despatx 98, 08003
Profession:	Actuarial Science		Barcelona, Spain
Membership:	--	**Telephone:**	34-93-319-08-18
Established:	1992	**Fax:**	34-93-319-08-18
		E-mail:	actuaris@actuaris.org
		Web:	www.actuaris.org

Instituto de Actuarios Españoles

Designation:	--	**Address:**	Victor Andrés Belaunde 36,
Designatory Letters:	--		28016 Madrid, Spain
Profession:	Actuarial Science	**Telephone:**	34-1457-8696
Membership:	--	**Fax:**	34-1457-1407
Established:	1943	**E-mail:**	--
		Web:	www.actuaries.org

Asociación de Técnicos de Informática

Designation:	--	**Address:**	Ciutat de Granada 131,
Designatory Letters:	--		Edifico ICT, ES-08018,
Profession:	Information Technology		Barcelona, Spain
Membership:	--	**Telephone:**	34-93-412-5235
Established:	--	**Fax:**	34-93-412-7713
		E-mail:	secregen@ati.es
		Web:	--

Instituto Español de Analistas Financieros (IEAF)

Designation:	--	**Address:**	Avenida del Brasil, 17-3° A y
Designatory Letters:	--		B, E-2820, Madrid, Spain
Profession:	Investment Management	**Telephone:**	34-91-563-1972
Membership:	--	**Fax:**	34-91-563-2575
Established:	--	**E-mail:**	ieaf@mad.servicom.es
		Web:	www.ieaf.es

Asociación Española de Empreseas de Consultoría (AEC)—Instituto de Consultores de Organización y Dirección

Designation:	--	**Address:**	Orfilia 5-Escalera 1-4 D,
Designatory Letters:	--		28010 Madrid, Spain
Profession:	Management Consulting	**Telephone:**	34-91-308-0161
Membership:	--	**Fax:**	34-91-308-2327
Established:	--	**E-mail:**	consultoras@consultoras.com
		Web:	www.consultoras.com

Federación Española de Marketing (FEM)

Designation:	--	**Address:**	Pena y Goni 2-1°D, E-20002,
Designatory Letters:	--		San Sebastian, Spain
Profession:	Marketing	**Telephone:**	34-43-272722
Membership:	--	**Fax:**	34-43-272788
		E-mail:	--
		Web:	--

Asociación Española de Tesoreros de Empresa – ASSET (Spanish Association of Corporate Treasurers)

Designation:	--	**Address:**	Aribau, 195 5 Derecha 08021
Designatory Letters:	--		Barcelona, Spain
Profession:	Treasury Management	**Telephone:**	34-93-414-1214
Membership:	--	**Fax:**	34-93-414-0106
Established:	--	**E-mail:**	asset@asset.es
		Web:	www.asset.es

SRI LANKA

Association of Accounting Technicians of Sri Lanka

Designation:	Accounting Technician	**Address:**	AAT Centre, No. 540
Designatory Letters:	MAAT (Member of the Association of Accounting Technicians)		Thimibirigasyaya Road, Narahenpita, Colombo – 05, Sri Lanka
Profession:	Accounting	**Telephone:**	94-1-559-669
Membership:	--	**Fax:**	94-1-559-299
Established:	1987	**E-mail:**	aatsled@sltnet.lk
		Web:	www.aatsl.lk

The Institute of Chartered Accountants of Sri Lanka

Designation:	Chartered Accountant	**Address:**	30 A, Malalasekera
Designatory Letters:	ACA (SL) (Associate Member of the Institute of Chartered Accountants of Sri Lanka)		Mawatha, Colombo 7, Sri Lanka
		Telephone:	94-1-585.451, 586-256
	FCA (SL) (Fellow Member of the Institute of Chartered Accountants of Sri Lanka)	**Fax:**	94-1-588-783
		E-mail:	technical@icasrilanka.com
		Web:	www.icasrilanka.com
Profession:	Accounting		
Membership:	--		
Established:	1959		

Society of Certified Management Accountants of Sri Lanka

Designation:	Certified Management Accountant	**Address:**	01, Bethesda Place (Off Dickmans Road), Colombo 5, Sri Lanka
Designatory Letters:	CMA (Certified Management Accountant)	**Telephone:**	94-011-250-1062
Profession:	Accounting	**Fax:**	94-011-250-7087
Membership:	--	**E-mail:**	--
Established:	2000	**Web:**	www.cma-srilanka.org

Institute of Bankers of Sri Lanka

Designation:	--	**Address:**	No. 5, Mile Post Avenue,
Designatory Letters:	AIB (Associate of the Institute of Bankers)		Colombo 3, Sri Lanka
		Telephone:	--
	FIB (Fellow of the Institute of Bankers)	**Fax:**	--
		E-mail:	--
Profession:	Banking	**Web:**	--
Membership:	--		
Established:	--		

The Computer Society of Sri Lanka (CSSL)

Designation:	--	**Address:**	Professional Centre, 275/75 Stanley Wijesundera Mawatha, Colombo 7, Sri Lanka
Designatory Letters:	--		
Profession:	Information Technology		
Membership:	--		
Established:	--	**Telephone:**	94-11-259-2762
		Fax:	94-11-250-8009
		E-mail:	cssisec@cssl.lk
		Web:	--

Sri Lanka Institute of Marketing

Designation:	--	**Address:**	5th Floor, Lakshmans Building, 321 Galle Road, Colombo 3, Sri Lanka
Designatory Letters:	--		
Profession:	Marketing		
Membership:	--	**Telephone:**	94-1-575658-564-220
Established:	1970	**Fax:**	94-1-575210
		E-mail:	--
		Web:	www.lanka.net/slim

SUDAN

The Sudanese Association of Certified Accountants

Designation:	--	**Address:**	Alekhawa Building, Albara Street, Khartoum, Sudan
Designatory Letters:	--		
Profession:	Accounting	**Telephone:**	--
Membership:	--	**Fax:**	249-11-772-980-782803-774536
Established:	--		
		E-mail:	zeinborai65@yahoo.com
		Web:	--

SWAZILAND

Swaziland Institute of Accountants

Designation:	Chartered Accountant	**Address:**	MTN Office Park, Smuts Street, Mbabane, Swaziland
Designatory Letters:	CA (S) (Chartered Accountant of Swaziland)		
		Telephone:	
Profession:	Accounting	**Fax:**	268-40-45566
Membership:	60	**E-mail:**	268-40-46827
Established:	1985	**Web:**	sia@realnet.co.sz
			--

SWEDEN

Föreningen Auktoriserade Revisorer (FAR) (The Swedish Institute of Authorised Public Accountants) Professional institute for authorised public accountants (*auktoriserade revisorer*)

Designation:	Auktoriserad Revisor/Godkäand Revisor (Authorized Public Accountant)	**Address:**	Box 6417, S-113 82, Stockholm, Sweden
		Telephone:	46-8-506-112-00
Designatory Letters:	--	**Fax:**	46-8-341-461
Profession:	Accounting	**E-mail:**	sekr@far.se
Membership:	--	**Web:**	www.far.se
Established:	1923		

Revisorsnämnden (The Supervisory Board of Public Accountants)

Designation:	--	**Address:**	PO Box 24014, S-104, 50 Stockholm, Sweden
Designatory Letters:	--		
Profession:	Accounting	**Telephone:**	468-783-1870
Membership:	--	**Fax:**	468-783-1871
Established:	1995	**E-mail:**	--
		Web:	--

Svenska Revisorsamfundet SRS (The Swedish Association of Auditor) Professional institute for
approved public accountants (*godkända revisorer*)

Designation:	--	**Address:**	Sibyellgatan 47, Stockholm,
Designatory Letters:	--		Sweden
Profession:	Accounting	**Telephone:**	46-8-663-2250
Membership:	--	**Fax:**	46-8-663-0248
Established:	1899	**E-mail:**	info@revisorsamfundet.se
		Web:	www.revisorsamfundet.se

Svenska Aktuarieforeningen

Designation:	--	**Address:**	c/o Swedish Insurance
Designatory Letters:	--		Federation, PO Box 1436,
Profession:	Actuarial Science		S-11184 Stockholm,
Membership:	--		Sweden
Established:	1904	**Telephone:**	46-0-8783-07211
		Fax:	46-0-8723-0308
		E-mail:	--
		Web:	www.aktuarieforeningen.se

Swedish Information Processing Society

Designation:	--	**Address:**	PO Box 45 153, S-104 30
Designatory Letters:	--		Stockholm, Sweden
Profession:	Information Technology	**Telephone:**	46-8-506-40400
Membership:	--	**Fax:**	46-8-506-40415
Established:	--	**E-mail:**	rolf.berndston@dfs.se
		Web:	www.dfs.se

The Swedish Society of Financial Analysts (SFF)

Designation:	--	**Address:**	S-111, 30 Stockholm,
Designatory Letters:	--		Sweden
Profession:	Investment Management	**Telephone:**	46-8-570-19702
Membership:	--	**Fax:**	46-8-570-19703
Established:	--	**E-mail:**	lindblad@finansanalyktiker.se
		Web:	www.finansanalytiker.se

Swedish Association of Management Consultants (SAMC)

Designation:	--	**Address:**	Box 7469, S-103 92
Designatory Letters:	--		Stockholm, Sweden
Profession:	Management Consulting	**Telephone:**	46-8-231-600
Membership:	--	**Fax:**	46-8-660-3378
Established:	--	**E-mail:**	info@samc.se
		Web:	www.samc.ce

Sveriges Marknadsförbund

Designation:	--	**Address:**	Sveavägen 17, 5 tr 11157,
Designatory Letters:	--		Stockholm, Sweden
Profession:	Marketing	**Telephone:**	46-8-215-863
Membership:	--	**Fax:**	46-8-215-819
Established:	--	**E-mail:**	kansli@svemarknad.se
		Web:	www.svemarknad.se

Svenskt Projecktforum (Swedish Project Management Society)

Designation:	--	**Address:**	Norr Mälarstrand 20, 11220
Designatory Letters:	--		Stockholm, Sweden
Profession:	Project Management	**Telephone:**	46-8-653-5635
Membership:	--	**Fax:**	46-8-651-5198
Established:	1989	**E-mail:**	info@projforum.se
		Web:	www.projforum.se

SWITZERLAND

Treuhand-Kammer—Swiss Institute of Certified Accountants and Tax Consultants

Designation:	Certified Accountant	**Address:**	Limmatquai 120, CH-8001,
Designatory Letters:	--		Zürich, Switzerland
Profession:	Accounting	**Telephone:**	41-1-267-7575
Membership:	--	**Fax:**	41-1-267-7585
Established:	--	**E-mail:**	dienste@treuhand-kammer.ch
		Web:	www.treuhand-kammer.ch

Association Suisse des Actuaires (Swiss Association of Actuaries)

Designation:	--	**Address:**	c/o Swiss Reinsurance
Designatory Letters:	--		Company, Mythenquai 50-
Profession:	Actuarial Science		60, 8022 Zurich,
Membership:	--		Switzerland
Established:	1905	**Telephone:**	1-285-2681
		Fax:	1-285-4754
		E-mail:	info@actuaries.ch
		Web:	www.actuaries.ch/

Information and Communication Technology

Designation:	--	**Address:**	PO Box 515, Kramgasse 5,
Designatory Letters:	--		CH-3000, Bern,
Profession:	Information Technology		Switzerland
Membership:	--	**Telephone:**	41-31-328-2720
Established:	--	**Fax:**	41-31-328-2730
		E-mail:	info@ictswitzerland.ch
		Web:	www.ictswitzerland.ch

Swiss Financial Analysts Association (SFAA)

Designation:	--	**Address:**	Feldstrasse 80, 8180 Buelach,
Designatory Letters:	--		Switzerland
Profession:	Investment Management	**Telephone:**	41-1-872-3540
Membership:	--	**Fax:**	41-1-872-3532
Established:	--	**E-mail:**	info@sfaa.ch
		Web:	www.sfaa.ch

Assocation Suisse des Conseils en Organisation et Gestion (ASCO)

Designation:	--	**Address:**	Weinbergstrasse 31, CH-
Designatory Letters:	--		8006, Zürich, Switzerland
Profession:	Management Consulting	**Telephone:**	410-43-343-9480
Membership:	--	**Fax:**	410-43-343-9481
Established:	--	**E-mail:**	office@asco.ch
		Web:	www.asco.ch

SMC Schweizerischer Marketing Club

Designation:	--	**Address:**	Parkweg 2, CH-4665
Designatory Letters:	--		Oftringen, Switzerland
Profession:	Marketing	**Telephone:**	--
Established:	--	**Fax:**	--
		E-mail:	--
		Web:	www.sms-biel.ch

SPM Swiss Project Management Association

Designation:	--	**Address:**	Flughofstrasse 50, CH-8152,
Designatory Letters:	--		Glattbrugg, Switzerland
Profession:	Project Management	**Telephone:**	41-44-809-1170
Membership:	1,000	**Fax:**	41-44-809-1140
Established:	1983	**E-mail:**	spm@spm.ch
		Web:	www.spm.ch

SYRIA

Association of Syrian Certified Accountants

Designation:	--	**Address:**	PO Box 40005, Damascus-
Designatory Letters:	--		Reknal dein – Shamdein
Profession:	Accounting		Square, Bahsa, Syria
Membership:	--	**Telephone:**	963-11-224-0663
Established:	--	**Fax:**	963-11-276-4750
		E-mail:	ASCASY@hotmail.com
		Web:	--

Syrian Computer Society (SCS)

Designation:	--	**Address:**	PO Box 33492, Damascus,
Designatory Letters:	--		Syria
Profession:	Information Technology	**Telephone:**	--
Membership:	--	**Fax:**	963-11-373-7558
Established:	--	**E-mail:**	scs@syriatel.net
		Web:	www.scs-syria.com

T

TAIWAN

Federation of CPA Associations of Chinese Taiwan

Designation:	--	**Address:**	9th Floor, 1 Nanhai Road, Taipei, Taiwan
Designatory Letters:	--		
Profession:	Accounting	**Telephone:**	886-2-2394-5291
Membership:	--	**Fax:**	886-2393-6216
Established:	--	**E-mail:**	james.wang@tw.ey.com
		Web:	www.nfcpaa.org.tw

The Actuarial Institute of the Republic of China (AIRC)

Designation:	--	**Address:**	c/o Cathay Life Insurance Company Ltd., 20F, 296, Jen-Ai Road, Section 4, Taipei, Taiwan
Designatory Letters:	--		
Profession:	Actuarial Science		
Membership:	--	**Telephone:**	886-2755-1399, X 2253
Established:	1969	**Fax:**	886-2755-9180
		E-mail:	--
		Web:	www.airc.org.tw

The Securities Analysts Association, Chinese Taipei

Designation:	--	**Address:**	15F, No.100, Sec 2, Roosevelt Road, Taipei, Taiwan 100
Designatory Letters:	--		
Profession:	Investment Management	**Telephone:**	886-2-2366-6085
Membership:	--	**Fax:**	886-2-2369-1302
Established:	--	**E-mail:**	tsaa@mail.gretai.org.tw
		Web:	www.saa.gretai.org.tw

Chinese Marketing Association R.O.C.

Designation:	--	**Address:**	3F-I No. 63, Nanking E.Rd., Sec 5, Taipei, Taiwan, R.O.C.
Designatory Letters:	--		
Profession:	Marketing	**Telephone:**	886-2-749-1789
Membership:	--	**Fax:**	886-2-753-3688
Established:	--	**E-mail:**	gpr@ms4.hinet.net
		Web:	--

Taiwan Project Management Association

Designation:	Certified Project Management Associate	**Address:**	12F No. 529 Po-Ai Road, Feng Shan City, Kaohsiiong County, Taiwan.
	Certified Project Manager		
	Certified Senior Project Manager	**Telephone:**	886-7-747-9681
		Fax:	886-7-743-4906
	Certified Project Director	**E-mail:**	allini@tpma-tw.org
Designatory Letters:	CPMA (Certified Project Management Associate)	**Web:**	www.tpma-tw.org
	CPM (Certified Project Manager)		
	CSPM (Certified Senior Project Manager)		
	CPD (Certified Project Director)		
Profession:	Project Management		
Membership:	--		
Established:	--		

TANZANIA

National Board of Accountants and Auditors (NBAA)

Designation:	Certified Public Accountant of Tanzania	**Address:**	Mhasibu House, Bibi Titi Mohamed Road, Ilala District, Dar es Salaam, Tanzania
	Certified Public Accountant Public Practice	**Telephone:**	255-51-151-745
		Fax:	255-51-151-746
	General Accountant	**E-mail:**	info@nbaa-tz.org
	Approved Accountant	**Web:**	www.nbaa-tz.org
	Accounting Technician		
Designatory Letters:	CPA (T) (Certified Public Accountant of Tanzania)		
	CPA-PP (Certified Public Accountant Public Practice)		
	GA (Graduate Accountant)		
	AP (Approved Accountant)		
	AT (Accounting Technician)		
Profession:	Accounting		
Membership:	--		
Established:	1972		

Tanzania Association of Accountants

Designation:	--	**Address:**	Mhasibu House, Bibi Titi Mohamed Road, PO Box 459, Dar es Salaam, Tanzania
Designatory Letters:	--		
Profession:	Accounting		
Membership:	--	**Telephone:**	255-51-151814, 112058
Established:	--	**Fax:**	255-51-114920, 151746
		E-mail:	ernst.young@twiga.com
		Web:	--

THAILAND

Federation of Accounting Professions

Designation:	--	**Address:**	444/1 Samsen Road, Dusit,
Designatory Letters:	--		Bangkok 10300, Thailand
Profession:	Accounting	**Telephone:**	66-2-668-8535-8
Membership:	--	**Fax:**	66-2-2241-8787
Established:	--	**E-mail:**	afarep@icaat.or.th
		Web:	--

The Society of Actuaries of Thailand (SAT)

Designation:	--	**Address:**	c/o The Thai Life Assurance
Designatory Letters:	--		Association, 36/1 Soi Sapanku,
Profession:	Actuarial Science		Rama 4 Road, BKK 10120,
Membership:	--		Thailand
Established:	1975	**Telephone:**	276-1025-7
		Fax:	276-1997
		E-mail:	--
		Web:	--

Thailand Internet Association

Designation:	--	**Address:**	Srisakdi Charmonman IT Centre,
Designatory Letters:	--		Assumption University Bangna
Profession:	Information Technology		Campus, Bangna-Trad. Km 26,
Membership:	--		Bang Sao Thong, Samutprakarn
Established:	--		10540, Thailand
		Telephone:	662-723-2891
		Fax:	662-723-2892
		E-mail:	charm@ksc.net.th
		Web:	--

Securities Analysts Association

Designation:	--	**Address:**	62 Stock Exchange of Thailand
Designatory Letters:	--		Building, 11th Fl. Room 1105,
Profession:	Investment Management		Ratchadapisek Rd., Klongtoey,
Membership:	--		Bangkok 10110, Thailand
Established:	--	**Telephone:**	662-229-2355-6
		Fax:	662-654-5034
		E-mail:	info@saa-thai.org
		Web:	www.saa-thai.org

Marketing Association of Thailand

Designation:	--	**Address:**	14th Floor, Lumpini Tower,
Designatory Letters:	--		1168/21 Rama IV Road,
Profession:	Marketing		Tungmhamek, Bangkok 10120,
Membership:	--		Thailand
Established:	--	**Telephone:**	662-285-5987-88
		Fax:	662-285-5989
		E-mail:	--
		Web:	--

TRINIDAD AND TOBAGO

Institute of Chartered Accountants of Trinidad & Tobago

Designation:	Chartered Accountant	**Address:**	2nd Floor, Professional Centre,
Designatory Letters:	CA (T) (Chartered Accountant of Trinidad and Tobago)		Wrightson Road Ext., PO Box 864, Port of Spain, Trinidad & Tobago
Profession:	Accounting	**Telephone:**	868-623-8000
Membership:	927	**Fax:**	868-623-8000
Established:	1970	**E-mail:**	icatt@tstt.net.tt
		Web:	www.icatt.org

TUNISIA

Ordre des Experts Comptables de Tunisie

Designation:	Certificat D'Etudes Superieures de Revisior-Comptable	**Address:**	Immeuble Lac des Cygnes, Bloc B, Appt B5 & B6, 3 eme Etage, Rue de Lac Victoria, Les Berges du
Designatory Letters:	CPA		Lac, 1053 Tunis, Tunisia
Profession:	Accounting	**Telephone:**	216-71-965-255; 963-290
Membership:	--	**Fax:**	216-71-964-204-965-323
Established:	--	**E-mail:**	oect@planet.tn
		Web:	www.oect.org.tn

Ordre Des Experts Comptables et des Commissaires aux Comptes de Tunisie

Designation:	--	**Address:**	33 Rue Dr. Burnet,
Designatory Letters:	--		Mutuelleville,Tunisia
Profession:	Accounting	**Telephone:**	216-1780-949, 282-979
Membership:	--	**Fax:**	--
Established:	--	**E-mail:**	--
		Web:	--

TURKEY

Expert Accountants' Association of Turkey

Designation:	--	**Address:**	Husrev Gerede Cad. 21, 80680-
Designatory Letters:	--		Tesvikiye, Instanbul, Turkey
Profession:	Accounting	**Telephone:**	90-212-236-1071
Membership:	--	**Fax:**	90-212-236-1715
Established:	--	**E-mail:**	pekdemir@turk.net
		Web:	www.tmud.org.tr

Union of Chambers of Certified Public Accountants of Turkey (TÜRMOB)

Designation:	--	**Address:**	65 Genclik Caddesi No: 107,
Designatory Letters:	--		Anittepe 06570, Ankara, Turkey
Profession:	Accounting	**Telephone:**	90-312-232-5065
Membership:	--	**Fax:**	90-312-232-5074
Established:	--	**E-mail:**	international@turmob.org.tr
		Web:	www.turmob.org.tr

Turkiye Aktuerler Dernegi

Designation:	--	**Address:**	Morbasan Sok.Koza Is Merkezi,
Designatory Letters:	--		B.Blok K.3 Balmumcu, Besiktas, Instanbul, Turkey
Profession:	Actuarial Science	**Telephone:**	--
Membership:	--	**Fax:**	--
Established:	1951	**E-mail:**	--
		Web:	--

Institute of Management Consultants of Turkey

Designation:	--	**Address:**	Dedeman Ticaret Merkezi, Yildiz Posta, Cad No. 52, Kat 3, 34340 Esentepe, Instanbul, Turkey
Designatory Letters:	--		
Profession:	Management Consulting		
Membership:	--	**Telephone:**	0-212-273-1863
Established:	--	**Fax:**	0-212-273-1867
		E-mail:	--
		Web:	--

Turkish Marketing Association

Designation:	--	**Address:**	Büyük Dere Caddesi Hürhan Kat: 5 No. 15/A, 34381 Sisli, Instanbul, Turkey
Designatory Letters:	--		
Profession:	Marketing		
Membership:	--	**Telephone:**	90-212-518-1620
Established:	--	**Fax:**	90-212-518-1615
		E-mail:	info@tpad.org.tr
		Web:	www.tpad.org.tr

Project Management Association Turkey

Designation:	--	**Address:**	Gulvenlik Caddesi Guven Sokak 28/1 Y. Ayrnci, 06540, Ankara, Turkey
Designatory Letters:	--		
Profession:	Project Management		
Membership:	--	**Telephone:**	312-468-0901
Established:	--	**Fax:**	312-426-7013
		E-mail:	denzig@venus.aselsan.com.tr
		Web:	--

U

UGANDA

Institute of Certified Public Accountants of Uganda

Designation:	Certified Public Accountant of Uganda	**Address:**	42 Bukoto Street, Kololo, PO Box 12464, Kampala, Uganda
Designatory Letters:	CPA (U) (Certified Public Accountant of Uganda)	**Telephone:**	256-41-540-125-6
		Fax:	256-41-540-389
Profession:	Accounting	**E-mail:**	icpau@infocom.co.ug
Membership:	560	**Web:**	--
Established:	1992		

UKRAINE

The Ukrainian Actuarial Society

Designation:	Certified Ukrainian Actuary	**Address:**	c/o Mathematical Department of the Kyiv National University, 64 Volodymyrska str., Kyiv 01033, Ukraine
Designatory Letters:	CUA (Certified Ukrainian Actuary)		
	FCUA (Fellow Certified Ukrainian Actuary)	**Telephone:**	380-44-266-2337
		Fax:	380-44-266-2337
Profession:	Actuarial Science	**E-mail:**	krvavych@yahoo.com
Membership:	--	**Web:**	--
Established:	1999		

Ukrainian Federation of Professional Accountants and Auditors

Designation:	--	**Address:**	Avenue Bazhana, 26, Office 166, Kiev, 02410, Ukraine
Designatory Letters:	--		
Profession:	Accounting	**Telephone:**	380-44-574-5537
Membership:	--	**Fax:**	380-44-574-5537
Established:	--	**E-mail:**	headoffice@ufpaa.org
		Web:	www.ufpaa.org

Ukraine Society of Financial Analysts

Designation:	--	**Address:**	PO 328, Kiev-1, 01001 Ukraine
Designatory Letters:	--	**Telephone:**	38-044-284-3081
Profession:	Investment Management	**Fax:**	38-044-205-3281
Membership:	--	**E-mail:**	usfa@nbi.org.ua
Established:	--	**Web:**	www.usfa.org.ua

Ukrainian Marketing Association

Designation:	--	**Address:**	Prospect Peremogy 54/1, Office 434, 436, Kiev 03057, Ukraine
Designatory Letters:	--		
Profession:	Marketing		
Membership:	--	**Telephone:**	38-044-459-6209
Established:	--	**Fax:**	38-044-456-0894
		E-mail:	uma@kneu.kiev.ua
		Web:	www.uam.iatp.org.ua

Ukraine Project Management Association (UKRNET)

Designation:	--	**Address:**	31 Povitnofloskiy pnosp., Kiev
Designatory Letters:	--		252252037, Ukraine
Profession:	Project Management	**Telephone:**	7-044-272-9400
Membership:	--	**Fax:**	7-044-245-4857
Established:	--	**E-mail:**	--
		Web:	--

UNITED ARAB EMIRATES

Accountants and Auditors Association

Designation:	--	**Address:**	PO Box 38881, Sharjah, United
Designatory Letters:	--		Arab Emirates
Profession:	Accounting	**Telephone:**	971-6-556-5555
Membership:	--	**Fax:**	971-6-556-5554
Established:	1997	**E-mail:**	aaauae@emirates.net.ae
		Web:	www.aaa.org.ae

UNITED KINGDOM and NORTHERN IRELAND

Association of Accounting Technicians

Designation:	Accounting Technician	**Address:**	154 Clerkenwell Road, London
Designatory Letters:	MAAT (Member of the		EC1R 5AD, England
	Association of	**Telephone:**	207-415-7501
	Accounting	**Fax:**	207-410-0904
	Technicians)	**E-mail:**	jane.scottpaul@aat.org.uk
	FMAAT (Fellow Member	**Web:**	www.aat.co.uk
	of the Association of		
	Accounting		
	Technicians)		
Profession:	Accounting		
Membership:	102,000 (including		
	students)		
Established:	1980		

Association of Authorised Public Accountants (AAPA)

Designation:	Authorised Public	**Address:**	10 Cornfield Road, Eastbourne,
	Accountant		East Sussex BN21 4QE, England
Designatory Letters:	AAPA (Associate of the	**Telephone:**	01323-410-412
	Association of	**Fax:**	01323-733-313
	Authorised Public	**E-mail:**	info@accaglobal.com
	Accountants)	**Web:**	www.accaglobal.com
	FAPA (Fellow of the		
	Association of		
	Authorised Public		
	Accountants)		
Profession:	Accounting		
Membership:	--		
Established:	1978		

Association of Chartered Certified Accountants

Designation:	Chartered Certified Accountant	**Address:**	29 Lincoln's Inn Fields, London WC2A, 3EE, England
	Certified Accounting Technician	**Telephone:**	44-207-059-5000
		Fax:	44-207-396-7070
Designatory Letters:	ACCA (Associate Member of the Association of Chartered Certified Accountants)	**E-mail:**	info@accaglobal.com
		Web:	www.accaglobal.com
	FCCA (Fellow Member of the Association of Chartered Certified Accountants)		
	CAT (Certified Accounting Technician)		
	DipFM (Diploma in Financial Management)		
	DipCG (Diploma in Corporate Governance)		
	DipIFR (Diploma in International Financial Reporting)		
Profession:	Accounting		
Membership:	370,000 (including 260,000 students)		
Established:	1904		

Association of Church Accountants and Treasurers (ACAT)

Designation:	NA	**Address:**	England
Designatory Letters:	NA	**Telephone:**	--
Profession:	Accounting	**Fax:**	--
Membership:	--	**E-mail:**	admin@acat.uk.com
Established:	1992	**Web:**	www.acat.com

Association of International Accountants

Designation:	International Accountant	**Address:**	Staithes 3, The Watermark, Metro Riverside, Newcastle-upon-Tyne, NE11 9SN, England
Designatory Letters:	AAIA (Associate Member of the Association of International Accountants)	**Telephone:**	44-0-191-482-4409
		Fax:	44-0-191-482-5578
	FAIA (Fellow Member of the Association of International Accountants)	**E-mail:**	aia@aia.org.uk
		Web:	www.aia.org.uk
Profession:	Accounting		
Membership:	15,000		
Established:	1928		

Association of On-line Accountants

Designation:	NA	**Address:**	5th Floor, 100 Victoria Street, Bristol BS1 6HZ, England
Designatory Letters:	NA	**Telephone:**	117-915-9604
Profession:	Accounting	**Fax:**	117-915-9638
Membership:	--	**E-mail:**	--
Established:	--	**Web:**	www.aola.co.uk

British Accounting Association (BAA)

Designation:	NA	**Address:**	Kathryn Hewitt, BAA Administrator,
Designatory Letters:	NA		Sheffield University Management
Profession:	Accounting		School, 9 Mappin Street,
Membership:	--		Sheffield S1 4DT, England
Established:	1947	**Telephone:**	0114-222-3462
		Fax:	0114-222-3348
		E-mail:	baa@sheffield.ac.uk
		Web:	www.baa.group.shef.ac.uk

British Association of Hospitality Accountants (BAHA)

Designation:	--	**Address:**	Merley House Business Centre,
Designatory Letters:	ABHA (Associate Member of the British Association of Hospitality Accountants)		Merley House Lane, Wimborne, Dorset, BH21 3AA, England
		Telephone:	1202-889-430
		Fax:	1202-887-967
	ABHA Cert. (Associate Member Certified of the British Association of Hospitality Accountants)	**E-mail:**	admin@baha-uk.org
		Web:	www.baha-uk.org
	FBHA (Fellow Member of the British Association of Hospitality Accountants)		
Profession:	Accounting		
Membership:	700		
Established:	1969		

Chartered Institute of Public Finance and Accountancy

Designation:	--	**Address:**	3 Robert Street, London
Designatory Letters:	IPFA (Member of the Chartered Institute of Public Finance and Accountancy)	**Telephone:**	WC2N 6BH, England
		Fax:	44-20-7543-5600
		E-mail:	44-2-7543-5700
		Web:	steve.freer@cipfa.org
	CPFA (Chartered Public Finance Accountant) (A new dual professional designation between the CIPFA and the CMA Canada)		www.cipfa.org.uk
Profession:	Accounting		
Membership:	15,000		
Established:	1885		

Financial Reporting Council (FRC) and the Professional Oversight Board for Accountancy

Designation:	NA	**Address:**	5th Floor, Aldwych House, 71-91
Designatory Letters:	NA		Aldwych, London WC2 4HN,
Profession:	Accounting		England
Established:	--	**Telephone:**	207-492-2300
		Fax:	207-492-2301
		E-mail:	A.Andrews@frc.org.uk
		Web:	www.frc.org.uk

Institute of Chartered Accountants in England & Wales

Designation:	Chartered Accountant	**Address:**	Chartered Accountants' Hall,
Designatory Letters:	ACA (Associate Member of the Institute of Chartered Accountants in England and Wales) FCA (Fellow Member of the Institute of Chartered Accountants in England and Wales)	**Telephone:** **Fax:** **E-mail:** **Web:**	Moorgate Place, London EC2P 2BJ, England 44-207-920-8403 44-207-628-1874 jean.ettridge@icaew.co.uk www.icaew.co.uk
Profession:	Accounting		
Membership:	128,000		
Established:	1880		

Institute of Chartered Accountants of Scotland

Designation:	Chartered Accountant	**Address:**	CA House, 21 Haymarket Yards,
Designatory Letters:	CA (Chartered Accountant)	**Telephone:**	Edinburgh EH12 5BH, Scotland 44-131-347-0100
Profession:	Accounting	**Fax:**	44-131-347-0105
Membership:	16,400	**E-mail:**	enquiries@icas.org.uk
Established:	1854	**Web:**	www.icas.org.uk

Institute of Financial Accountants

Designation:	Financial Accountant	**Address:**	Burford House, 44 London Road,
Designatory Letters:	AFA (Associate Member of the Institute of Financial Accountants) FFA (Fellow Member of Institute of Financial Accountants)	**Telephone:** **Fax:** **E-mail:** **Web:**	Sevenoaks, Kent TN13 1AS, England 01732-458-080 01732-455-848 mail@ifa.org.uk www.ifa.org.uk
Profession:	Accounting		
Membership:	--		
Established:	1916		

International Network of Professional Accountants (INPACT)

Designation:	NA	**Address:**	Inpact International, Tavistock
Designatory Letters:	NA		House South, Tavistock Square,
Profession:	Accounting		London WC1H 9LG, England
Membership:	--	**Telephone:**	207-387-4741
Established:	--	**Fax:**	207-387-4715
		E-mail:	inpact@inpactint.com
		Web:	www.inpactint.com

The International Accounting Standards Board (IASB)

Designation:	NA	**Address:**	30 Cannon Street, London EC4M
Designatory Letters:	NA		6XH, UK
Profession:	Accounting	**Telephone:**	44-207-246-6410
Membership:	NA	**Fax:**	44-207-246-6411
Established:	1973	**E-mail:**	iasb@iasb.org
		Web:	www.iasb.org

National Association of Specialist Dental Accountants

Designation:	NA	**Address:**	England
Designatory Letters:	NA	**Telephone:**	0870-601-0230
Profession:	Accounting	**Fax:**	--
Membership:	--	**E-mail:**	frances.clark@keswickaccountants.co.uk
Established:	--	**Web:**	www.nasda.org.uk

Society of Law Accountants of Scotland

Designation:	NA	**Address:**	7 Sidlaw Terrace, Birkhill, Angus DD2 5PY, Scotland
Designatory Letters:	NA		
Profession:	Accounting	**Telephone:**	01382-580-131
Membership:	--	**Fax:**	01382-580-131
Established:	1910	**E-mail:**	solas.admin@hotmail.co.uk
		Web:	www.solas.co.uk

Society of International Accounting Technicians

Designation:	International Accounting Technician	**Address:**	South Bank Building, Kingsway, Team Valley, Gateshead, Tyne-and-Wear NE11 0JS, England
Designatory Letters:	SIAT (Associate Membership) SIAT (Fellow Membership)	**Telephone:**	0870-750-3132
		Fax:	0191-482-5578
		E-mail:	siat@siatglobal.com
Profession:	Accounting	**Web:**	www.siatglobal.com
Membership:	--		
Established:	--		

Society of Professional Accountants

Designation:	NA	**Address:**	95 High Street, Great Missenden, Buckinghamshire HP16 0AL, England
Designatory Letters:	NA		
Profession:	Accounting		
Membership:	--	**Telephone:**	01494-864414
Established:	1996	**Fax:**	01494-864454
		E-mail:	mail@spa.org.uk
		Web:	www.spa.org.uk

Society of Turnaround Professionals

Designation:	--	**Address:**	8th Floor, 120 Aldersgate St, London EC1A 4JQ, England
Designatory Letters:	--		
Profession:	Accounting, Restructuring	**Telephone:**	207-566-4222
		Fax:	207-566-4224
Membership:	--	**E-mail:**	info@stp.org.uk
Established:	2000	**Web:**	www.stp.org.uk

Institute of Social and Ethical Accounting and Ethics

Designation:	Certified Sustainability Assurance Practitioner	**Address:**	Unit A, 137 Shepherdess Walk, London N1 7RQ, England
	CSAP (Certified Sustainability Assurance	**Telephone:**	207-549-0400
		Fax:	207-253-7440
Designatory Letters:	Practitioner)	**E-mail:**	secretariat@account.org.uk
Profession:	Accounting, Social	**Web:**	www.account.org.uk
Membership:	--		
Established:	1995		

The Faculty of Actuaries

Designation:	--	**Address:**	Maclaurin House, 18 Dublin Street, Edinburgh EH1 3AP, Scotland
Designatory Letters:	FFA (Fellow of the Faculty of Actuaries)	**Telephone:**	0131-240-1300
Profession:	Actuarial Science	**Fax:**	0131-240-1313
Membership:	--	**E-mail:**	faculty@actuaries.org.uk
Established:	1856	**Web:**	www.actuaries.org.uk

Institute of Actuaries

Designation:	--	**Address:**	Staple Inn Hall, High Holborn, London WC1V 7QJ, England
Designatory Letters:	AIA (Associate Member of the Institute of Actuaries)	**Telephone:**	207-632-2100
		Fax:	207-632-2111
	FIA (Fellow Member of the Institute of Actuaries)	**E-mail:**	institute@actuaries.org
		Web:	www.actuaries.org.uk
Profession:	Actuarial Science		
Membership:	--		
Established:	1848		

Staple Inn Actuarial Society

Designation:	NA	**Address:**	Staple Inn Hall, High Holborn, London WC1V 7QJ, England
Designatory Letters:	NA		
Profession:	Actuarial Science	**Telephone:**	--
Membership:	--	**Fax:**	--
Established:	1910	**E-mail:**	chairman@sias.org.uk
		Web:	www.sias.org.uk

Chartered Institute of Arbitrators

Designation:	Chartered Arbitrator, Accredited Mediator	**Address:**	International Arbitration Centre, 12 Bloomsbury Square, London WC1A 2LP, England
Designatory Letters:	ACIarb (Associate of the Chartered Institute of Arbitrators)	**Telephone:**	44-0-207-421-7444
	MCIarb (Member of the Chartered Institute of Arbitrators)	**Fax:** **E-mail:** **Web:**	44-0-207-404-4023 info@arbitrators.org www.arbitrators.org
	FCIArb (Fellow of the Chartered Institute of Arbitrators)		
Profession:	Arbitration, Adjudication, Mediation		
Membership:	11,000		
Established:	1915		

Chartered Institute of Bankers in Scotland

Designation:	Chartered Banker	**Address:**	Drumsheugh House, 38b Drumsheugh Gardens, Edinburgh, EH3 7SW, Scotland
Designatory Letters:	CB (Chartered Banker) PMA (Professional Mortgage Adviser)	**Telephone:**	131-473-7777
Profession:	Banking	**Fax:**	131-473-7788
Membership:	--	**E-mail:**	info@ciobs.org.uk
Established:	1875	**Web:**	www.ciobs.org.uk

The Chartered Institute of Banking (CIB)

Designation: Chartered Banker

Designatory Letters:
ACIB (Associateship of the Chartered Institute of Bankers)
FCIB (Fellowship of the Chartered Institute of Bankers)
CeFS (Certificate in Financial Studies)
DipFS (Diploma in Financial Studies)
CeFA (Certificate for Financial Advisers)
CeMAP (Certificate in Mortgage Advice and Practice)
CeRGI (Certificate of Regulated General Insurance)
CeLTM (Certificate in Lifetime Mortgages)
CDCS (Certified Documentary Credit Specialist)
CSP (Customer Service Professional)
CeLTCI (Certificate in Long-Term Care Insurance)
CeRCC (Certificate in Regulated Customer Care)
Adv CeMAP (Advanced Certificate in Mortgage Advice and Practice)
CeCM (Certificate in Commercial Mortgages)
CeSRE (Certificate in Supervising in a Regulated Environment)
Professional DFSM (Professional Diploma in Financial Services Management)
Applied DFSM (Corporate – Applied Diploma in Corporate Banking)
Applied DFSM (Applied Diploma in Retailing Financial Services)
BSc/ACIB (BSc [Hons] Degree in Financial Services and Associateship)
BSc/RIM (BSc [Hons] Degree in Financial Services and Associateship – Risk and Insurance Management)
BSc/RFS (BSc [Hons] Degree in Financial Services and Associateship – Retailing Financial Services)
BSc/CB (BSc [Hons] Degree in Financial Services and Associateship – Corporate Banking)
ADCB for RBS Group (Applied Diploma in Corporate Banking for RBS Group)
Applied DFSM – Corporate for HSBC (Applied Diploma in Corporate Banking for HSBC)
Applied DFSM –Retail for HSBC (Applied Diploma in Retailing Financial Services for HSBC)
DipCRM for Barclays Africa (Diploma in Customer Relationship for Barclays Africa)
DipCRM for RBS Group (Diploma in Customer Relationship Management for RBS Group)
DipFDA (Factors & Discounters Association Diploma)

Profession:	Banking	**Address:**	IFS House, 4-9 Burgate Lane, Canterbury, Kent CT1 2XJ, England
Membership:	--		
Established:	1879	**Telephone:**	01227-762600
		Fax:	01227-763788
		E-mail:	customerservice@ifslearning.com
		Web:	www.ifslearning.com

Institute of Certified Book-keepers (ICB)

Designation: Certified Bookkeeper

Designatory Letters:
AICB (Associate Member of the Institute of Certified Book-keepers)
FICB (Fellow Member of the Institute of Certified Book-keepers)

Profession: Bookkeeping

Membership: 150,000

Established: 1996

Address: 1 Northumberland Avenue, Trafalgar Square, London WC2N 5BW, England

Telephone: 0845-060-2345

Fax: --

E-mail: info@bookkeepers.uk

Web: www.bookkeepers.uk

International Association of Book-keepers (IAB)

Designation:	--	**Address:**	Burford House, 44 London Road,
Designatory Letters:	AIAB (Associate of the	**Telephone:**	Sevenoaks, Kent TN13 1AS,
	International	**Fax:**	England
	Association of Book-	**E-mail:**	01732-458-080
	keepers)	**Web:**	01732-455-848
	MIAB (Member of the		mail@iab.org.uk
	International		www.iab.org.uk
	Association of Book-		
	keepers)		
	FIAB (Fellow of the		
	International		
	Association of Book-		
	keepers)		
Profession:	Bookkeeping		
Membership:	--		
Established:	1972		

Institute of Business Advisers (IBA)

Designation:	--	**Address:**	Response House, Queen Street N,
Designatory Letters:	AIBA (Associate of the		Chesterfield, S41 9AB, England
	Institute of Business	**Telephone:**	1246-453-322
	Advisers)	**Fax:**	1246-453-300
	MIBA (Member of the	**E-mail:**	info@iba.org.uk
	Institute of Business	**Web:**	www.iba.org.uk
	Advisers)		
	FIBA (Fellow of the		
	Institute of Business		
	Advisers)		
	CIBA (Companion of the		
	Institute of Business		
	Advisers)		
Profession:	Business Advising		
Membership:	--		
Established:	1989--as the Institute of		
	Business Counsellors.		
	Changed to IBA in 1997		

Association of Business Executives (ABE)

Designation:	--	**Address:**	William House, 14 Worple Road,
Designatory Letters:	AMABE (Associate		Wimbledon, London SW19
	Member of the		4DD, England
	Association of Business	**Telephone:**	44-20-8879-1973
	Executives)	**Fax:**	44-20-8946-7153
	MABE (Member of the	**E-mail:**	info@abeuk.com
	Association of Business	**Web:**	www.abeuk.org
	Executives)		
	FABE (Fellow Member of		
	the Association of		
	Business Executives)		
Profession:	Business/Management		
Membership:	--		
Established:	1973		

Institute of Chartered Secretaries and Administrators (ICSA)

Designation:	Chartered Secretary	**Address:**	16 Park Crescent, London W1N
Designatory Letters:	ACIS (Associate Member		4AH, England
	of the Institute of	**Telephone:**	207-580-4741
	Chartered Secretaries	**Fax:**	207-323-1132
	and Administrators)	**E-mail:**	icsa@icsa.org.uk
	FCIS (Fellow Member of	**Web:**	www.icsa.org.uk
	the Institute of		
	Chartered Secretaries		
	and Administrators)		
Profession:	Corporate Governance		
Membership:	71,000 (44,000 members		
	and 27,000 students)		
Established:	1891		

International Records Management Trust (IRMT)

Designation:	NA	**Address:**	4th Floor, 7 Hatton Gardens, London
Designatory Letters:	NA		EC1 8AD, England
Profession:	Corporate Governance	**Telephone:**	44-20-7831-4101
Membership:	--	**Fax:**	44-20-7831-6303
Established:	1989	**E-mail:**	info@irmt.org
		Web:	www.irmt.org

Institute of Credit Management (ICM)

Designation:	--	**Address:**	The Water Mill, Station Road, South
Designatory Letters:	AICM (Associate Member		Luffenham, Oakham,
	of the Institute of Credit		Leicestershire, LE15 8NB,
	Management)	**Telephone:**	England
	MICM (Member of the	**Fax:**	01780-722-900
	Institute of Credit	**E-mail:**	01780-721-333
	Management)	**Web:**	info@icm.org.uk
	FICM (Fellow of the		www.icm.org.uk
	Institute of Credit		
	Management)		
Profession:	Credit Management		
Membership:	--		
Established:	1939		

Institute of Environmental Management and Assessment

Designation:	Chartered Environmentalist	**Address:**	St. Nicholas Home, 70 Newport, Lincoln LN1 3DP, England
Designatory Letters:	AIEMA (Associate Member of the Institute of Environmental Management and Assessment)	**Telephone:**	44-0-1522-540-069
		Fax:	44-0-1522-540-090
		E-mail:	info@iema.net
		Web:	www.iema.net
	MIEMA (Full Member of the Institute of Environmental Management and Assessment)		
	FIEMA (Fellow Member of the Institute of Environmental Management and Assessment)		
Profession:	Environmental Management		
Membership:	10,000		
Established:	1999		

The Academy of Executive and Administrators

Designation:	--	**Address:**	Academy House, Warwick Corner, 42 Warwick Road, Kenilworth, Warwickshire CV8 1HE, England
Designatory Letters:	Stud.A.E.A.(Cert.AEA) (Student Member of the Academy of Executive and Administrators)	**Telephone:**	44-01926-855-498
	M.A.E.A.(Dip.AEA) (Full Member of the Academy of Executive and Administrators)	**Fax:**	44-01926-513100
		E-mail:	info@group-ims.com
		Web:	www.group-ims.com
	F.A.E.A.(Dip.AEA) (Fellow Member of the Academy of Executive and Administrators)		
	C.A.E.A.(Dip.AEA) (Companion Member of the Academy of Executive and Administrators)		
Profession:	Executive and Administration		
Membership:	--		
Established:	2002		

The Finance and Leasing Association

Designation:	NA	**Address:**	15-19 Kingsway, London WC2B 6UN, England
Designatory Letters:	NA		
Profession:	Finance/Leasing	**Telephone:**	207-836-6511
Membership:	--	**Fax:**	207-420-9600
Established:	1945	**E-mail:**	info@fla.org.uk
		Web:	www.fla.org.uk

Healthcare Financial Management Association

Designation:	--	**Address:**	Suite 32, Albert House,
Designatory Letters:	--		111 Victoria Street, Bristol BS1
Profession:	Financial Management		6A1, England
Membership:	--	**Telephone:**	117-929-4789
Established:	--	**Fax:**	117-929-4844
		E-mail:	info@hfma.org.uk
		Web:	www.hfma.org.uk

Institute of Professional Financial Managers (IPFM)

Designation:	Professional Financial Manager	**Address:**	40 Pembroke Square, London W8 6PE, England
Designatory Letters:	TIPFM (Technician of the Institute of Professional Financial Managers)	**Telephone:**	020-7460-5362
		Fax:	0870-831-9379
		E-mail:	ipfm1992@yahoo.co.uk
	AIPFM (Associate of the Institute of Professional Financial Managers)	**Web:**	www.ipfm.org
	FIPFM (Fellow of the Institute of Professional Financial Managers)		
	DIPFM (Doctoral Fellow of the Institute of Professional Financial Managers)		
Profession:	Financial Management		
Membership:	10,000		
Established:	1992		

The Personal Finance Society

Designation:	--	**Address:**	42-48 High Road, South Woodford, London E18 2JP, England
Designatory Letters:	CertPFS (Member of the Personal Finance Society by Certificate)	**Telephone:**	208-530-0852
		Fax:	--
	DipPFS (Member of the Personal Finance Society by Diploma)	**E-mail:**	Customer.serv@thepfs.org
		Web:	www.thepfs.org
	APFS (Associate Member of the Personal Finance Society)		
	FPFS (Fellow Member of the Personal Finance Society)		
Profession:	Financial Management		
Membership:	85,000		
Established:	1991		

Institute of Financial Planning

Designation:	Certified Financial Planner	**Address:**	Whitefriars Centre, Lewins Mead, Bristol BS1 2NT, England
Designatory Letters:	CFP(R) (Certified Financial Planner)	**Telephone:**	0117-945-2470
		Fax:	0117-929-2214
	FIFP (Fellow of the Institute of Financial Planning)	**E-mail:**	enquiries@financialplanning.org.uk
		Web:	www.financialplanning.org.uk
Profession:	Financial Planning		
Membership:	1,500		
Established:	1986		

National Network of Independent Forensic Accountants

Designation:	NA	**Address:**	England
Designatory Letters:	NA	**Telephone:**	0845-609-6091
Profession:	Forensic Accounting	**Fax:**	--
Membership:	--	**E-mail:**	enquiries@nifa.co.uk
Established:	--	**Web:**	www.nifa.co.uk

Institute of Personnel and Development

Designation:	--	**Address:**	151 The Broadway, London SW19
Designatory Letters:	MCIPD (Member of the Chartered Institute of Personnel and Development)	**Telephone:**	1JQ, England
		Fax:	0208-612-6200
		E-mail:	0208-612-6201
		Web:	--
	FCIPD (Fellow Member of the Chartered Institute of Personnel and Development)		www.cipd.co.uk
	CCIPD (Companion of the Chartered Institute of Personnel and Development)		
Profession:	Human Resources Management		
Membership:	--		
Established:	--		

Institute for the Management of Information Systems (IMIS)

Designation:	--	**Address:**	5 Kingfisher House, New Mill
Designatory Letters:	LIMIS (Licentiate Member of the Institute for the Management of Information Systems)		Road, Orpington, Kent BR5 3QG, England
		Telephone:	700-00-23456
		Fax:	700-00-23023
	AIMIS (Associate Member of the Institute for the Management of Information Systems)	**E-mail:**	central@imis.org.uk
		Web:	www.imis.org.uk
	MIMIS (Full Member of the Institute for the Management of Information Systems)		
	FIMIS (Fellow Member of the Institute for the Management of Information Systems)		
Profession:	Information Technology		
Membership:	12,000		
Established:	1978		

Institution of Analysts and Programmers (IAP)

Designation:	--	**Address:**	Charles House, 36 Culmington
Designatory Letters:	GradIAP (Graduate of the		Road, London W13 9NH,
	Institution of Analysts		England
	and Programmers)	**Telephone:**	208-567-2118
	AMIAP (Associate	**Fax:**	208-567-4379
	Member, Institution of	**E-mail:**	dg@iap.org.uk
	Analysts and	**Web:**	www.iap.org.uk
	Programmers)		
	MIAP (Member,		
	Institution of Analysts		
	and Programmers)		
	FIAP (Fellow, Institution		
	of Analysts and		
	Programmers)		
Profession:	Information Technology		
Membership:	--		
Established:	1981		

Insolvency Practitioners' Association (IPA)

Designation:	--	**Address:**	Valiant House, 4-10 Heneage Lane,
Designatory Letters:	MIPA (Member of the		London EC3A 5OQ, UK
	Insolvency Practitioners	**Telephone:**	207-623-5105
	Association	**Fax:**	207-623-5122
	FIPA (Fellow Member of	**E-mail:**	secretariat@insolvency-
	the Insolvency		practitioners.org.uk
	Practitioners	**Web:**	www.insolvency-
	Association)		practitioners.org.uk
Profession:	Insolvency		
Membership:	--		
Established:	1961		

The Chartered Insurance Institute (CII)

Designation:	--	**Address:**	42-48 High Road, South Woodford,
Designatory Letters:	Dip CII (Member of the		London E18 2JP, England
	Chartered Insurance	**Telephone:**	208-989-8464
	Institute by Diploma)	**Fax:**	208-530-3052
	Cert CII (Member of the	**E-mail:**	customer.serv@cii.co.uk
	Chartered Insurance	**Web:**	www.cii.co.uk
	Institute by Certificate)		
	Cert CII (MP) (Certificate		
	Member of the Society		
	of Mortgage		
	Professionals)		
	FAIQ (CII) (Holder of the		
	Financial Advisers'		
	International		
	Qualification)		
	ACII (Associate of the		
	Chartered Insurance		
	Institute)		
	FCII (Fellow of the		
	Chartered Insurance		
	Institute)		
Profession:	Insurance		
Membership:	--		
Established:	1897		

Institute of Internal Auditors - UK and Ireland

Designation:	--	**Address:**	13 Abbeville Mews, 88 Clapham Park Road, London SW4 7BX, England
Designatory Letters:	CertIA (Certificate in Internal Audit and Business Risk)	**Telephone:**	020-7498-0101
	MIIA (Member of the Institute of Internal Auditors)	**Fax:**	020-7978-2492
		E-mail:	info@iia.org.uk
	QiCA (Qualification in Computer Auditing)	**Web:**	www.iia.org.uk
	FIIA (Fellow Member of the Institute of Internal Auditors)		
	PIIA (Practitioner of the Institute of Internal Auditors)		
Profession:	Internal Auditing		
Membership:	7,500		
Established:	1948		

The Institute of Investment Management and Research (IIMR)

Designation:	--	**Address:**	211-213 High Street, Bromley, Kent BR1 1NY, England
Designatory Letters:	AIIMR (Associate Member of the Institute of Investment Management and Research)	**Telephone:**	0181-464-0811
		Fax:	0181-313-0587
		E-mail:	--
	FIIMR (Fellow Member of the Institute of Investment Management and Research)	**Web:**	--
Profession:	Investment Management		
Membership:	--		
Established:	1955		

Information Security Forum

Designation:	NA	**Address:**	Southwark Towers, Level 14, 32 London Bridge St., London SE1 9SY, England
Designatory Letters:	NA		
Profession:	Information Systems		
Membership:	NA	**Telephone:**	44-20-7212-5346
Established:	1989	**Fax:**	44-2-7213-4813
		E-mail:	isinfo@securityforum.org
		Web:	www.securityforum.org

British Computer Society (BCS)

Designation:	--	**Address:**	1st Floor, Block D, North Star House, North Star Avenue, Swindon, Wiltshire SN2 1FA, England
Designatory Letters:	AMBCS (Associate Member of the British Computer Society)		
	MBCS (Member of the British Computer Society)	**Telephone:**	0845-300-4417
		Fax:	01793-417444
	FBCS (Fellow Member of the British Computer Society)	**E-mail:**	bcshq@org.uk
		Web:	www.bcs.org
	CITP (Chartered Information Technology Professional)		
	CEng (Chartered Engineer)		
	IEng (Incorporated Engineer)		
	CSc (Chartered Scientist)		
Profession:	Information Technology		
Membership:	--		
Established:	1957 (Incorporated by Royal Charter in 1984)		

Institute of Export

Designation:	--	**Address:**	Export House, Minerva Business Park, Lynch Wood, Peterborough, PE2 8EH, England
Designatory Letters:	AMIEx (Associate Member of the Institute of Export)		
	MIEx (Grad) (Graduate Member of the Institute of Export)	**Telephone:**	01733-4044400
		Fax:	01733-404444
		E-mail:	institute@export.org.uk
	MIEx (Member of the Institute of Export)	**Web:**	www.export.org.uk
Profession:	International Trade		
Membership:	--		
Established:	1935		

Chartered Management Institute (CMI)

Designation:	Chartered Manager	**Address:**	Management House, Cottingham Road, Corby, Northants NN17 1TT, England
Designatory Letters:	ACMI (Associate Member of the Chartered Management Institute)		
	MCMI (Member of the Chartered Management Institute)	**Telephone:**	01536-204222
		Fax:	01536-201651
		E-mail:	enquiries@managers.org.uk
	FCMI (Fellow of the Chartered Management Institute)	**Web:**	www.managers.org.uk
Profession:	Management		
Membership:	--		
Established:	The CMI was established in 1992 from a merger of the British Institute of Management (BIM) and the Institution of Industrial Managers (IIMD).		

Financial Executives Group

Designation:	--	**Address:**	PO Box 30, Blacknest, Alton,
Designatory Letters:	--		Hampshire GU34 4PX, England
Profession:	Management	**Telephone:**	0171-580-2491
Membership:	--	**Fax:**	0171-580-2493
Established:	--	**E-mail:**	fen@cima.org.uk
		Web:	--

Institute of Directors

Designation:	--	**Address:**	116 Pall Mall, London SW1Y 5ED,
Designatory Letters:	--		England
Profession:	Management	**Telephone:**	207-839-1233
Membership:	--	**Fax:**	207-930-1949
Established:	1903	**E-mail:**	membership@iod.com
		Web:	www.iod.com

Institute of Administrative Management (IAM)

Designation:	--	**Address:**	40 Chatsworth Parade, Petts Wood,
Designatory Letters:	A InstAM (Associate Member of the Institute of Administrative Management)		Orpington, Kent BR5 1RW, England
		Telephone:	207-8841-7100
	M InstAM (Member of the Institute of Administrative Management)	**Fax:**	207-841-1119
		E-mail:	info@instam.org
		Web:	www.instam.org
	F InstAM (Fellow Member of the Institute of Administrative Management)		
Profession:	Management		
Membership:	--		
Established:	1915		

The Institute of Management Specialists

Designation:	--	**Address:**	Academy House, Warwick Corner,
Designatory Letters:	Stud.I.M.S.(Cert.IMS)		42 Warwick Road, Kenilworth,
	(Student Member of the		Warwickshire CV8 1HE,
	Institute of Management		England
	Specialists)	**Telephone:**	44-01926-855-498
	A.M.I.M.S.(Dip.IMS)	**Fax:**	44-01926-513100
	(Associate Member of	**E-mail:**	info@group-ims.com
	the Institute of	**Web:**	www.group-ims.com
	Management		
	Specialists)		
	M.I.M.S.(Dip.IMS) (Full		
	Member of the Institute		
	of Management		
	Specialists)		
	F.I.M.S.(Dip.IMS) (Fellow		
	Member of the Institute		
	of Management		
	Specialists)		
	Comp. I.M.S. (Dip. IMS)		
	(Companion Member of		
	the Institute of		
	Management		
	Specialists)		
Profession:	Management		
Membership:	--		
Established:	1971		

Oxford Association of Management

Designation:	--	**Address:**	Oxford Centre for Innovation, Mill
Designatory Letters:	CMBA (Certified Master		Street, Oxford OX2 0JX,
	of Business		England
	Administration)	**Telephone:**	44-0-1865-812072
	CDBA (Certified Doctor	**Fax:**	44-0-1863-793165
	of Business	**E-mail:**	admin@oxim.org
	Administration)	**Web:**	www.oxim.org
Profession:	Management		
Membership:	--		
Established:	1990		

Professional Business and Technical Management

Designation:	--	**Address:**	Academy House, Warwick Corner,
Designatory Letters:	Stud.Prof.BTM(Cert.BTM)		42 Warwick Road, Kenilworth,
	(Student Member of		Warwickshire CV8 1HE,
	Professional Business		England
	and Technical	**Telephone:**	44-01926-855-498
	Management)	**Fax:**	44-01926-513100
	A.M.Prof.BTM(Cert.BTM)	**E-mail:**	info@group-ims.com
	(Associate Member of	**Web:**	www.group-ims.com
	Professional Business		
	and Technical		
	Management)		
	M.Prof.BTM(Dip.BTM)		
	(Full Member of		
	Professional Business		
	and Technical		
	Management)		
	F.Prof.BTM(Cert.BTM)		
	(Fellow Member of		
	Professional Business		
	and Technical		
	Management)		
	C.Prof.BTM(Cert.BTM)		
	(Companion Member of		
	Professional Business		
	and Technical		
	Management)		
Profession:	Management		
Membership:	--		
Established:	1983		

The Strategic Planning Society

Designation:	NA	**Address:**	Buxton House, 7 Highbury Hill,
Designatory Letters:	NA		N5 1SU, England
Profession:	Management	**Telephone:**	845-056-3663
Membership:	--	**Fax:**	870-751-8216
Established:	1967	**E-mail:**	membership@sps.org.uk
		Web:	sps.org.uk

Chartered Institute of Management Accountants

Designation:	Chartered Management	**Address:**	26 Chapter Street, London SW1P
	Accountant	**Telephone:**	4NP, England
Designatory Letters:	ACMA (Associate	**Fax:**	44-208-849-2206
	Member of the	**E-mail:**	44-208-849-2454
	Chartered Institute of	**Web:**	cima.contact@cimaglobal.com
	Management		www.cimaglobal.com
	Accountants)		
	FCMA (Fellow Member		
	of the Chartered		
	Institute of Management		
	Accountants)		
Profession:	Management Accounting		
Membership:	155,000 (including		
	students)		
Established:	1919		

Institute of Management Consultancy (IMC)

The IMC merged with the Chartered Management Institute in 2005

Designation:	--	**Address:**	3rd Floor, 17-18 Hayward's Place, London EC1R 0EQ, England
Designatory Letters:	AMIMC (Associate Member of the Institute of Management Consultancy)	**Telephone:**	--
		Fax:	44-0-20-7566-5220
	MIMC (Member of the Institute of Management Consultancy)	**E-mail:**	consult@imc.co.uk
		Web:	www.imc.co.uk/
	CMC (Certified Management Consultant. The Institute has determined that the CMC designation cannot be used on its own, without being linked to FIMC or MIMC)		
	FIMC (Fellow of the Institute of Management Consultancy)		
Profession:	Management Consulting		
Membership:	4,000		
Established:	1962		

Management Consultancies Association (MCA)

Designation:	NA	**Address:**	60 Trafalgar Square, London WC2N 5DS, England
Designatory Letters:	NA	**Telephone:**	44-207-321-3990
Profession:	Management Consulting	**Fax:**	44-207-321-3991
Membership:	--	**E-mail:**	mca@mca.org.uk
Established:	--	**Web:**	www.mca.org.uk

The Institute of Manufacturing

Designation:	--	**Address:**	Academy House, Warwick Corner, 42 Warwick Road, Kenilworth, Warwickshire CV8 1HE, England
Designatory Letters:	Stud.I.Manf.(Cert.I.Manf.) (Student Member of the Institute of Manufacturing)		
	A.M.I.Manf.(Dip.I.Manf.) (Associate Member of the Institute of Manufacturing)	**Telephone:**	44-01926-855-498
		Fax:	44-01926-513100
		E-mail:	info@group-ims.com
	M.I.Manf.(Dip.I.Manf.) (Full Member of the Institute of Manufacturing)	**Web:**	www.group-ims.com
	F.I.Manf.(Dip.I.Manf.) (Fellow Member of the Institute of Manufacturing)		
	Comp.I.Manf.(Dip.I.Manf.) (Companion Member of the Institute of Manufacturing)		
Profession:	Manufacturing and Manufacturing Management		
Membership:	--		
Established:	1978		

Chartered Institute of Marketing

Designation:	Chartered Marketer	**Address:**	Moor Hall, Cookham, Berkshire, SL6 9QH, England
Designatory Letters:	ACIM (Associate of the Chartered Institute of Marketing)	**Telephone:**	1628-427500
		Fax:	1628-427499
	MCIM (Member of the Chartered Institute of Marketing)	**E-mail:**	membership@cim.co.uk
		Web:	www.cim.co.uk
	FCIM (Fellow of the Chartered Institute of Marketing)		
Profession:	Marketing		
Membership:	--		
Established:	1911		

Pension Research Accountants Group

Designation:	NA	**Address:**	c/o David Slade, Deloitte & Touche, Four Brindleyplace, Birmingham B1 2HZ, England
Designatory Letters:	NA		
Profession:	Pension Accounting		
Membership:	--	**Telephone:**	0121-695-5541
Established:	1978	**Fax:**	0121-695-5311
		E-mail:	feedback@prag.org.uk
		Web:	www.prag.org.uk

Pensions Management Institute (PMI)

Designation:	--	**Address:**	PMI House, 4/10 Artillery Lane, London E1 7LS, England
Designatory Letters:	APMI (Associateship of the Pensions Management Institute)	**Telephone:**	207-247-1452
	MPMI (Ordinary Membership of the Pensions Management Institute)	**Fax:**	207-375-0603
		E-mail:	enquiries@pension-pmi.org.uk
	Dip.IEB (Diploma in International Employee Benefits)	**Web:**	www.pension-pmi.org.uk
	FPMI (Fellowship of the Pensions Management Institute)		
Profession:	Pensions Management		
Membership:	--		
Established:	1976		

Association of Project Management

Designation:	--	**Address:**	150 West Wycombe Road, High Wycombe, Buckinghamshire, England HP12 3AE
Designatory Letters:	MAPM (Member of the Association of Project Management)	**Telephone:**	0845-458-1944
	FAPM (Fellow of the Association of Project Management)	**Fax:**	01494-528-937
		E-mail:	info@apm.org.uk
		Web:	www.apm.org.uk
Profession:	Project Management		
Membership:	15,000		
Established:	1972		

Chartered Institute of Purchasing and Supply

Designation:	Member of the Chartered Institute of Purchasing and Supply	**Address:**	Easton House, Church Street, Easton-on-the-Hill, Stamford, Lincolnshire PE9 3NZ, England
Designatory Letters:	MCIPS (Member of the Chartered Institute of Purchasing and Supply)	**Telephone:**	01780-56777
	FCIPS (Fellow of the Chartered Institute of Purchasing and Supply)	**Fax:**	01780-51610
		E-mail:	--
		Web:	www.cips.org
Profession:	Purchasing		
Membership:	40,000		
Established:	1932		

The British Quality Foundation

Designation:	--	**Address:**	32-34 Great Peter Street, London SW1P 2Q2, England
Designatory Letters:	--	**Telephone:**	020-7654-5000
Profession:	Quality Management	**Fax:**	020-7654-5001
Membership:	--	**E-mail:**	mail@quality-foundation.co.uk
Established:	--	**Web:**	www.quality-foundation.co.uk

Institute of Quality Assurance (IQA)

Designation:	--	**Address:**	12 Grosvenor Crescent, London SW1X 7EE, England
Designatory Letters:	LicIQA (Licentiate of the Institute of Quality Assurance) AMIQA (Associate Member of the Institute of Quality Assurance) MIQA (Member of the Institute of Quality Assurance) FIQA (Fellow of the Institute of Quality Assurance)		
Profession:	Quality Management	**Telephone:**	207-245-6722
Membership:	--	**Fax:**	207-245-6788
Established:	1919	**E-mail:**	iqa@iqa.org
		Web:	www.iqa.org

Institute of Risk Management

Designation:	--	**Address:**	4 Lloyd's House, 6 Lloyd's Avenue, London EC3N 3AX, England
Designatory Letters:	MIRM (Member of the Institute of Risk Management) FIRM (Fellow of the Institute of Risk Management)	**Telephone:**	44-020-7709-9808
		Fax:	44-020-7709-0716
		E-mail:	enquiries@theirm.org
		Web:	www.theirm.org
Profession:	Risk Management		
Membership:	--		
Established:	--		

The Society of Sales and Marketing

Designation:	--	**Address:**	40 Archdale Road, East Dulwich, London SE22 9HJ, England
Designatory Letters:	ASSAM (Associate Member of the Society of Sales and Marketing) GSSAM (Graduate of the Society of Sales and Marketing) FSSAM (Fellow of the Society of Sales and Marketing)	**Telephone:**	44-0208-693-0555
		Fax:	44-0709-234-2170
		E-mail:	info@ssam.co.uk
		Web:	www.ssam.co.uk
Profession:	Sales and Marketing Management		
Membership:	--		
Established:	1980		

Institute of Chartered Shipbrokers

Designation:	Chartered Shipbroker	**Address:**	85 Gracechurch Street, London, EC 3V 0AA, England
Designatory Letters:	MICS (Member of the Institute of Chartered Shipbrokers) FICS (Fellow of the Institute of Chartered Shipbrokers)	**Telephone:**	020-7623-1111
		Fax:	020-7623-8118
		E-mail:	info@ics.org.uk
		Web:	www.ics.org.uk
Profession:	Shipping		
Membership:	3,600		
Established:	1911		

The Academy of Multi-Skills

Designation:	--	**Address:**	Academy House, Warwick Corner, 42 Warwick Road, Kenilworth, Warwickshire CV8 1HE, England
Designatory Letters:	Stud.A.M.S.(Cert.Ms) (Student Member of the Academy of Multi-Skills)		
	Aff.A.M.S.(Cert.Ms) (Affiliate Member of the Academy of Multi-Skills)	**Telephone:**	44-01926-855-498
		Fax:	44-01926-513100
		E-mail:	info@group-ims.com
	A.M.A.M.S.(Dip.Ms) (Associate Member of the Academy of Multi-Skills)	**Web:**	www.group-ims.com
	M.A.M.S.(Dip.Ms) (Full Member of the Academy of Multi-Skills)		
	F.A.M.S.(Dip.Ms) (Fellow Member of the Academy of Multi-Skills)		
	C.A.M.S.(Dip.Ms) (Companion Member of the Academy of Multi-Skills)		
Profession:	Skilled Trades, Crafts, and Professions		
Membership:	--		
Established:	1995		

Association of Taxation Technicians

Designation:	--	**Address:**	12 Upper Belgrave Street, London SW1X 8BB, England
Designatory Letters:	ATT (Member of the Association of Taxation Technicians [ATT])	**Telephone:**	0171-235-2544
		Fax:	0171-235-2562
Profession:	Taxation	**E-mail:**	--
Membership:	--	**Web:**	--
Established:	1989		

Chartered Institute of Taxation

Designation:	Chartered Tax Adviser	**Address:**	12 Upper Belgrave Street, London SW1X 8BB, England
Designatory Letters:	CTA (Chartered Tax Adviser)	**Telephone:**	0171-235-9381
	ATII (Associate Member of the Chartered Institute of Taxation)	**Fax:**	0171-235-2562
		E-mail:	post@tax.org.uk
	FTII (Fellow Member of the Chartered Institute of Taxation)	**Web:**	www.tax.org.uk
Profession:	Taxation		
Membership:	--		
Established:	1930		

Institute of Indirect Taxation

Designation:	--
Designatory Letters:	AIIT (Associate Member of the Institute of Indirect Taxation) Hon. AIIT(Honourary Associate Member of the Institute of Indirect Taxation) FIIT (Fellow Member of the Institute of Indirect Taxation) Hon.FIIT (Honourary Fellow Member of the Institute of Indirect Taxation)
Profession:	Taxation
Membership:	600
Established:	1991

Address:	St. G1, The Stables, Station Road West, Oxted, Surrey RH8 9EE, England
Telephone:	1833-730658
Fax:	1833-717-778
E-mail:	enquiries@theiit.org.uk
Web:	www.theiit.org.uk

Association of Corporate Treasurers (ACT)

Designation:	--
Designatory Letters:	AMCT (Associate Member of the Association of Corporate Treasurers) MCT (Member of the Association of Corporate Treasurers) FCT (Fellow of the Association of Corporate Treasurers)
Profession:	Treasury Management
Membership:	--
Established:	1979

Address:	Ocean House, 10/12 Little Trinity Lane, London, EC4V 2DJ, England
Telephone:	020-7213-9728
Fax:	020-7248-2591
E-mail:	dcreed@treasurers.co.uk
Web:	www.treasurers.org

Society of International Treasurers

Designation:	--
Designatory Letters:	--
Profession:	Treasury Management
Membership:	--
Established:	1977

Address:	2 Tereslake Green, Westbury on Trym, Bristol BS10 6LT, England
Telephone:	44-117-950-8019
Fax:	44-117-950-8019
E-mail:	mail@socintrs.com
Web:	www.socintrs.com

Society of Trust and Estate Practitioners

Designation:	Trust and Estate Practitioner
Designatory Letters:	TEP (Trust and Estate Practitioner)
Profession:	Trusts, Estates, and Related Legal and Financial Matters Pertaining to Inheritance, Generational Change, and Financial Planning
Membership:	12,000
Established:	1991

Address:	26 Grosvenor Garden, London SW1W 0GT, England
Telephone:	207-838-4890
Fax:	207-838-4886
E-mail:	STEP@step.org
Web:	www.step.org

UNITED STATES

Academy of Accounting Historians

Designation:	NA	**Address:**	c/o Tiffany Welch, Academy
Designatory Letters:	NA		Administrator, Weatherhead
Profession:	Accounting		School of Management, 10900
Membership:	--		Euclid Avenue, Cleveland, Ohio
Established:	--		44106-7235 USA
		Telephone:	--
		Fax:	--
		E-mail:	twelch@gmail.com
		Web:	www.rutgers.edu/raw/aah/

The American Accounting Association (AAA)

Designation:	NA	**Address:**	5717 Bessie Drive, Sarasota,
Designatory Letters:	NA		Florida 34233-2399 USA
Profession:	Accounting	**Telephone:**	941-921-7747
Established:	1916	**Fax:**	941-923-4093
		E-mail:	office@aahq.org
		Web:	www.aahq.org

American Association of Attorney-Certified Public Accountants

Designation:	NA	**Address:**	3921 Old Lee Highway, Suite 71A,
Designatory Letters:	NA		Fairfax, Virginia 22030 USA
Profession:	Accounting	**Telephone:**	888-ATTY-CPA or 703-288-9272
Membership:	--	**Fax:**	703-352-8073
Established:	1964	**E-mail:**	cmulligan@attorney-cpa.com
		Web:	www.attorney-cpa.com

American Association of Finance and Accounting

Designation:	NA	**Address:**	USA
Designatory Letters:	NA	**Telephone:**	314-878-2270
Profession:	Accounting	**Fax:**	61-3-9349-5076
Membership:	--	**E-mail:**	srb@exechunter.com
Established:	1978	**Web:**	www.aafa.com

American Institute of Certified Public Accountants

Designation:	Certified Public Accountant	**Address:**	1211 Avenue of the Americas, New York, New York 10036-8775 USA
Designatory Letters:	CPA (Certified Public Accountant)		
	PFS (Personal Financial Specialist)	**Telephone:**	212-596-6200
		Fax:	212-596-6213
	CITP (Certified Information Technology Professional)	**E-mail:**	aanderson@aicpa.org
		Web:	www.aicpa.org/
	ABV (Accredited in Business Valuation)		
Profession:	Accounting		
Membership:	327,000		
Established:	1896		

American Society of Women Accountants (ASWA)

Designation:	NA	**Address:**	8405 Greensboro Drive, Suite 800,
Designatory Letters:	NA		McLean, Virginia 22102 USA
Profession:	Accounting	**Telephone:**	800-326-2163/703-506-3265
Membership:	--	**Fax:**	703-506-3266
Established:	1938	**E-mail:**	aswa@aswa.org
		Web:	www.aswa.org

American Women's Society of Certified Public Accountants (AWSCPA)

Designation:	NA	**Address:**	136 South Keowee Street, Dayton,
Designatory Letters:	NA		Ohio 45402 USA
Profession:	Accounting	**Telephone:**	937-222-1872
Membership:	900	**Fax:**	937-222-5794
Established:	1933	**E-mail:**	info@awscpa.org
		Web:	www.awscpa.org

Asociación de Contadores de Cuba en el exilio
(Association of Cuban Accountants in Exile)

Designation:	NA	**Address:**	42 S.W. 34th Av., Miami, Florida
Designatory Letters:	NA		33145 USA
Profession:	Accounting	**Telephone:**	305-569-0109
Membership:	--	**Fax:**	305-649-2898
Established:	1961	**E-mail:**	ramoncitomar@aol.com
		Web:	--

Association for Accounting Administration

Designation:	--	**Address:**	136 South Keowee Street, Dayton,
Designatory Letters:	--		Ohio 45402 USA
Profession:	Accounting	**Telephone:**	937-222-0030
Membership:	--	**Fax:**	937-222-5794
Established:	1984	**E-mail:**	aaainfo@cpaadmin.org
		Web:	www.cpaadmin.org

Association of Chartered Accountants in the United States (ACAUS)

Designation:	NA	**Address:**	341 Lafayette St., Suite 4246,
Designatory Letters:	NA		New York, New York
Profession:	Accounting		10012-2417 USA
Membership:	5,000	**Telephone:**	212-334-2078
Established:	1980	**Fax:**	--
		E-mail:	president@acaus.org
		Web:	www.acaus.org

Association of Insolvency and Restructuring Advisors (AIRA)

Designation:	Certified Insolvency and Restructuring Accountant	**Address:**	221 Stewart Avenue, Ste 207, Medford, Oregon 97501 USA
	Certified in Distressed Business Valuation	**Telephone:**	541-858-1665
		Fax:	541-858-9187
Designatory Letters:	CIRA (Certified Insolvency and Restructuring Accountant)	**E-mail:**	aira@airacira.org
		Web:	www.airacira.org
	CIDBV (Certified in Distressed Business Valuation)		
Profession:	Accounting		
Membership:	--		
Established:	1981		

Association of Latino Professionals in Finance and Accounting (ALPFA)

Designation:	NA	**Address:**	801 South Grand Avenue, Suite 400, Los Angeles, California 90017 USA
Designatory Letters:	NA		
Profession:	Accounting		
Membership:	--	**Telephone:**	213-243-0004
Established:	1972	**Fax:**	213-243-0006
		E-mail:	info@national.alpfa.org
		Web:	www.alpfa.org

Cuban American CPAs Association

Designation:	NA	**Address:**	PO Box 442061, Miami, Florida 33144 USA
Designatory Letters:	NA		
Profession:	Accounting	**Telephone:**	305-220-3771
Membership:	--	**Fax:**	305-220-2363
Established:	--	**E-mail:**	cacpa@cacpa.org
		Web:	www.cacpa.org

Federal Accounting Standards Advisory Board (FASAB)

Designation:	NA	**Address:**	441 G Street, N.W., Suite 6814, Washington, D.C. 20548 USA
Designatory Letters:	NA		
Profession:	Accounting	**Telephone:**	202-512-7310
Established:	--	**Fax:**	202-512-7366
		E-mail:	fasab@fasab.org
		Web:	www.fasab.gov

The Financial Accounting Foundation—comprising The Financial Accounting Standards Board (FASB) and the Governmental Accounting Standards Board (GASB)

Designation:	NA	**Address:**	401 Merritt, PO Box 5116, Norwalk, Connecticut 06856-5116 USA
Designatory Letters:	NA		
Profession:	Accounting	**Telephone:**	203-847-0700
Established:	1973	**Fax:**	203-849-9714
		E-mail:	fasbpubs@fasb.org
		Web:	www.fasb.org

Government Finance Officers Association

Designation:	Certified Public Finance Officer	**Address:**	203 N. LaSalle St., Suite 2700, Chicago, Illinois 60601-1210
Designatory Letters:	CPFO (Certified Public Finance Officer)	**Telephone:**	USA
		Fax:	312-977-9700
Profession:	Accounting	**E-mail:**	312-977-4806
Membership:	--	**Web:**	Inquiry@gfoa.org
Established:	1906		www.gfoa.org

International Association for Accounting Education and Research (IAAER)

Designation:	NA	**Address:**	c/o Gary Sundem, University of Washington, School of Business Administration, Box 353200, Seattle, Washington 98195 USA
Designatory Letters:	NA		
Profession:	Accounting		
Membership:	--		
Established:	1984	**Telephone:**	206-543-9390
		Fax:	206-685-9825
		E-mail:	glsundem@u.washington.edu
		Web:	www.iaaer.org

National Association of Accountants

Designation:	NA	**Address:**	1010 N. Fairfax St. Alexandria, Virginia 22314 USA
Designatory Letters:	NA		
Profession:	Accounting	**Telephone:**	800-966-6679
Membership:	--	**Fax:**	703-549-2984
Established:	1945	**E-mail:**	members@nsacct.org
		Web:	www.nsacct.org

National Association of Black Accountants (NABA)

Designation:	NA	**Address:**	7249-A Hanover Parkway, Greenbelt, Maryland 20770 USA
Designatory Letters:	NA		
Profession:	Accounting	**Telephone:**	301-474-NABA
Membership:	--	**Fax:**	301-474-3114
Established:	1969	**E-mail:**	--
		Web:	www.nabainc.org

National Council of Philippine American Canadian Accountants (NCPACA)

Designation:	NA	**Address:**	97-45 Queen's Blvd., Suite 1030, Rego Park, New York 11374-2101 USA
Designatory Letters:	NA		
Profession:	Accounting		
Membership:	--	**Telephone:**	718-275-1422
Established:	--	**Fax:**	718-275-6762
		E-mail:	--
		Web:	www.ncpaca-intl.org

US General Accounting Office (GAO)

Designation:	NA	**Address:**	441 G Street, Washington, D.C. 20548 USA
Designatory Letters:	NA		
Profession:	Accounting	**Telephone:**	202-512-4800
Established:	--	**Fax:**	202-512-4400
		E-mail:	beckers@gao.gov
		Web:	www.gao.gov

Public Company Accounting Oversight Board (PCAOB)

Designation:	NA	**Address:**	1666 K Street, N.W., Washington, D.C. 20006-2803 USA
Designatory Letters:	NA		
Profession:	Accounting/Auditing	**Telephone:**	202-207-9100
Membership:	--	**Fax:**	202-862-8430
Established:	2002	**E-mail:**	info@pcaobus.org
		Web:	www.pcaobus.org

Institute of Certified Management Accountants (ICMA)

Designation:	Certified Management Accountant	**Address:**	10 Paragon Drive, Montvale, New Jersey 07645-1760 USA
	Certified in Financial Management	**Telephone:**	201-573-9000 or 800-638-4427
		Fax:	201-474-1608
Designatory Letters:	CMA (Certified Management Accountant)	**E-mail:**	cmacfm@imanet.org
		Web:	www.imanet.org
	CFM (Certified in Financial Management)		
Profession:	Accounting/Corporate Finance		
Membership:	65,000		
Established:	1972 by the Institute of Management Accountants which was founded in 1919		

Accreditation Council for Accountancy and Taxation (ACAT)

Designation:	International Accredited Business Accountant	**Address:**	1010 N. Fairfax St. Alexandria, Virginia 22314 USA
Designatory Letters:	ECS (Elder Care Specialist)	**Telephone:**	888-289-7763
		Fax:	703-519-2512
	ATA (Accredited Tax Advisor)	**E-mail:**	info@acatcredentials.org
	ATP (Accredited Tax Preparer)	**Web:**	www.acatcredentials.org
	ABA (Accredited Business Accountant)		
	ABA (Accredited Business Advisor)		
Profession:	Accounting/Taxation		
Membership:	--		
Established:	1973		

American Academy of Actuaries

Designation:	--	**Address:**	1100 17th St NW, 7th Floor, Washington, D.C. 20036 USA
Designatory Letters:	--		
Profession:	Actuarial Science	**Telephone:**	202-223-8196
Membership:	--	**Fax:**	202-872-1948
Established:	1948	**E-mail:**	webmaster@actuary.org
		Web:	www.actuary.org

American Society of Pension Actuaries (ASPA)

Designation:	--	**Address:**	4245 North Fairfax Drive, Suite # 750, Arlington, Virginia 22203-1619 USA
Designatory Letters:	APM (Associate Professional Member, Society of Pension Actuaries)		
		Telephone:	703-516-9300
	QPFC (Qualified Plan Financial Consultant)	**Fax:**	703-516-9308
		E-mail:	asppa@asppa.org
	QKA (Qualified 401K Administrator)	**Web:**	www.asppa.org
	QPA (Qualified Pension Administrator)		
	CPC (Certified Pension Consultant)		
	MSPA (Member, Society of Pension Actuaries)		
	FSPA (Fellow, Society of Pension Actuaries)		
Profession:	Actuarial Science		
Membership:	--		
Established:	1966		

American Society of Pension Professionals and Actuaries

Designation:	Qualified Plan Financial Consultant	**Address:**	4245 North Fairfax Drive, Ste 750, Arlington, Virginia 22203 USA
Designatory Letters:	QPFC (Qualified Plan Financial Consultant)	**Telephone:**	703-516-9300
		Fax:	703-516-9308
Profession:	Actuarial Science	**E-mail:**	asppa@asppa.org
Membership:	--	**Web:**	www.asppa.org
Established:	--		

Casualty Actuarial Society (CAS)

Designation:	--	**Address:**	4350 North Fairfax Drive, Suite # 250, Arlington, Virginia 22203 USA
Designatory Letters:	ACAS (Associate, Casualty Actuarial Society)		
		Telephone:	703-276-3100
	FCAS (Fellow, Casualty Actuarial Society)	**Fax:**	703-276-3108
		E-mail:	office@asact.org
Profession:	Actuarial Science	**Web:**	www.casact.org
Membership:	--		
Established:	1914		

Conference of Consulting Actuaries

Designation:	NA	**Address:**	1110 W. Lake Cook Road, Suite 235, Buffalo Grove, Illinois 60089-1968 USA
Designatory Letters:	NA		
Profession:	Actuarial Science		
Membership:	--	**Telephone:**	847-419-9090
Established:	1950	**Fax:**	847-419-9091
		E-mail:	conference@ccactuaries.org
		Web:	www.ccactuaries.org

Society of Actuaries

The program is sponsored by the Joint Board for the Enrollment of Actuaries, American Society of Pension Professionals & Actuaries (ASPPA) and the Society of Actuaries (SOA)

Designation:	Enrolled Actuary	**Address:**	475 N. Martingale, Suite 800,
Designatory Letters:	EA (Enrolled Actuary)		Schaumburg, Illinois 60173-2226
Profession:	Actuarial Science		USA
Membership:	4,138	**Telephone:**	847-706-3500
Established:	SOA—1949. Joint Board	**Fax:**	847-706-3599
	for the Enrollment of	**E-mail:**	webmaster@soa.org
	Actuaries (1974)	**Web:**	www.soa.org

Society of Actuaries (SoA)

Designation:	--	**Address:**	475 N. Martingale Road,
Designatory Letters:	ASA (Associate Member		Schaumburg, Illinois 60173 USA
	of the Society of	**Telephone:**	847-706-3500
	Actuaries)	**Fax:**	847-706-3599
	FSA (Fellow Member of	**E-mail:**	djay@soa.org
	the Society of	**Web:**	www.soa.org
	Actuaries)		
Profession:	Actuarial Science		
Membership:	--		
Established:	1949		

International Association of Administrative Professionals

Designation:	Certified Professional	**Address:**	10502 NW Ambassador Drive, PO
	Secretary	**Telephone:**	Box 20404, Kansas City, Missouri
	Certified Administrative	**Fax:**	64195-0404 USA
	Personnel	**E-mail:**	816-891-6600
Designatory Letters:	CPS (Certified	**Web:**	816-891-9118
	Professional Secretary)		service@iaap-hq.org
	CAP (Certified		www.iaap-hq.org
	Administrative		
	Personnel)		
Profession:	Administrative Personnel		
Membership:	40,000		
Established:	1942		

Society of Certified Senior Advisors

Designation:	Certified Senior Advisor	**Address:**	1777 S. Bellaire Street, Suite 235,
Designatory Letters:	CSA (Certified Senior		Denver, Colorado 80222 USA
	Advisor)	**Telephone:**	888-290-7315
Profession:	Aging, Advice on	**Fax:**	303-757-7677
Membership:	13,000	**E-mail:**	dand@csa.us--
Established:	1997	**Web:**	www.csa-csa.com

Association of Airport Auditors Inc. (AAIA)

Designation:	NA	**Address:**	AAIA, c/o HCAA, PO Box 22287,
Designatory Letters:	NA		Tampa, Florida 33622 USA
Profession:	Airport Auditing	**Telephone:**	--
Membership:	350	**Fax:**	--
Established:	1989	**E-mail:**	dwhitworth@tampaairport.com
		Web:	www.airport-auditors.org

Association of Certified Anti-Money Laundering Specialists

Designation:	Certified Anti-Money Laundering Specialist	**Address:**	Brickwell Bayview Center, 80 Southwest 8th Street, Ste 2350, Miami, Florida 33130 USA
Designatory Letters:	CAMS (Certified Anti-Money Laundering Specialist)	**Telephone:**	305-373-0020
		Fax:	305-373-7788
Profession:	Anti-Money Laundering	**E-mail:**	info@acams.org
Membership:	--	**Web:**	www.acams.org
Established:	--		

American Society of Appraisers

Designation:	--	**Address:**	555 Herdon Parkway, Ste 125, Herndon, Virginia 20170 USA
Designatory Letters:	ASA (Accredited Senior Appraiser)	**Telephone:**	703-478-2228
	AM (Accredited Member)	**Fax:**	703-742-8471
		E-mail:	asainfo@appraisers.org
	FASA (Fellow, American Society of Appraisers)	**Web:**	www.appraisers.org
Profession:	Appraising		
Membership:	--		
Established:	1936		

The Appraisal Foundation

Designation:	NA	**Address:**	1155 15th St., NW, Ste. 1111, Washington, D.C. 20005 USA
Designatory Letters:	NA	**Telephone:**	202-347-7722
Profession:	Appraising	**Fax:**	202-347-7727
Membership:	--	**E-mail:**	paula@appraisalfoundation.org
Established:	1987	**Web:**	www.appraisalfoundation.org

National Association of Certified Valuation Analysts

Designation:	--	**Address:**	1111 E. Brickyard Road, Ste 200, Salt Lake City, Utah 84105 USA
Designatory Letters:	CVA (Certified Valuation Analyst)	**Telephone:**	801-486-0600
	AVA (Accredited Valuation Analyst)	**Fax:**	801-486-7500
	CFD (Certified Fraud Deterrence Analyst)	**E-mail:**	nacva@nacva.com
		Web:	www.nacva.com
	CFFA (Certified Forensic Financial Analyst)		
Profession:	Appraising		
Membership:	--		
Established:	1990		

The Fiduciary and Investment Risk Management Association (FIRMA)

Designation:	--	**Address:**	PO Box 48297, Athens, Georgia 30604 USA
Designatory Letters:	CTA (Certified Trust Auditor)	**Telephone:**	706-354-0083
	CTCP (Certified Trust Compliance Professional)	**Fax:**	706-353-3994
		E-mail:	thefirma@negia.net
		Web:	www.thefirma.org
Profession:	Auditing		
Membership:	--		
Established:	1985		

International Association of Auto Theft Investigators

Designation:	NA	**Address:**	PO Box 223, Clinton, New York,
Designatory Letters:	NA		New York 13323-0223 USA
Profession:	Auto Theft Investigations	**Telephone:**	315-853-1913
Membership:	--	**Fax:**	315-793-0048
Established:	1952	**E-mail:**	--
		Web:	www.iaati.org

Independent Community Bankers of America

Designation:	--	**Address:**	1615 L St., NW, Suite 900,
Designatory Letters:	CCBIA (Certified Community Bank Internal Auditor)		Washington, D.C. 20036-5623 USA
	CCBCO (Certified Community Bank Compliance Officer)	**Telephone:**	800-422-8439/202-659-9216
		Fax:	--
		E-mail:	info@icba.org
	CCBSO (Certified Community Bank Security Officer)	**Web:**	www.icba.org
	CCBTO (Certified Community Bank Technology Officer)		
Profession:	Bank Auditing		
Membership:	5,000		
Established:	1930		

Institute of Certified Bankers

Designation:	--	**Address:**	1120 Connecticut Ave. NW, Suite 600, Washington, D.C. 20036 USA
Designatory Letters:	CRCM (Certified Regulatory Compliance Manager)		
		Telephone:	202-663-5092
	CCSR (Certified Customer Service Representative)	**Fax:**	202-828-4540
		E-mail:	ICB@aba.com
		Web:	www.aba.com
	CPB (Certified Personal Banker)		
	CBT (Certified Bank Teller)		
	CLBB (Certified Lender Business Banker)		
	CCTS (Certified Corporate Trust Specialist)		
	CTFA (Certified Trust and Financial Advisor)		
	CRSP (Certified Retired Services Professional)		
	CSOP (Certified Securities Operation Professional)		
	CISP (Certified IRA Services Professional)		
	CFMP (Certified Financial Marketing Professional)		
	CFSSP (Certified Financial Services Security Professional)		
Profession:	Banking		
Membership:	8,000		
Established:	1990		

Cannon Financial Institute

Designation:	--	**Address:**	PO Box 6447, Athens, Georgia 30604 USA
Designatory Letters:	AFIM (Accredited Fiduciary Investment Manager)	**Telephone:**	706-353-3346
		Fax:	706-353-3994
	CFIRS (Certified Fiduciary and Investment Risk Specialist)	**E-mail:**	--
		Web:	www.cannonfinancial.com
Profession:	Banking/Investment		
Membership:	--		
Established:	1960		

American Bankruptcy Institute

Designation:	--	**Address:**	44 Canal Center Plaza, Suite 404, Alexandria, Virginia 22314 USA
Designatory Letters:	--		
Profession:	Bankruptcy Management	**Telephone:**	703-739-0800
Membership:	--	**Fax:**	703-739-1060
Established:	--	**E-mail:**	info@abiworld.org
		Web:	www. abiworld.org

American Board of Certification

Designation:	Certified Consumer Bankruptcy Attorney	**Address:**	44 Canal Center Plaza, Suite 404, Alexandria, Virginia 22314 USA
Designatory Letters:	CCBA (Certified Consumer Bankruptcy Attorney)	**Telephone:**	703-739-1023
		Fax:	415-986-4905
Profession:	Bankruptcy Management	**E-mail:**	certification@abcworld.org
Membership:	--	**Web:**	www. abcworld.org
Established:	--		

American Institute of Professional Bookkeepers

Designation:	Certified Bookkeeper	**Address:**	Suite 500, 6001 Montrose Road, Rockville, Maryland 20852 USA
Designatory Letters:	CB (Certified Bookkeeper)	**Telephone:**	800-622-0121
Profession:	Bookkeeping	**Fax:**	800-541-0066
Membership:	--	**E-mail:**	info@aipb.org
Established:	1987	**Web:**	www.aipb.org

The International Association of Business Communicators

Designation:	Accredited Business Communicator	**Address:**	One Hallidie Plaza, Suite 600, San Francisco, California 94102 USA
Designatory Letters:	ABC (Accredited Business Communicator)	**Telephone:**	415-544-4700, 800-776-4222
		Fax:	415-544-4747
		E-mail:	servicecenter@iabc.com
Profession:	Business Communication	**Web:**	www.iabc.com
Membership:	--		
Established:	--		

Institute of Business Appraisers

Designation:	Business Appraiser	**Address:**	PO Box 17410, Plantation, Florida 33318 USA
Designatory Letters:	CBA (Certified Business Appraiser)	**Telephone:**	954-584-1144
	AIBA (Accredited, Institute of Business Appraisers)	**Fax:**	954-584-1184
		E-mail:	ibahq@go-iba.org
	BVAL (Business Valuator Accredited in Litigation)	**Web:**	www.instbusapp.org
Profession:	Business Valuation		
Membership:	--		
Established:	1978		

Association of College & University Auditors

Designation:	NA	**Address:**	342 North Main St., West Hartford, Connecticut 06117-2507 USA
Designatory Letters:	NA		
Profession:	College and University Internal Auditing	**Telephone:**	860-586-7561
		Fax:	860-586-7550
Membership:	--	**E-mail:**	acua@acua.org
Established:	1958	**Web:**	www.acua.org

International Guild of Professional Consultants (IGPC)

Designation:	Certified Professional Consultant	**Address:**	5703 Red Bug Lake Road, # 403, Winter Springs, Florida 32708
Designatory Letters:	CPC (Certified Professional Consultant)	**Telephone:**	USA
			407-678-7853
Profession:	Consulting	**Fax:**	407-678-8173
Membership:	--	**E-mail:**	info@igpc.org
Established:	1982	**Web:**	www.igpc.org

Professional and Technical Consultants Association (PATCA)

Designation:	--	**Address:**	PO Box 2261, Santa Clara,
Designatory Letters:	--		California 95055 USA
Profession:	Consulting	**Telephone:**	800-747-2822 or 408-971-5902
Membership:	--	**Fax:**	866-746-1053
Established:	--	**E-mail:**	info@patca.org
		Web:	www.patca.org

Financial Executives International

Designation:	NA	**Address:**	200 Campus Drive, PO Box 674,
Designatory Letters:	NA		Florham Park, New Jersey 07932
Profession:	Corporate Governance		USA
Membership:	--	**Telephone:**	973-765-1023
Established:	1931	**Fax:**	973-765-1023
		E-mail:	ccunningham@fei.org
		Web:	www.fei.org

The Internal Control Center of Excellence

Designation:	Certified Internal Control Specialist	**Address:**	2102 Park Center Drive, Suite 200, Orlando, Florida 32835-7614 USA
Designatory Letters:	CICS (Certified Internal Control Specialist)	**Telephone:**	407-472-4424
		Fax:	407-363-1112
Profession:	Corporate Governance	**E-mail:**	pwarner@internalcontrolinstitute.org
Membership:	--	**Web:**	www.internalcontrolinstitute.org
Established:	2006		

Society of Corporate Compliance and Ethics

Designation:	NA	**Address:**	6500 Barrie Road, Suite 250,
Designatory Letters:	NA		Minneapolis, Minnesota 55435
Profession:	Corporate Governance		USA
Membership:	500	**Telephone:**	888-277-4977
Established:	2003	**Fax:**	952-988-0146
		E-mail:	info@corporatecompliance.org
		Web:	www.corporatecompliance.org

Society of Corporate Secretaries and Governance Professionals

Designation:	NA	**Address:**	521 Fifth Avenue, New York,
Designatory Letters:	NA		New York 10175 USA
Profession:	Corporate Governance	**Telephone:**	212-681-2000
Membership:	--	**Fax:**	212-681-2005
Established:	1946	**E-mail:**	research@governanceprofessionals.org
		Web:	www. governanceprofessionals.org

Society of Competitive Intelligence Professionals

Designation:	NA	**Address:**	1700 Diagonal Road, Ste 520,
Designatory Letters:	NA		Alexandria, Virginia 22314 USA
Profession:	Corporate Intelligence	**Telephone:**	703-739-0696
	Gathering	**Fax:**	703-739-2524
Membership:	--	**E-mail:**	info@scip.org
Established:	--	**Web:**	www.scip.org

American Association of Cost Engineering International (AACE International)
(Association for the Advancement of Cost Engineering)

Designation:	--	**Address:**	209 Prairie Avenue, Suite 100,
Designatory Letters:	CCC (Certified Cost Consultant)		Morgantown, West Virginia 26501 USA
	CCE (Certified Cost Engineer)	**Telephone:**	800-858-2678; 304-296-8444
	EVP (Earned Value Professional)	**Fax:**	304-291-5728
		E-mail:	info@aacei.org
	PSP (Planning & Scheduling Professional)	**Web:**	www.aacei.org
	ICC (Interim Cost Consultant)		
Profession:	Cost Management		
Membership:	5,100		
Established:	1956		

Credit Union National Association

Designation:	Credit Union Compliance Expert	**Address:**	601 Pennsylvania Ave., NW, South Bldg., Washington, D.C. 20004-2601 USA
Designatory Letters:	CUCE (Credit Union Compliance Expert)	**Telephone:**	202-638-5777
Profession:	Credit Union Auditing	**Fax:**	202-638-7734
Membership:	--	**E-mail:**	dorothy@cuna.org
Established:	--	**Web:**	www.cuna.org

National Association of Federal Credit Unions

Designation:	Certified Compliance Officer	**Address:**	3138 10th Street, North Arlington, Virginia 22201-2149 USA
Designatory Letters:	CCO (Certified Compliance Officer)	**Telephone:**	800-336-4644/703-522-4770
		Fax:	703-524-1082
Profession:	Credit Union Auditing	**E-mail:**	--
Membership:	--	**Web:**	www.nafcu.org
Established:	1934		

Association of Credit Union Internal Auditors Inc.

Designation:	NA	**Address:**	PO Box 1926, Columbus, Ohio 43216-1926 USA
Designatory Letters:	NA		
Profession:	Credit Union Internal Auditing	**Telephone:**	614-221-9702
		Fax:	--
Membership:	--	**E-mail:**	--
Established:	--	**Web:**	www.acuia.org

Credit Union Internal Auditors' Association

Designation:	NA	**Address:**	USA
Designatory Letters:	NA	**Telephone:**	619-980-9831
Profession:	Credit Union Internal Auditing	**Fax:**	--
		E-mail:	--
Membership:	--	**Web:**	www.cuiaa.org
Established:	1986		

Institute for Customer Relationship Management (iCRM)

Designation:	--	**Address:**	3505 Koger Boulevard, Suite 210, Duluth, Georgia 30096 USA
Designatory Letters:	--		
Profession:	Customer Relations	**Telephone:**	678-280-0300
Membership:	--	**Fax:**	678-280-0311
Established:	--	**E-mail:**	info@institutecrm.com
		Web:	www.institutecrm.com

Investment Training and Consulting Institute Inc.

Designation:	Certified Investments and Derivatives Auditor	**Address:**	140 E. 9th Street, Auburn, Kansas 66402 USA
Designatory Letters:	CIDA (Certified Investments and Derivatives Auditor)	**Telephone:**	785-256-2800
		Fax:	785-256-2840
		E-mail:	investci@aol.com
Profession:	Derivatives Auditing	**Web:**	www.investci.com
Membership:	--		
Established:	--		

Financial Engineering Institute

Designation:	Chartered Financial Engineer	**Address:**	25400 US Highway 19 North, Ste 226, Clearwater, Florida 33763 USA
Designatory Letters:	ChFE (Chartered Financial Engineer)	**Telephone:**	727-797-9120
Profession:	Engineering Finance	**Fax:**	727-797-9150
Membership:	--	**E-mail:**	nickg@thefei.com
Established:	--	**Web:**	www.thefei.com

The Academy of Board Certified Environmental Professionals

Designation:	Certified Environmental Professional	**Address:**	PO Box 1598, Winter Park, Florida 32790 USA
Designatory Letters:	CEP (Certified Environmental Professional)	**Telephone:**	866-767-8073
		Fax:	407-425-7427
		E-mail:	office@abcep.org
Profession:	Environmental Auditing	**Web:**	www.abcep.org
Membership:	500		
Established:	1979		

Board of Environmental, Health and Safety Auditor Certifications

Designation:	Health and Safety Certified Professional Environmental Auditor	**Address:**	247 Maitland Avenue, Altamonte Springs, Florida 32701-4201
		Telephone:	USA
Designatory Letters:	CPEA (Certified Professional Environmental Auditor) [The CPEA can be one or more of five specialty areas: EMS 14000+, Environmental Compliance, Health & Safety, Management System, and Responsible Care]	**Fax:**	407-831-7727
		E-mail:	407-830-7495
		Web:	beac@theiia.org
			www.beac.org
Profession:	Environmental, Health, and Safety Auditing		
Membership:	1,400		
Established:	1997		

California Escrow Association (CEA)

Designation:	--	**Address:**	2520 Venture Oaks Way, Suite 150, Sacramento, California 95833 USA
Designatory Letters:	CEO (Certified Escrow Officer)	**Telephone:**	
	CSEO (Certified Senior Escrow Officer)	**Fax:**	--
	CMHS (Certified Mobile Home Specialist)	**E-mail:**	--
	CBSS (Certified Bulk Sales Specialist)	**Web:**	cea@camgmt.com
	CEI (Certified Escrow Instructor)		www.ceaescrow.org
	CET (Certified Escrow Technician)		
Profession:	Escrow and Sales		
Membership:	--		
Established:	--		

Estate Planning Institute

Designation:	Chartered Estate Planning Practitioner	**Address:**	5 Learning Park, PO Box 669, Luray, Virginia 22835 USA
Designatory Letters:	CEPP (Chartered Estate Planning Practitioner)	**Telephone:**	800-232-6465
		Fax:	703-852-4444
Profession:	Estate Planning	**E-mail:**	reg@cepp-epi.com
Membership:	--	**Web:**	www.cepp-epi.com
Established:	--		

National Association of Estate Planners and Councils (NAEPC)

Designation:	Accredited Estate Planner	**Address:**	1120 Chester Avenue, Suite 470, Cleveland, Ohio 44114 USA
Designatory Letters:	AEP (Accredited Estate Planner)	**Telephone:**	866-266-2224
Profession:	Estate Planning	**Fax:**	216-696-2582
Membership:	1,400	**E-mail:**	admin@naepc.org
Established:	1962	**Web:**	www.naepc.org

National Institute of Certified Estate Planners

Designation:	Certified Estate Planner	**Address:**	3811 Southland Ave., Kokomo, Indiana 46902 USA
Designatory Letters:	CEP (Certified Estate Planner)	**Telephone:**	765-453-4300
Profession:	Estate Planning	**Fax:**	--
Membership:	--	**E-mail:**	--
Established:	--	**Web:**	www.nicep.org

Ethics and Compliance Officer Association

Designation:	--	**Address:**	411 Waverley Oaks Road, Suite 324, Waltham, Massachusetts 02452 USA
Designatory Letters:	--		
Profession:	Ethics	**Telephone:**	781-647-9333
Membership:	--	**Fax:**	781-647-9399
Established:	1992	**E-mail:**	Support@theecoa.org
		Web:	www.theecoa.org

The Coaches Training Institute

Designation:	Certified Professional Co-Active Coach	**Address:**	4000 Civic Center Drive, Suite 500, San Rafael, California 94903 USA
Designatory Letters:	CPCC (Certified Professional Co-Active Coach)	**Telephone:**	
		Fax:	415-451-6000/800-691-6008
		E-mail:	415-472-1204
Profession:	Executive Coaching	**Web:**	CTInfo@thecoaches.com
Membership:	--		www.thecoaches.com
Established:	1992		

International Coach Federation (ICF)

Designation:	--	**Address:**	2365 Harrodsburg Road, Suite A325, Lexington, Kentucky 40504 USA
Designatory Letters:	ACC (Associate Certified Coach)		
	PCC (Professional Certified Coach)	**Telephone:**	888-423-3131/859-219-3580
		Fax:	859-226-4411
	MCC (Master Certified Coach)	**E-mail:**	icfoffice@coachfederation.org
		Web:	www.coachfederation.org
Profession:	Executive Coaching		
Membership:	--		
Established:	--		

Advisor Certification Series

Designation:	Certified Annuity Advisor	**Address:**	8657 Douglas Ave., Ste 385, Des Moines, Iowa 503224 USA
Designatory Letters:	CAA (Certified Annuity Advisor)	**Telephone:**	866-299-8368
		Fax:	641-755-4034
Profession:	Finance	**E-mail:**	caa@annuityadvisor.org
Membership:	--	**Web:**	www.annuityadvisor.org
Established:	--		

Annuity National Brokerage Inc.

Designation:	Certified Annuity Consultant	**Address:**	USA
		Telephone:	--
Designatory Letters:	CAC (Certified Annuity Consultant)	**Fax:**	--
		E-mail:	anbc@anbc.com
Profession:	Finance	**Web:**	www.anbc.com
Membership:	--		
Established:	--		

Christian Financial Professional Network

Designation:	Christian Financial Professionals Network Certified Member	**Address:**	5605 Glenridge Drive, Ste 845, Atlanta, Georgia 30342 USA
		Telephone:	404-497-7680
Designatory Letters:	CFPN (Christian Financial Professionals Network Certified Member)	**Fax:**	404-497-7685
		E-mail:	--
		Web:	www.cfpn.org
Profession:	Finance		
Membership:	--		
Established:	--		

Society of Financial Service Professionals

Designation:	NA	**Address:**	17 Campus Boulevard, Suite 201, Newtown Square, Pennsylvania 19073-3230 USA
Designatory Letters:	NA		
Profession:	Finance		
Membership:	--	**Telephone:**	610-526-2500
Established:	1928	**Fax:**	610-527-1499
		E-mail:	Custserv@financialpro.org
		Web:	www.financialpro.org

Society of Financial Examiners

Designation:	Certified Financial Examiner	**Address:**	174 Grace Blvd., Altamonte Springs, Florida 32714 USA
	Accredited Financial Examiner	**Telephone:**	407-682-4930
	Automated Examination Specialist	**Fax:**	407-682-3175
		E-mail:	pkeyes@sofe.org
Designatory Letters:	CFE (Certified Financial Examiner)	**Web:**	www.sofe.org
	AFE (Accredited Financial Examiner)		
	AES (Accredited Examination Specialist)		
Profession:	Financial Auditing		
Membership:	--		
Established:	--		

International Association of Registered Financial Consultants

Designation:	Registered Financial Associate	**Address:**	The Financial Planning Building, PO Box 42506, Middletown, Ohio 45042-0506 USA
	Registered Financial Consultant	**Telephone:**	800-532-9060
Designatory Letters:	RFA (Registered Financial Associate)	**Fax:**	513-424-5752
		E-mail:	director@iarfc.org
	RFC (Registered Financial Consultant)	**Web:**	www.iarfc.org
Profession:	Financial Consulting		
Membership:	--		
Established:	--		

Heartland Institute of Financial Education

Designation:	Certified Financial Educator	**Address:**	2851 S. Parker Road, Ste 1100, Aurora, Colorado 80014 USA
Designatory Letters:	CFEd (Certified Financial Educator)	**Telephone:**	303-597-0197/888-517-7115
		Fax:	303-369-3900
		E-mail:	--
Profession:	Financial Education	**Web:**	www.heartlandfinancialeducation.com
Membership:	300		
Established:	2004		

American Academy of Financial Management

Designation:	Chartered Asset Manager	**Address:**	245 Glendale Drive, Ste 1, Metaire, Louisiana 70001 USA [Offices in Dubai, UAE, Singapore, Beijing, Mexico, Taiwan, and Hong Kong]
	Master Financial Professional		
	Financial Analyst Designate		
	Registered Financial Specialist	**Telephone:**	--
		Fax:	419-828-4923
	Chartered Portfolio Manager	**E-mail:**	info@financialanalyst.org
		Web:	www.financialanalyst.org
	Chartered Trust and Estate Planner		
	Chartered Wealth Manager		
	Chartered Risk Analyst		
Designatory Letters:	CAM (Chartered Asset Manager)		
	MFP (Master Financial Professional)		
	FAD (Financial Analyst Designate)		
	RFS (Registered Financial Specialist)		
	CPM (Chartered Portfolio Manager)		
	CTEP (Chartered Trust and Estate Planner)		
	CWM (Chartered Wealth Manager)		
	CRA (Chartered Risk Analyst)		
Profession:	Financial Management		
Membership:	35,000		
Established:	1996		

Institute for Divorce Financial Analysts

Designation:	Certified Divorce Financial Analyst	**Address:**	24901 Northwestern Highway, Ste 710, Southfield, Michigan 48075
Designatory Letters:	CDFA (Certified Divorce Financial Analyst) (Offered in Canada as well)		USA
		Telephone:	800-875-1760
		Fax:	248-223-0199
		E-mail:	shar@institutedfa.com
Profession:	Financial Management	**Web:**	www.institutedfa.com
Membership:	1,700		
Established:	1993		

International Association of Financial Engineers

Designation:	NA	**Address:**	560 Lexington Avenue, 9th Floor,
Designatory Letters:	NA		New York, New York 10022
Profession:	Financial Management		USA
Membership:	--	**Telephone:**	212-317-7479
Established:	1992	**Fax:**	212-527-2927
		E-mail:	main@iafe.org
		Web:	www.iafe.org

Association of Chartered Senior Financial Planners

Designation:	Chartered Senior Financial Planner	**Address:**	8174 South Holly St, # 253, Centennial, Colorado 80122
Designatory Letters:	CSFP (Chartered Senior Financial Planner)		USA
		Telephone:	866-942-2737
Profession:	Financial Planning	**Fax:**	303-379-6483
Membership:	1,000	**E-mail:**	info@acsfp.com
Established:	2003	**Web:**	www.acsfp.com

Association for Financial Counseling and Planning Education

Designation:	Certified Housing Counselor	**Address:**	1500 W 3rd Ave., Suite 223, Columbus, Ohio 43212 USA
	Accredited Financial Counselor	**Telephone:**	614-485-9650
		Fax:	614-485-9650
Designatory Letters:	CHC (Certified Housing Counselor)	**E-mail:**	411@afcpe.org
	AFC (Accredited Financial Counselor)	**Web:**	www.afcpe.org
Profession:	Financial Planning		
Membership:	--		
Established:	--		

The Certified Financial Planner Board of Standards (CFP Board)

Designation:	Certified Financial Planner	**Address:**	1670 Broadway, Suite # 600, Denver, Colorado 80202-4809
Designatory Letters:	CFP (Certified Financial Planner)		USA
		Telephone:	303-830-7500
Profession:	Financial Planning	**Fax:**	303-860-7388
Membership:	--	**E-mail:**	mail@CFPBoard.org
Established:	1985	**Web:**	www.cfp.net

College for Financial Planning

Designation:	Registered Paraplanner	**Address:**	8000 E. Maplewood Ave., Ste 200, Greenwood Village, Colorado 80111 USA
	Chartered Retirement Plan Specialist		
	Accredited Wealth Management Advisor	**Telephone:**	800-237-9990
		Fax:	303-220-1200
		E-mail:	cffpstudentservicecenter@apollogrp.edu
	Accredited Asset Management Specialist	**Web:**	www.cffp.edu
	Chartered Retirement Planning Counselor		
	Chartered Retirement Plans Specialist		
	Chartered Mutual Fund Counselor		
Designatory Letters:	RP (Registered Paraplanner)		
	CRPS (Chartered Retirement Plan Specialist)		
	AWMA (Accredited Wealth Management Advisor)		
	AAMS (Accredited Asset Management Specialist)		
	CRPC (Chartered Retirement Planning Counselor)		
	CRPS (Chartered Retirement Plans Specialist)		
	CMFC (Chartered Mutual Fund Counselor)		
Profession:	Financial Planning		
Membership:	100,000		
Established:	1972		

Financial Service Standards

Designation:	Professional Plan Consultant	**Address:**	2652 Hidden Valley Drive, Ste 100A, Pittsburgh, Pennsylvania 15241 USA
Designatory Letters:	PPC (Professional Plan Consultant)	**Telephone:**	412-977-9304
Profession:	Financial Planning	**Fax:**	724-942-4196
Membership:	--	**E-mail:**	info@financialservicestandards.com
Established:	--	**Web:**	www.financialservicestandards.com

International Association of Qualified Financial Planners

Designation:	Qualified Financial Planner	**Address:**	PO Box 7007, Beverly Hills, California 90212-7007 USA
Designatory Letters:	QFP (Qualified Financial Planner)	**Telephone:**	877-346-3037
		Fax:	303-379-6483
Profession:	Financial Planning	**E-mail:**	info@acsfp.com
Membership:	--	**Web:**	www.iaqfp.org
Established:	2003		

National Association of Financial and Estate Planning

Designation:	Certified Estate Advisor	**Address:**	Salt Lake City, Utah 84107 USA
	CEA (Certified Estate	**Telephone:**	801-266-9900
Designatory Letters:	Advisor)	**Fax:**	801-266-1019
Profession:	Financial Planning	**E-mail:**	--
Membership:	--	**Web:**	www.nafep.org
Established:	--		

National Institute of Certified College Planners

Designation:	Certified College	**Address:**	PO Box 15278, Syracuse, New
	Planning Specialist		York 13215-0278 USA
Designatory Letters:	CCPS (Certified College	**Telephone:**	800-765-2031
	Planning Specialist)	**Fax:**	406-765-2060
Profession:	Financial Planning	**E-mail:**	staff@niccp.com
Membership:	1,024	**Web:**	www.niccp.com
Established:	2002		

Registered Financial Planners Institute

Designation:	Registered Financial	**Address:**	2001 Cooper Foster Park Road,
	Planner		Amherst, Ohio USA
	Senior Registered	**Telephone:**	440-282-7176
	Financial Planner	**Fax:**	--
Designatory Letters:	RFP (Registered Financial	**E-mail:**	info@rfpi.com
	Planner)	**Web:**	www.rfpi.com
	SRFP (Senior Registered		
	Financial Planner)		
Profession:	Financial Planning		
Membership:	2,500		
Established:	1983		

The American College

Designation:	--	**Address:**	270 S. Bryn Mawr Avenue, Bryn Mawr, Pennsylvania 1910-2196 USA
Designatory Letters:	CAP (Chartered Advisor in Philanthropy)	**Telephone:**	888-263-7265
		Fax:	610-526-1465
	CASL (Chartered Advisor in Senior Living)	**E-mail:**	studentservices@theamericancollege.edu
		Web:	www.theamericancollege.edu
	ChFC (Chartered Financial Consultant)		
	CLF (Chartered Leadership Fellow)		
	CLU (Chartered Life Underwriter)		
	FSS (Financial Services Specialist)		
	LUTF (Life Underwriter Training Council Fellow) (Administered jointly by the American College and the National Association of Insurance and Financial Advisors)		
	REBC (Registered Employee Benefit Consultant)		
	RHU (Registered Health Underwriter)		
Degrees:	MSM (Master of Science in Management)		
	MSFS (Master of Science in Financial Services)		
Profession:	Financial Services		
Membership:	150,000		
Established:	1927 (American College)		

Bank Administration Institute (BAI)

Designation:	Certified Bank Auditor Certified Risk Professional	**Address:**	One North Franklin Street, Chicago, Illinois 60606-0943 USA
Designatory Letters:	CBA (Certified Bank Auditor)	**Telephone:**	312-553-4600 or 800-224-9889
	CRP (Certified Risk Professional)	**Fax:**	312-683-2373
		E-mail:	info@bai.org
Profession:	Financial Services Auditing	**Web:**	www.bai.org
Membership:	--		
Established:	1914		

Institute of Forensic Science
(The American College of Forensic Examiners Institute – ACFEI)

Designation:	--	**Address:**	2750 East Sunshine St.,
Designatory Letters:	CHS (Certified in Homeland Security)		Springfield, Missiouri 65804 USA
	CFC (Certified Forensic Consultant)	**Telephone:**	417-881-3818 or 800-423-9737
		Fax:	417-881-4702
	CMI (Certified Medical Investigator)	**E-mail:**	--
		Web:	www.acfei.org
	Cr.FA (Certified Forensic Accountant)		
	CFN (Certified Forensic Nurse)		
Profession:	Forensic Studies		
Membership:	--		
Established:	--		

The International Franchise Association

Designation:	Certified Franchise Executive	**Address:**	1501 K. Street, N.W., Suite 200, Washington, D.C. 20005 USA
Designatory Letters:	CFE (Certified Franchise Executive)	**Telephone:**	202-628-8000
		Fax:	202-628-0812
Profession:	Franchising	**E-mail:**	--
Membership:	--	**Web:**	www.franchise.org
Established:	--		

Association of Certified Fraud Examiners (ACFE)

Designation:	Certified Fraud Examiner	**Address:**	716 West Avenue, Austin, Texas 78701 USA
Designatory Letters:	CFE (Certified Fraud Examiner)	**Telephone:**	512-478-9000 or 800-245-3321
Profession:	Fraud Investigation	**Fax:**	512-478-9297
Membership:	37,000	**E-mail:**	info@cfenet.com
Established:	1988	**Web:**	www.cfenet.com

Association of Certified Fraud Specialists Inc.

Designation:	Certified Fraud Specialist	**Address:**	8124 Ardenness Drive, Sacramento, California 95829 USA
Designatory Letters:	CFS (Certified Fraud Specialist)		
Profession:	Fraud Investigation	**Telephone:**	916-419-6319
Membership:	--	**Fax:**	916-419-6318
Established:	--	**E-mail:**	acfs@almccoskey.com
		Web:	www.acfs.net

Association of Government Accountants (AGA)

Designation:	Certified Government Financial Manager	**Address:**	2208 Mt. Vernon Avenue, Alexandria, Virginia 22301-1314 USA
Designatory Letters:	CGFM (Certified Government Financial Manager)	**Telephone:**	703-684-6931
		Fax:	703-548-9367
Profession:	Government Accounting	**E-mail:**	--
Membership:	14,000	**Web:**	www.agacgfm.org
Established:	1994		

National Association of Local Government Auditors (NALGA)

Designation:	NA	**Address:**	449 Lewis Hargett Circle,
Designatory Letters:	NA		Suite 290, Lexington, Kentucky
Profession:	Government (Local)		40503-3590 USA
	Internal Auditing	**Telephone:**	859-276-0686
Membership:	--	**Fax:**	--
Established:	--	**E-mail:**	--
		Web:	www.nalga.org

National Institute of Governmental Purchasing Inc.

Designation:	--	**Address:**	151 Spring St., Herndon, Virginia
Designatory Letters:	CPPB (Certified		20170-5223 USA
	Professional Public	**Telephone:**	800-367-6447/703-736-8900
	Buyer)	**Fax:**	703-736-2818
	CPPO (Certified Public	**E-mail:**	kcampbell@nigp.org
	Purchasing Officer)	**Web:**	www.nigp.org
Profession:	Government Purchasing		
Membership:	--		
Established:	1944		

Healthcare Financial Management Association

Designation:	--	**Address:**	1301 Connecticut Ave., NW,
Designatory Letters:	CHFP – Certified	**Telephone:**	Ste 300, Washington D.C.
	Healthcare Financial	**Fax:**	20036-3417 USA
	Professional	**E-mail:**	202-296-2920
	FHFMA – Fellow of the	**Web:**	202-223-9771
	Healthcare Financial		--
	Management		www.hfma.org
	Association		
Profession:	Healthcare Financial		
	Management		
Membership:	--		
Established:	--		

Association of Healthcare Internal Auditors

Designation:	NA	**Address:**	900 Fox Valley Drive, Ste # 204,
Designatory Letters:	NA		Longwood, Florida 32779 USA
Profession:	Healthcare Internal	**Telephone:**	407-786-8200
	Auditing	**Fax:**	--
Membership:	--	**E-mail:**	--
Established:	--	**Web:**	--

American Healthcare Executives

Designation:	Certified Healthcare	**Address:**	Ste. 1700, One North Franklin St.,
	Executive		Chicago, Illinois 60606-3424
Designatory Letters:	CHE (Certified Healthcare		USA
	Executive)	**Telephone:**	312-424-2820
	FACHE (Fellow of the	**Fax:**	312-424-0023
	American College of	**E-mail:**	geninfo@ache.org
	Healthcare Executives)	**Web:**	www.ache.org
Profession:	Healthcare Management		
Membership:	--		
Established:	--		

Hospitality Financial and Technology Professionals

Designation:	--	**Address:**	11709 Boulder Lane, Suite # 110, Austin, Texas 78726 USA
Designatory Letters:	CHAE (Certified Hospitality Accountant Executive)	**Telephone:**	512-249-5333 or 800-646-4387
		Fax:	512-249-1533
	CHTP (Certified Hospitality Technology Professional)	**E-mail:**	certification@hftp.org
		Web:	www.hftp.org
Profession:	Hospitality Management and/or Hospitality Technology		
Membership:	4,600		
Established:	1952		

American Hotel and Lodging Educational Institute

Designation:	--	**Address:**	800 N. Magnolia Avenue, Suite 1800, Orlando, Florida 32803 USA
Designatory Letters:	CHA (Certified Hotel Administrator)		
	CHRM (Certified Hotel Revenue Manager)	**Telephone:**	407-999-8100
	CHI (Certified Hospitality Instructor)	**Fax:**	407-236-7848
	CLM (Certified Lodging Manager)	**E-mail:**	eiinfo@ahla.com
	CLSD (Certified Lodging Security Director)	**Web:**	www.ei-ahla.org

CRDE (Certified Rooms Division Executive)

CFBE (Certified Food and Beverage Executive)

CHHE (Certified Hospitality Housekeeping Executive)

CHRE (Certified Human Resources Executive)

CEOE (Certified Engineering Operations Executive)

CHSP (Certified Hospitality Sales Professional)

CHDT (Certified Hospitalty Department Trainer)

CHS (Certified Hospitality Supervisor)

CLSS (Certified Lodging Security Supervisor)

MHS (Master Hotel Supplier)

CHE (Certified Hospitality Educator)

CGS (Certified Gaming Supervisor)

CGPS (Certified Government Property Supervisor)

CGPT (Certified Government Property Technician)

CGPM (Certified Government Property Manager)

CHT (Certified Hospitality Trainer)

HFTP (Hospitality Financial & Technology Professional)

Profession:	Hotel Management
Membership:	--
Established:	--

International Association for Human Resource Inc.

Designation:	Certified Human Resources Service Professional	**Address:**	PO Box 1086, Burlington, Massachusetts 01803-6806 USA
		Telephone:	800-804-3983/781-791-9488
Designatory Letters:	CHRSP (Certified Human Resources Professional)	**Fax:**	781-998-8011
		E-mail:	moreinfo@ihrim.org
Profession:	Human Resource Management	**Web:**	www.ihrim.org
Membership:	--		
Established:	--		

International Foundation of Employee Benefits Plans

Designation:	--	**Address:**	18700 Bluemound Road, Brookfield, Wisconsin 53045 or PO Box 69, Brookfield, Wisconsin 53008-0069 USA
Designatory Letters:	ATMS (Advanced Trustee Management Standards)		
	CAPP (Certificate of Achievement in Public Plan Policy)	**Telephone:**	888-334-3327
	RPA (Retirement Plans Associate)	**Fax:**	--
	CEBS (Certified Employee Benefits Specialist)	**E-mail:**	--
		Web:	www.ifebp.org
	TMP (Trustee Masters Program)		
Profession:	Human Resource Management		
Membership:	--		
Established:	1954		

Society for Human Resource Management

Designation:	--	**Address:**	1800 Duke Street, Alexandria, Virginia 22314 USA
Designatory Letters:	PHR (Professional in Human Resource Management)	**Telephone:**	703-548-6999
		Fax:	703-535-6490
	SPHR (Senior Professional in Human Resource Management)	**E-mail:**	shrm@shrm.org
		Web:	www.shrm.org
Profession:	Human Resource Management		
Membership:	205,000		
Established:	1948		

American Society for Industrial Security

Designation:	Certified Protection Professional	**Address:**	1625 Prince Street, Alexandria, Virginia 22314-2818 USA
Designatory Letters:	CPP (Certified Protection Professional)	**Telephone:**	703-519-6200
		Fax:	703-519-6299
	PCI (Professional Certified Investigator)	**E-mail:**	asis@asisonline.org
		Web:	asisonline.org
	PSP (Physical Security Professional)		
Profession:	Industrial Security		
Membership:	34,000		
Established:	1955		

Cisco Systems Inc.

Designation:	--	**Address:**	United States
Designatory Letters:	CCDA (Cisco Certified Design Associate)		800-553-6387/408-526-4000
	CCNA (Cisco Certified Network Associate)	**Telephone:**	--
	CPCC (Cisco IP Contact Center Express Specialist)	**Fax:**	--
		E-mail:	www.cisco.com
	CCDP (Cisco Certified Design Professional)	**Web:**	
	CCIP (Cisco Certified Internetwork Professional)		
	CCNP (Cisco Certified Network Professional)		
	CCVP (Cisco Certified Voice Professional)		
	CCSI (Certified Cisco Systems Instructor)		
	CCIE (Cisco Certified Internetwork Expert)		
	CCSP (Cisco Certified Security Professional)		
Profession:	Information Technology		
Membership:	--		
Established:	--		

The Computer Security Institute (CSI)

Designation:	--	**Address:**	600 Community Drive, Manhasset,
Designatory Letters:	--		New York 11030 USA
Profession:	Information Technology	**Telephone:**	800-250-2429
Membership:	--	**Fax:**	847-763-9606/9602
Established:	1974	**E-mail:**	csimemberservice@gocsi.com
		Web:	www.gocsi.com

The Computing Technology Industry Association (CTIA)

Designation:	--	**Address:**	1815 S. Meyers Road, Ste. 300,
Designatory Letters:	CompTIA A+		Oakbrook Terrace, Illinois
	CompTIA Network+		60181-5228 USA
	CompTIA Server+	**Telephone:**	630-678-8300
	CompTIA CTII+	**Fax:**	630-678-8384
	CompTIA LINUX+	**E-mail:**	--
	CompTIA Convergence+	**Web:**	www.comptia.org
	CompTIA i-Net+		
	CompTIA Project+		
	CompTIA e-Biz+		
	CompTIA HTII+ (Certified Home and Technology Integration)		
	CompTIA RFID (Radio Frequency Identification)		
	CompTIA CDIAA+ (Certified Document Imaging Architect)		
Profession:	Information Technology		
Membership:	--		
Established:	1982		

Disaster Recovery Institute (DRI)

Designation:	Business Continuity Planner	**Address:**	1400 I Street NW, Washington, D.C. 20005 USA
Designatory Letters:	ABCP (Associate Business Continuity Planner)	**Telephone:**	202-962-3979
	CBCP (Certified Business Continuity Planner)	**Fax:**	202-962-3939
		E-mail:	driinfo@drii.org
	CFCP (Certified Functional Continuity Professional)	**Web:**	www.drii.org
	MBCP (Master Business Continuity Planner)		
Profession:	Information Technology		
Membership:	--		
Established:	1988		

IEEE Computer Society

Designation:	NA	**Address:**	1730 Massachusetts Ave., N.W., Washington, D.C. 20036-1992 USA
Designatory Letters:	NA		
Profession:	Information Technology		
Membership:	--	**Telephone:**	202-371-0101
Established:	--	**Fax:**	202-296-2187
		E-mail:	amkelly@computer.org
		Web:	www.computer.org

Information Resources Management Association (IRMA)

Designation:	NA	**Address:**	701 E-Chocolate Avenue, Suite 200, Hershey, Pennsylvania 17033 USA
Designatory Letters:	NA		
Profession:	Information Technology	**Telephone:**	717-533-8879
Membership:	--	**Fax:**	717-533-8661
Established:	--	**E-mail:**	member@irma-international.org
		Web:	www.irma-international.org

Institute for Certification of Computing Professionals (ICCP)

Designation:	--	**Address:**	2350 E. Devon Avenue, Suite 115, Des Plaines, Illinois 60018-4503 USA
Designatory Letters:	ACP (Associate Computing Professional)		
	CCP (Certified Computing Professional)	**Telephone:**	847-299-4227
		Fax:	847-299-4280
	CBIP (Certified Business Intelligence Professional)	**E-mail:**	office@iccp.org
		Web:	www.iccp.org
	CDMP (Certified Data Management Professional)		
	ISA (Information Systems Professional)		
	ISP (Information Systems Professional [Canada])		
Profession:	Information Technology		
Membership:	--		
Established:	1973		

Novell

Designation:	--	**Address:**	USA
Designatory Letters:	CNI (Certified Novell Instructor)	**Telephone:**	800-529-3400/801-861-1329
		Fax:	--
	CNE (Certified Novell Engineer)	**E-mail:**	crc@novell.com
		Web:	www.novell.com
	CNA (Certified Novell Administrator)		
	CLP (Certified Linux Professional)		
	CLE (Certified Linux Engineer)		
	Master CNE (Master Certified Novell Engineer)		
	NAI (Novell Authorized Instructor)		
Profession:	Information Technology		
Membership:	--		
Established:	--		

Office Automation Society International (OASI)

Designation:	--	**Address:**	5170 Meadow Wood Blvd., Lyndhurst, Ohio 44124-3724 USA
Designatory Letters:	COAP (Certified Office Automation Professional)	**Telephone:**	216-461-4803
Profession:	Information Technology	**Fax:**	216-461-4803
Membership:	--	**E-mail:**	JBDyke@aol.com
Established:	1982	**Web:**	--

Professional Association of Certified Domain Appraisers (ACDA)

Designation:	Certified Domain Appraiser	**Address:**	USA
Designatory Letters:	CDA (Certified Domain Appraiser)	**Telephone:**	--
		Fax:	--
		E-mail:	--
Profession:	Information Technology	**Web:**	www.the-office.com/ appraiser/aboutACDA.htm
Membership:	--		
Established:	--		

Vingo Publishing LLC.

Designation:	Converged Solutions Provider	**Address:**	3300 N. Central, Suite 300, Phoenix, Arizona 85012 USA
Designatory Letters:	CSP (Converged Solutions Provider)	**Telephone:**	--
		Fax:	--
Profession:	Information Technology	**E-mail:**	cspcertification@vpico.com
Membership:	--	**Web:**	www.cspcertification.com
Established:	--		

Information Systems Audit and Control Association (ISACA)

Designation:	Certified Information Systems Auditor Certified Information Security Manager	**Address:**	3701 Algonquin Road, Suite 1010, Rolling Meadows, Illinois 60008 USA
Designatory Letters:	CISM (Certified Information Security Manager) CISA (Certified Information Systems Auditor)	**Telephone:** **Fax:** **E-mail:** **Web:**	647-253-1545 647-253-1443 -- www.isaca.org
Profession:	Information Technology Auditing		
Membership:	50,000		
Established:	1969		

IT Financial Management Association

Designation:	--	**Address:**	PO Box 30188, Santa Barbara, California 93130 USA
Designatory Letters:	FMC (IT Financial Management Controllership Certificate) FMA (IT Financial Management Accounting Certificate) AM (IT Asset Management Certificate) CABC (IT Chargeback and Activity Based Costing Certificate) PMB (IT Performance Management and Benchmarking Certificate) GFM (Government IT Financial Management Certificate)	**Telephone:** **Fax:** **E-mail:** **Web:**	805-687-7390 805-687-7382 info@itfma.com www.itfma.com
Profession:	Information Technology Financial Management		
Membership:	--		
Established:	1988		

Global Information Assurance Certification (GIAC)

Designation:	--
Designatory Letters:	GISF (GIAC Information Security Fundamentals)
	GSEC (GIAC Security Essentials Certification)
	GCFW (GIAC Certified Firewall Analyst)
	GCIA (GIAC Certified Intrusion Analyst)
	GCIH (GIAC Certified Incident Handler)
	GCWN (GIAC Certified Windows Security Administrator)
	GCUX (GIAC Certified UNIX Security Administrator)
	GCFA (GIAC Certified Forensics Analyst)
	GAWN (GIAC Assessing Wireless Networks)
	GSIP (GIAC Secure Internet Presence)
	GCSC (GIAC Certified Security Consultant)
	GCLC (GIAC Security Leadership Certification)
	GOEC (GIAC Operations Essentials)
	GSAE (GIAC Security Audit Essentials)
	G7799 (GIAC Certified ISO-17799 Specialist)
	GSNA (GIAC Systems and Network Auditor)
Profession:	Information Technology Security
Membership:	--
Established:	1999

Address:	United States
Telephone:	--
Fax:	--
E-mail:	info@giac.org
Web:	www.giac.org

International Information System Security Certification Consortium (ISC)²

Designation:	--	**Address:**	USA
Designatory Letters:	CISSP (Certified Information Systems Security Professional)	**Telephone:**	703-891-6781/866-462-477
		Fax:	703-356-7977
	SSCP (Systems Security Certified Practitioner)	**E-mail:**	institute@isc2.org
		Web:	www.isc2.org
	CAP (Certified and Accreditation Professional)		
	ISSAP (Information Systems Security Architecture Professional)		
	ISSMP (Information Systems Security Management Professional)		
	ISSEP (Information Systems Security Engineering Professional)		
Profession:	Information Technology Security		
Membership:	--		
Established:	1989		

Institute of Internal Auditors

Designation:	Certified Internal Auditor	**Address:**	249 Maitland Avenue, Altamonte Springs, Florida 32701-4201 USA
	Certification in Control Self-Assessment		
	Certified Financial Services Auditor	**Telephone:**	407-937-1111
		Fax:	407-937-1101
	Certified Government Auditing Professional	**E-mail:**	custserv@theiia.org
		Web:	www.theiia.org
Designatory Letters:	CIA (Certified Internal Auditor)		
	CCSA (Certification in Control Self-Assessment)		
	CFSA) Certified Financial Services Auditor)		
	CGAP (Certified Government Auditing Professional)		
Profession:	Internal Auditing		
Membership:	122,000		
Established:	1941		

Academy of Life Underwriting (ALU)

Designation:	--	**Address:**	2901 Telestar Court, Falls Church, Virginia 22042 USA
Designatory Letters:	AALU (Associate, Academy of Life Underwriting)	**Telephone:**	703-641-9400/888-275-0092
		Fax:	703-641-9885
	FALU (Fellow, Academy of Life Underwriting)	**E-mail:**	stertzer@aalu.org
		Web:	www.aalu.org
Profession:	Insurance		
Membership:	--		
Established:	1948		

American Institute for Chartered Property Casualty Underwriters/Insurance Institute of America

Designation:	--	**Address:**	720 Providence Road, PO Box 3016, Malvern, Pennsylvania 19355-0716 USA
Designatory Letters:	AAI (Accredited Adviser in Insurance)		
	AAM (Associate in Automation Management)	**Telephone:**	610-644-2100
	AFSB (Associate in Fidelity and Surety Bonding)	**Fax:**	610-725-1000
		E-mail:	lewis@cpcuiia.org
	AIAF (Associate in Insurance Accounting and Finance)	**Web:**	www.aicpcu.org
	AIC (Associate in Claims)		
	AIM (Associate in Management)		
	AIS (Associate in Insurance Services)		
	AIT (Associate in Information Technology)		
	AMIM (Associate in Marine Insurance Management)		
	APA (Associate in Premium Auditing)		
	API (Associate in Personal Insurance)		
	ARC (Associate in Regulation and Compliance)		
	ARe (Associate in Reinsurance)		
	ARM (Associate in Risk Management)		
	ASLI (Associate in Surplus Life Insurance)		
	AU (Associate in Underwriting)		
	CPCU (Chartered Property Casualty Underwriter)		
	RMPE (Risk Management for Public Entities)		
Profession:	Insurance		
Membership:	--		
Established:	1942/1909		

Insurance Accounting and Systems Association

Designation:	--	**Address:**	3511 Shannon Road, Suite 160,
Designatory Letters:	--		PO Box 51340, Durham, North
Profession:	Insurance		Carolina 27707 USA
Membership:	--	**Telephone:**	919-489-0991
Established:	1928	**Fax:**	919-489-1994
		E-mail:	info@iasa.org
		Web:	www.iasa.org

Insurance Data Management Association (IDMA)

Designation:	--	**Address:**	85 John Street, New York,
Designatory Letters:	CIDM (Certified Insurance		New York 10038 USA
	Data Manager)	**Telephone:**	212-669-0496
	AIDM (Associate	**Fax:**	212-669-0535
	Insurance Data	**E-mail:**	rpenbarthy@idma.org
	Manager)	**Web:**	www.idma.org
Profession:	Insurance		
Membership:	--		
Established:	1984		

Insurance Educational Association

Designation:	--	**Address:**	100 California Street, Suite 650,
Designatory Letters:	CPDM (Certified		San Francisco, California 94111
	Professional Disability		USA
	Management)	**Telephone:**	800-655-4432
Profession:	Insurance	**Fax:**	415-986-4905
Membership:	--	**E-mail:**	Info@ieatraining.com
Established:	1876	**Web:**	www. ieatraining.com

Insurance Regulatory Examiners Society (IRES)

Designation:	--	**Address:**	12710 S. Pflumm Road, Suite 200,
Designatory Letters:	C.I.E. (Certified Insurance		Olathe, Kansas 66062 USA
	Examiner)	**Telephone:**	913-768-4700
	A.I.E. (Accredited	**Fax:**	913-768-4900
	Insurance Examiner)	**E-mail:**	ireshq@swbell.net
Profession:	Insurance	**Web:**	www.go-ires.org
Membership:	--		
Established:	1987		

International Institute of Loss Adjusters, Inc. (IILA)

Designation:	NA	**Address:**	J. Shaw & Co., 1100 Main Street,
Designatory Letters:	NA		Lombard, Illinois 60148-3971
Profession:	Insurance		USA
Membership:	--	**Telephone:**	630-932-0707
Established:	1965	**Fax:**	630-932-1392
		E-mail:	info@iila.com
		Web:	www.iila.com

Life Office Management Association Inc. (LOMA)

Designation:	--	**Address:**	2300 Windy Ridge Parkway,
Designatory Letters:	AAPA (Associate,		Suite 600, Atlanta, Georgia
	Annuity Products and		30339-8443 USA
	Administration)	**Telephone:**	770-951-1770
	ACS (Associate, Customer	**Fax:**	770-984-0441
	Service)	**E-mail:**	education@loma.org
	AFSB (Associate in	**Web:**	www.loma.org
	Fidelity and Surety		
	Bonding)		
	AFSI (Associate, Financial		
	Services Institute)		
	AIAA (Associate,		
	Insurance Agency		
	Administration)		
	AIAF (Associate in		
	Insurance Accounting		
	and Finance)		
	AIRC (Associate,		
	Insurance Regulatory		
	Compliance)		
	ALMI (Associate, Life		
	Management Institute)		
	ARA (Associate,		
	Reinsurance		
	Administration)		
	CPFS (Certified		
	Professional in Financial		
	Services)		
	CPLHI (Certified		
	Professional Life and		
	Health Insurance		
	Program)		
	FFSI (Fellow, Financial		
	Services Institute)		
	FLMI (Fellow, Life		
	Management Institute)		
	PFSL (Programa de		
	Formación en Seguros		
	de LOMA)		
	PFLP (Programa de		
	Foração LOMA em		
	Português)		
Profession:	Insurance		
Membership:	--		
Established:	1924		

Life Office Management Association Inc. (LOMA) under the direction of the International Claim Association (ICA)

Designation:	--	**Address:**	2300 Windy Ridge Parkway,
Designatory Letters:	ALHC - Associate, Life		Suite 600, Atlanta, Georgia
	and Health Claims		30339-8443 USA
Profession:	Insurance	**Telephone:**	770-951-1770
Membership:	--	**Fax:**	770-984-0441
Established:	1924 (LOMA)	**E-mail:**	education@loma.org
		Web:	www.loma.org

National Alliance for Insurance Education and Research

Designation:	--	**Address:**	3630 North Hills Drive, Austin, Texas 78755-2027 USA
Designatory Letters:	CIC (Certified Insurance Counsellor)	**Telephone:**	800-633-2165
	CISR (Certified Insurance Service Representative)	**Fax:**	512-349-6194
		E-mail:	alliance@scic.com
Profession:	Insurance	**Web:**	www. scic.com
Membership:	--		
Established:	--		

Professional Liability Underwriting Society

Designation:	Registered Professional Liability Underwriter	**Address:**	5353 Wayzata Blvd., Suite 600, Minneapolis, Minnesota 55146 USA
Designatory Letters:	RPLU (Registered Professional Liability Underwriter)	**Telephone:**	800-845-0778/952-746-2580
		Fax:	952-746-2599
Profession:	Insurance	**E-mail:**	sjohnson@plusweb.org
Membership:	--	**Web:**	www.plusweb.org
Established:	--		

Society of Certified Insurance Counselors

Designation:	Certified Insurance Counsellor	**Address:**	3630 North Hills Drive, PO Box 27027, Austin, Texas 78731 USA
Designatory Letters:	CIC (Certified Insurance Counsellor)	**Telephone:**	800-633-2165
Profession:	Insurance	**Fax:**	512-349-6194
Membership:	--	**E-mail:**	alliance@scic.com
Established:	1969	**Web:**	www.scic.com

3 Dimensional Wealth International

Designation:	3 Dimensional Wealth Planner	**Address:**	168 Forest Avenue, Locust Valley, New York 11560 USA
Designatory Letters:	C3DWP (3 Dimensional Wealth Planner)	**Telephone:**	877-339-3258
		Fax:	--
Profession:	Investment Management	**E-mail:**	info@3DWealth.org
Membership:	--	**Web:**	www.3dwealth.org
Established:	--		

Center for Fiduciary Studies

Designation:	Accredited Investment Fiduciary Analyst Accredited Investment Fiduciary	**Address:**	Fiduciary 360, 438 Division St., Sewickley, Pennsylvania 15143 USA
Designatory Letters:	AIFA (Accredited Investment Fiduciary Analyst) AIF (Accredited Investment Fiduciary)	**Telephone:**	412-741-8140
		Fax:	212-681-2005
		E-mail:	info@fi360.com
		Web:	www.fi360.com
Profession:	Investment Management		
Membership:	--		
Established:	--		

The CFA Institute

Designation:	Chartered Financial Analyst	**Address:**	PO Box 3668, Charlottesville, Virginia 22903-0668, or 560 Ray C. Hunt Drive, Charlottesville, Virginia 22903-0668 USA
Designatory Letters:	CIPM (Certificate in Investment Performance) [Formerly the CGIPS – Certificate in Global Investment Performance] CFA (Chartered Financial Analyst)	**Telephone:**	434-951-5499 or 800-247-8132
		Fax:	434-951-5262
		E-mail:	info@cfainstitute.org
		Web:	www.cfainstitute.org
Profession:	Investment Management		
Membership:	86,000		
Established:	1990 (Merger of the Financial Analysts Federation and the Institute of Chartered Financial Analysts which was established in 1963).		

Chartered Alternative Investment Analysts Association

Designation:	Chartered Alternative Investment Analyst	**Address:**	29 South Pleasant St., Amherst, Massachusetts 01002 USA
Designatory Letters:	CAIA (Chartered Alternative Investment Analyst)	**Telephone:**	413-253-7373
		Fax:	413-253-4494
		E-mail:	info@caia.org
Profession:	Investment Management	**Web:**	www.caia.org
Membership:	--		
Established:	1999		

Institute of Business and Finance

Designation:	Certified Fund Specialist Board Certified in Annuities Board Certified in Estate Planning Board Certified in Mutual Funds Certified Annuity Specialist Board Certified in Asset Allocation Board Certified in Securities Certified Senior Consultant Retired Income Specialist	**Address:** **Telephone:** **Fax:** **E-mail:** **Web:**	USA 800-848-2029 858-454-4660 -- www.icfs.com
Designatory Letters:	CFS (Certified Fund Specialist) BCA (Board Certified in Annuities) BCEP (Board Certified in Estate Planning) BCMF (Board Certified in Mutual Funds) CAS (Certified Annuity Specialist) BCAA (Board Certified in Asset Allocation) BCS (Board Certified in Securities) CSC (Certified Senior Consultant) RIS (Retired Income Specialist)		
Profession:	Investment Management		
Membership:	10,000		
Established:	1991		

Investment Adviser Association

Designation:	Chartered Investment Counsellor	**Address:**	1050 17th Street, NW, Ste 725, Washington, D.C. 20036-5503 USA
Designatory Letters:	CIC (Chartered Investment Counsellor)	**Telephone:**	202-293-4222
Profession:	Investment Management	**Fax:**	202-293-4223
Membership:	--	**E-mail:**	iaa@investmentadviser.org
Established:	1937	**Web:**	www.icaa.org

Investment Management Consultants Association (IMCA)

Designation:	Certified Investment Management Analyst Certified Investment Management Consultant	**Address:**	5619 DTC Parkway, Suite 500, Greenwood Village, Colorado 80111 USA
Designatory Letters:	CIMA (Certified Investment Management Analyst) CIMC (Certified Investment Management Consultant)	**Telephone:** **Fax:** **E-mail:** **Web:**	303-770-3377 303-770-1812 certification@imca.org www.imca.org
Profession:	Investment Management		
Membership:	--		
Established:	1985		

Merrill Lynch

Designation:	Certified Financial Manager	**Address:**	4 World Financial Center, 250 Vessey Street, New York, New York 10080 USA
Designatory Letters:	CFM (Certified Financial Manager)	**Telephone:**	212-449-1000
Profession:	Investment Management	**Fax:**	--
Membership:	--	**E-mail:**	--
Established:	--	**Web:**	www.ml.com

The Wealth Preservation Group

Designation:	Certified Wealth Preservation Planner Certified Asset Protection Planner Accredited Investment Fiduciary Auditor	**Address:**	378 River Run Dr., St. Joseph, Michigan 49085 USA
		Telephone:	269-408-1841
		Fax:	269-983-67917
		E-mail:	roccy@thewpi.org
		Web:	www.thewpi.org
Designatory Letters:	CWPP (Certified Wealth Preservation Planner) CAPP (Certified Asset Protection Planner) AIFA (Accredited Investment Fiduciary Auditor)		
Profession:	Investment Management		
Membership:	--		
Established:	--		

American Society of Association Executives

Designation:	Certified Association Executive	**Address:**	1575 I St, NW, Washington D.C. 20005-1168 USA
Designatory Letters:	CAE (Certified Association Executive)	**Telephone:** **Fax:**	202-626-2723 800-622-2723
Profession:	Management	**E-mail:**	ASAE@asaecenter.org
Membership:	--	**Web:**	www.asaecenter.org
Established:	--		

American Management Association (AMA)

Designation:	--	**Address:**	1601 Broadway, New York, New York 10019 USA
Designatory Letters:	--		
Profession:	Management	**Telephone:**	212-586-8100
Membership:	--	**Fax:**	212-903-8168
Established:	1923	**E-mail:**	customerservice@amanet.org
		Web:	www.amanet.org

Association of Professionals in Business Management Inc.

Designation:	--	**Address:**	8033 Sunset Blvd., Ste # 826,
Designatory Letters:	CBM (Certified Business Manager)		Los Angeles, California 90046 USA
	CABM (Certified Associate Business Manager)	**Telephone:**	312-214-3520
		Fax:	310-657-8996
		E-mail:	info@apbm.org
Profession:	Management	**Web:**	www.apbm.org
Membership:	3,000		
Established:	2000		

Institute of Certified Professional Managers (ICPM)

Designation:	Certified Manager	**Address:**	James Madison University,
Designatory Letters:	Certified Manager of Animal Resources		MSC 5504, Harrisonburg, Virginia 22807 USA
	CM (Certified Manager)	**Telephone:**	800-568-4120/540-568-3247
	CMAR (Certified Manager of Animal Resources)	**Fax:**	540-801-8650
		E-mail:	icpmcm@jmu.edu
Profession:	Management	**Web:**	www. //cob.jmu.edu//edu/
Membership:	--		
Established:	--		

National Association of Corporate Directors

Designation:	Certificate of Director Education	**Address:**	Two Lafayette Center, 1133 21st Street, N.W., Ste 700,
Designatory Letters:	NA		Washington, D.C. 20036 USA
Profession:	Management	**Telephone:**	202-775-0509
Membership:	--	**Fax:**	202-775-4857
Established:	--	**E-mail:**	info@nacdonline.org
		Web:	www.nacdonline.org

Institute of Certified E-Commerce Consultants (ICEC)

Designation:	Certified E-Commerce Consultant	**Address:**	2346 Camp Street, New Orleans, Louisiana 70130 USA
Designatory Letters:	CEC (Certified E-Commerce Consultant)	**Telephone:**	--
		Fax:	--
		E-mail:	enquiry@institutecec.org
Profession:	Management Consulting	**Web:**	www.institutecec.org
Membership:	--		
Established:	--		

Institute of Management Consultants (IMC) - USA

Designation:	Certified Management Consultant	**Address:**	Suite 800, 2025 M Street, Washington, D.C. 20036-3309
Designatory Letters:	CMC (Certified Management Consultant)		USA
		Telephone:	202-367-1134 or 800-221-2557
		Fax:	202-367-2134
Profession:	Management Consulting	**E-mail:**	office@imcusa.org
Membership:	--	**Web:**	www.imcusa.org/
Established:	1968		

American Marketing Association

Designation:	NA	**Address:**	311 South Wacker Drive, Ste 5800,
Designatory Letters:	NA		Chicago, Illinois 60606 USA
Profession:	Marketing	**Telephone:**	312-542-9000
Membership:	38,000	**Fax:**	312-542-9001
Established:	--	**E-mail:**	info@ama.org
		Web:	www.marketingpower.com

Microsoft Learning

Designation:	--	**Address:**	Redmond, Washington USA
Designatory Letters:	MCITP (Microsoft Certified Information Technology Professional)	**Telephone:**	--
		Fax:	--
		E-mail:	msft@msft.com
	MCPD (Microsoft Certified Professional Developer)	**Web:**	www.microsoft.com
	MCTS (Microsoft Certified Technology Specialist)		
	MCDST (Microsoft Certified Desktop Technician)		
	MCSA (Microsoft Certified Systems Administrator)		
	MCP (Microsoft Certified Professional)		
	MCSE (Microsoft Certified Systems Engineer)		
	MCDBA (Microsoft Certified Database Administrator)		
	MCAD (Microsoft Certified Application Developer)		
	MCSD (Microsoft Certified Solution Developer)		
	MCT (Microsoft Certified Trainer)		
	MCLC (Microsoft Certified Learning Consultant)		
	MOS (Microsoft Office Specialist)		
Profession:	Marketing		
Membership:	--		
Established:	--		

Connected International Meeting Professionals Association (CIMPA)

Designation:	Certified Global Meeting Planner	**Address:**	P9200 Bayard Place, Fairfax, Virginia 22052 USA
Designatory Letters:	CGMP (Certified Global Meeting Planner)	**Telephone:**	6512-684-0889
		Fax:	6267-390-5193
Profession:	Meeting and Conference Planning	**E-mail:**	Susan2@cimpa.org
		Web:	www.cimpa.org
Membership:	4,000		
Established:	1982		

Convention Industry Council

Designation:	Certified Meeting Professional	**Address:**	1620 I St. NW, 6th Floor, Washington, D.C. 20006 USA
Designatory Letters:	CMP (Certified Meeting Professional)	**Telephone:** **Fax:**	877-429-8634, 202-429-8634 202-463-8498
Profession:	Meeting and Conference Planning	**E-mail:** **Web:**	mpower@conventionindustry.org www.conventionindustry.org
Membership:	--		
Established:	1949		

American Society of Military Comptrollers

Designation:	Certified Defense Financial Manager	**Address:**	415 North Alfred St., Suite 3, Alexandria, Virginia 22314 USA
Designatory Letters:	CDFM (Certified Defense Financial Manager)	**Telephone:** **Fax:**	800-462-5637/703-549-0360 703-549-3181
Profession:	Military Comptrollership	**E-mail:**	--
Membership:	--	**Web:**	www.asmcertification.com
Established:	--		

Association of News Media Internal Auditors (NMIAA)

Designation:	NA	**Address:**	c/o Michele Bourne, The E.W. Scripps Company, 312 Walnut Street, Suite 2800, Cincinatti, Ohio 45202 USA
Designatory Letters:	NA		
Profession:	News Media Auditing		
Membership:	--		
Established:	1977	**Telephone:**	--
		Fax:	--
		E-mail:	ttrice@plaind.com
		Web:	www.nmiaa.org

American Production and Inventory Control Society (APICS)

Designation:	--	**Address:**	5301 Shawnee Road, Alexandria, Virginia 22312-2317 USA
Designatory Letters:	CSCP (Certified Supply Chain Personnel)	**Telephone:**	703-354-8851 or 800-444-2742
	CIRM (Certified in Integrated Resource Management)	**Fax:** **E-mail:** **Web:**	703-354-8106 service@apicshq.org www.apics.org
	CPIM (Certified in Production and Inventory Management)		
	CFPIM (Certified Fellow in Production and Inventory Management)		
Profession:	Operations Management		
Membership:	48,000		
Established:	1973		

American Payroll Association (APA)

Designation:	Fundamental Payroll Certificate Certified Payroll Professional	**Address:**	1025 Connecticut Avenue NW, Suite 1000, Washington, D.C. USA
Designatory Letters:	FPC (Fundamental Payroll Certificate)	**Telephone:** **Fax:**	202-817-1476 --
	CPP (Certified Payroll Certificate)	**E-mail:** **Web:**	apa@americanpayroll.org www.americanpayroll.org
Profession:	Payroll Management		
Membership:	--		
Established:	--		

Association of Public Pension Fund Auditors

Designation:	NA	**Address:**	PO Box 2407, ESP Station,
Designatory Letters:	NA		Albany, New York 12220 USA
Profession:	Pension Fund Auditing	**Telephone:**	--
Membership:	70 Pension Funds	**Fax:**	--
Established:	1991	**E-mail:**	webmaster@appfa.org
		Web:	appfa.org

The National Institute for Excellence in Professional Education, LLC

Designation:	--	**Address:**	237 Lancaster Avenue, Ste 500,
Designatory Letters:	CSEP (Certified Specialist in Estate Planning)		Devon, Pennsylvania 19333 USA
		Telephone:	610-688-4574
	CSRP (Certified Specialist in Retirement Planning)	**Fax:**	610-688-3395
		E-mail:	info@niepe.org
Profession:	Professional Business Education	**Web:**	www.niepe.org
Membership:	--		
Established:	--		

Project Management Institute

Designation:	Project Management Professional	**Address:**	Newtown Square, Pennsylvania USA
Designatory Letters:	PMP (Project Management Professional)	**Telephone:**	610-356-4600
		Fax:	610-356-4647
	CAPM (Certified Associate in Project Management)	**E-mail:**	customercare@pmi.org
		Web:	www.pmi.ca
Profession:	Project Management		
Membership:	--		
Established:	1969		

Institute for Supply Management (ISM)

Designation:	Certified Purchasing Manager	**Address:**	2055 East Centennial Circle, PO Box 22160, Tempe, Arizona 85285-2160 USA
	Accredited Purchasing Manager		
		Telephone:	480-752-6276 or 800-888-6276
	Certified Professional in Supply Management	**Fax:**	480-752-7890
		E-mail:	ashaw@ism.ws
Designatory Letters:	C.P.M. (Certified Purchasing Manager.)	**Web:**	www.ism.ws
	A.P.P. (Accredited Purchasing Manager)		
	CPSM (Certified Professional in Supply Management)		
Profession:	Purchasing and Supply Management		
Membership:	--		
Established:	1915		

American Society for Quality (ASQ)

Designation:	--	**Address:**	600 North Plankinton Ave.,
Designatory Letters:	SSGB (Six Sigma Green Belt Certificate)		Milwaukee, Wisconsin 53203 PO Box 3005, Milwaukee,
	SSBB (Six Sigma Black Belt Certificate)	**Telephone:**	Wisconsin 53201-3005 USA 414-272-8575
	CQE (Certified Quality Engineer)	**Fax:**	414-272-1734
	CQA (Certified Quality Auditor)	**E-mail:** **Web:**	help@asq.org www.asq.org
	CMQ/OE (Certified Manager of Quality/Organizational Effectiveness)		
	CQPA (Certified Quality Process Analyst)		
	CQIA (Certified Quality Improvement Associate)		
Profession:	Quality		
Membership:	100,000		
Established:	1946		

Quality Assurance Institute (QAI)

Designation:	--	**Address:**	2101 Parkbiter Drive, #200,
Designatory Letters:	CSQA (Certified Software Quality Analyst)		Orlando, Florida 32835-7614 USA
	CSTE (Certified Software Tester)	**Telephone:** **Fax:**	407-363-1111 407-363-1112
	CSPM (Certified Software Project Manager)	**E-mail:** **Web:**	-- www.qaiusa.com
Profession:	Quality Management		
Membership:	--		
Established:	1980		

California Association of Realtors

Designation:	Graduate Realtor Institute	**Address:**	525 South Virgil, Los Angeles,
Designatory Letters:	GRI (Graduate Realtor Institute)	**Telephone:**	California 90020 USA 213-739-8200
Profession:	Real Estate Management	**Fax:**	213-480-7724
Membership:	--	**E-mail:**	--
Established:	--	**Web:**	www.cae.org

CCIM Institute

Designation:	Certified Commercial Investment Member	**Address:**	430 North Michigan Ave., Chicago, Illinois, 60611-4092
Designatory Letters:	CCIM (Certified Commercial Investment Member)	**Telephone:** **Fax:**	USA 312-321-4460 312-321-4530
Profession:	Real Estate Management	**E-mail:**	sprice@ccim.net
Membership:	--	**Web:**	www.ccim.com
Established:	1954		

Council of Real Estate Brokerage Managers

Designation:	Certified Real Estate Brokerage Manager	**Address:**	430 North Michigan Ave., Chicago, Illinois 60611 USA
Designatory Letters:	CRB (Certified Real Estate Brokerage Manager)	**Telephone:**	800-621-8738
		Fax:	312-329-8882
		E-mail:	info@crb.com
Profession:	Real Estate Management	**Web:**	www.crb.com
Membership:	--		
Established:	1933		

Council of Residential Specialists

Designation:	Certified Residential Specialist	**Address:**	430 North Michigan Ave., Chicago, Illinois 60611 USA
Designatory Letters:	CRS (Certified Residential Specialist)	**Telephone:**	800-462-8841
		Fax:	312-329-8882
Profession:	Real Estate Management	**E-mail:**	--
Membership:	--	**Web:**	www.crs.com
Established:	1976		

Institute of Real Estate Managers

Designation:	--	**Address:**	430 North Michigan Ave., Chicago, Illinois 60611 USA
Designatory Letters:	AMO (Accredited Management Organization)	**Telephone:**	800-837-0706
	ARM (Accredited Residential Manager)	**Fax:**	800-338-4736
	CPM (Certified Property Manager)	**E-mail:**	custserv@irem.org
	ACM (Accredited Commercial Manager)	**Web:**	www.irem.org
Profession:	Real Estate Management		
Membership:	--		
Established:	1933		

Society of Industrial and Office Realtors

Designation:	--	**Address:**	1201 New York Ave., NW, Suite 350, Washington, D.C. 20005-6126 USA
Designatory Letters:	SIOR (Specialist Industrial and Office Real Estate)		
Profession:	Real Estate Management	**Telephone:**	202-449-8200
Membership:	--	**Fax:**	202-216-9325
Established:	--	**E-mail:**	admin@sior.com
		Web:	www.sior.com

Institute of Certified Records Managers

Designation:	--	**Address:**	5818 Molloy Road, Syracuse, New York 13211 USA
Designatory Letters:	CRM (Certified Records Manager)	**Telephone:**	877-244-3128
Profession:	Records Management	**Fax:**	315-474-1784
Membership:	872	**E-mail:**	admin@icrm.org
Established:	1975	**Web:**	www.icrm.org

International Foundation for Retirement Education

Designation:	Certified Retirement Administrator	**Address:**	PO Box 1860, Lubbock, Texas 79408-1860 USA
Designatory Letters:	CRA (Certified Retirement Administrator)	**Telephone:**	806-742-6100
		Fax:	806-742-6102
Profession:	Retirement Planning	**E-mail:**	--
Membership:	--	**Web:**	www.nfre.org
Established:	--		

Society of Certified Retirement Financial Advisers

Designation:	Certified Retirement Financial Advisor	**Address:**	1700 North Broadway, Ste 405, Walnut Creek, California 94596 USA
Designatory Letters:	CRFA (Certified Retirement Financial Advisor)	**Telephone:**	888-880-2732
		Fax:	425-660-2211
Profession:	Retirement Planning	**E-mail:**	info@crfa.org
Membership:	--	**Web:**	www.crfa.org
Established:	--		

Global Association of Risk Professionals

Designation:	Financial Risk Manager	**Address:**	100 Pavonia Ave., Ste 405, Jersey City, New Jersey 07310 USA
Designatory Letters:	FRM (Financial Risk Manager)		
Profession:	Risk Management	**Telephone:**	201-222-0054
Membership:	58,100	**Fax:**	201-222-5022
Established:	--	**E-mail:**	frm@garp.com
		Web:	www.garp.com

Professional Risk Managers' International Association (PRMIA)

Designation:	Certified Risk Manager	**Address:**	3630 North Hills Drive, Austin, Texas 78755 USA
Designatory Letters:	CRM (Certified Risk Manager)	**Telephone:**	800-633-2165
Profession:	Risk Management	**Fax:**	512-343-2167
Membership:	--	**E-mail:**	--
Established:	2002	**Web:**	www.prmia.org

Council of Supply Chain Management Professionals

Designation:	NA	**Address:**	333 East Butterfield Road, Suite 140, Lombard, Illinois 60148 USA
Designatory Letters:	NA		
Profession:	Supply Chain Management/ Logistics Management	**Telephone:**	630-574-0985
		Fax:	630-574-0989
Membership:	9,500	**E-mail:**	cscmpadmin@cscmp.org
Established:	1963	**Web:**	www.cscmp.org

American Society of Transportation and Logistics

Designation:	--	**Address:**	1700 N. Moore Street, Suite 1900,
Designatory Letters:	PLS (Professional Designation in Supply Management)		Arlington, Virginia 22209 USA
		Telephone:	703-524-5011
		Fax:	703-524-5017
	CTL (Certification in Transportation and Logistics)	**E-mail:**	astl@nitl.org
		Web:	www. astl.org
	DLP (Distinguished Logistics Professional)		
Profession:	Supply Management		
Membership:	--		
Established:	1946		

Internal Revenue Service (IRS)

Designation:	Enrolled Agent	**Address:**	Office of the Director of Practice,
Designatory Letters:	EA (Enrolled Agent).		PC:E:P, Internal Revenue
Profession:	Taxation		Service, 1111 Constitution Ave.,
Membership:	--		N.W., Washington, D.C. 20224
Established:	1913		USA
		Telephone:	202-376-1418
		Fax:	206-376-1420
		E-mail:	--
		Web:	www.irs.gov

Communications Fraud Control Association

Designation:	Certified Communication Security Professional	**Address:**	3030 N. Central Avenue, Ste 707,
			Phoenix, Arizona 85012 USA
Designatory Letters:	CCSP (Certified Communication Security Professional)	**Telephone:**	602-265-2322
		Fax:	602-265-1015
		E-mail:	fraud@cfca.org
Profession:	Telecommunications Fraud	**Web:**	www.cfca.org
Membership:	--		
Established:	1985		

Association of Chartered Treasury Managers

Designation:	Chartered Treasury Manager	**Address:**	835 Blossom Hill Road, Suite 206,
			San Jose, California 95123 USA
Designatory Letters:	CTM (Chartered Treasury Manager)	**Telephone:**	408-972-1348
		Fax:	408-972-1349
Profession:	Treasury Management	**E-mail:**	--
Membership:	--	**Web:**	www.actm.org
Established:	--		

Association for Financial Professionals

Designation:	--	**Address:**	7315 Wisconsin Ave., Suite 600 W,
Designatory Letters:	CTP (Certified Treasury Professional)		Bethesda, Maryland 20074 USA
		Telephone:	301-907-2862
	CCM (Certified Cash Manager)	**Fax:**	301-907-2864
		E-mail:	access@AFPonline.org
Profession:	Treasury Management	**Web:**	www.afponline.org
Membership:	--		
Established:	1979		

Appraisers Association of America

Designation:	--	**Address:**	386 Park Avenue South (Between 27 and 28 Streets), Suite 2000, New York, New York 10016 USA
Designatory Letters:	--		
Profession:	Valuation		
Membership:	--		
Established:	1949	**Telephone:**	212-889-5404
		Fax:	212-889-5503
		E-mail:	aaa@appraisersassoc.org
		Web:	appraisersassoc.org

The Heritage Institute

Designation:	Certified Wealth Consultant	**Address:**	Williamette, 205 Corporate Center, 1800 Blankenship Road, Ste 310, West Linn, Oregon 92068 USA
Designatory Letters:	CWC (Certified Wealth Consultant)	**Telephone:**	877-477-1659
Profession:	The Institute has advised that the certification is on "Wealth Management" as in the total wealth of the family, including values and human capital.	**Fax:**	503-650-2246
		E-mail:	info@theheritageinstitute.com
		Web:	www.theheritageinstitute.com
Membership:	--		
Established:	2003		

Kaplan University

Designation:	Wealth Management Specialist	**Address:**	USA
		Telephone:	866-523-3473
Designatory Letters:	WMS (Wealth Management Specialist)	**Fax:**	866-527-5268
		E-mail:	infowmb2b@kaplan.edu
Profession:	Wealth Management	**Web:**	www.kaplan.edu
Membership:	--		
Established:	--		

The Wealth Preservation Institute

Designation:	Certified Wealth Preservation Planner	**Address:**	St. Joseph, Michigan USA
		Telephone:	269-408-1841
Designatory Letters:	CWPP (Certified Wealth Preservation Planner)	**Fax:**	--
		E-mail:	--
Profession:	Wealth Management	**Web:**	www.thewpi.org
Membership:	--		
Established:	--		

URUGUAY

Colegio de Contadores, Economistas y Administradores del Uruguay

Designation:	--	**Address:**	Avda. Libertador 170, Piso 3°, Montevideo CP 11.100, Uruguay
Designatory Letters:	--		
Profession:	Accounting	**Telephone:**	5982-903-1000
Membership:	--	**Fax:**	5982-902-6639
Established:	--	**E-mail:**	ccea@ccea.com.uy
		Web:	www.ccea.com.uy

Centro LatinoAmericano de Estudios Informatica (CLEI)

Designation:	--	**Address:**	Escuela de Ingenieria, Universidad
Designatory Letters:	--		ORT-Uruguay, Cuareim 1451,
Profession:	Information Technology		Montevideo CP 11.100, Uruguay
Membership:	--	**Telephone:**	5982-902-1505 ext 228
Established:	--	**Fax:**	5982-908-1370
		E-mail:	corbo@athenea.ort.edu.uy
		Web:	www.clei.cl

UZBEKISTAN

National Association of Professional Accountants and Auditors of Uzbekistan

Designation:	--	**Address:**	Mavlyanov Street 1A, 700084
Designatory Letters:	--		Tashkent, Uzbekistan
Profession:	Accounting/Auditing	**Telephone:**	998-71-134-1890/134-0187
Membership:	--	**Fax:**	998-71-13039-44
Established:	--	**E-mail:**	minovar@albatros.uz
		Web:	--

V

VENEZUELA

Federación de Colegios de Contadores Públicos de Venezuela

Designation:	Contador Publico	**Address:**	Calle este 2 cruce con calle sur 25
Designatory Letters:	Colegiado		Edifico Rosalinda Piso No. 2-3-
	CPC - Contador Publico		4, Entre el Edifcio CTV y la
	Colegiado		Torre Viasa, La Candeleria,
Profession:	Accounting		Caracas 1060 A, Venezuela
Membership:	--	**Telephone:**	582-12-578-3234-1761-2807;
Established:	--		58255-622-4445-664-6560
		Fax:	582.12-578-3132
		E-mail:	federacion@fccpv.org
		Web:	www.fccpv.org

VIETNAM

Vietnam Accounting Association

Designation:	--	**Address:**	192 Giai Phong Road, Thanh xuan
Designatory Letters:	--		District, Hanoi, Vietnam
Profession:	Accounting	**Telephone:**	844-868-6714, 868-6721
Membership:	--	**Fax:**	844-868-6722
Established:	--	**E-mail:**	hktvn@hn.vnn.vn
		Web:	--

Z

ZAMBIA

Zambia Institute of Chartered Accountants

Designation:	Chartered Accountant	**Address:**	No. 24 Joseph Mwilwa Road, Plot No. 284a, Rhodes Park, Lusaka, Zambia
Designatory Letters:	AZICA (Associate Member of the Zambia Institute of Chartered Accountants) FZICA (Fellow Member of the Zambia Institute of Chartered Accountants)	**Telephone:** **Fax:** **E-mail:** **Web:**	222-773-224-489 224-490-236-5930 zica@coppernet.zm www.zica.co.zm
Profession:	Accounting		
Membership:	--		
Established:	1982		

Computer Society of Zambia

Designation:	--	**Address:**	Afriswitch PVT Ltd., 6 Lagos Road, Rhodes Park, Lusaka, Zambia
Designatory Letters:	--		
Profession:	Information Technology		
Membership:	--	**Telephone:**	260-1-257-270
Established:	--	**Fax:**	--
		E-mail:	--
		Web:	www.prmia.org

Institute of Management

Designation:	--	**Address:**	PO Box 31735, Lusaka, Zambia
Designatory Letters:	--	**Telephone:**	--
Profession:	Management	**Fax:**	--
Membership:	--	**E-mail:**	--
Established:	--	**Web:**	--

Zambia Institute of Marketing

Designation:	--	**Address:**	PO Box 230138, Ndola, Zambia
Designatory Letters:	--	**Telephone:**	--
Profession:	Marketing	**Fax:**	--
Membership:	--	**E-mail:**	--
Established:	--	**Web:**	--

ZIMBABWE

Institute of Chartered Accountants of Zimbabwe

Designation:	Chartered Accountant	**Address:**	PO Box CY 1079, Causeway,
Designatory Letters:	CA (Z) Chartered Accountant of Zimbabwe		Harare, Belgavia Harare, Zimbabwe
		Telephone:	263-4-793-950
Profession:	Accounting	**Fax:**	263-4-706.245
Membership:	1,300	**E-mail:**	faithfulm@icaz.org.zw
Established:	1918	**Web:**	www.icaz.org.zw

Institute of Chartered Secretaries and Administrators of Zimbabwe (Public Accountant and Auditors Board)

Designation:	Chartered Secretary Registered Public Accountant	**Address:**	PO Box CY 172, Causeway, Harare, Zimbabwe
Designatory Letters:	ACIS (Associate Member of the Institute of Chartered Secretaries & Administrators of Zimbabwe)	**Telephone:**	700555
		Fax:	700624
		E-mail:	cis@africaonline.co.zw
		Web:	www.icsaz.co.zw
	FCIS (Fellow Member of the Institute of Chartered Secretaries & Administrators of Zimbabwe)		
	RPAcc (Registered Public Accountant)		
Profession:	Corporate Management Accountant		
Membership:	--		
Established:	1902		

Computer Society of Zimbabwe

Designation:	NA	**Address:**	PO Box CY 164, Causeway,
Designatory Letters:	NA		Harare, Zimbabwe
Profession:	Information Technology	**Telephone:**	263-4-250-489
Membership:	1,000	**Fax:**	263-4-708-861
Established:	1974	**E-mail:**	membership@csz.org.zw
		Web:	www.csz.org.zw

APPENDIX
UMBRELLA ORGANIZATIONS

AUSTRIA

Designation:	NA	**Address:**	Hofrstraße 3, Laxenburg, Austria.
Designatory Letters:	NA	**Telephone:**	43-2236-73616
Administering Body:	International Federation	**Fax:**	43-2236-73616/19
	for Information	**E-mail:**	ifip@ifip.org
	Processing (IFIP)	**Web:**	www.ifip.org
Profession:	Information Technology		
Membership:	--		
Established:	--		

BAHRAIN

Designation:	NA	**Address:**	P.O. Box 1176, 603 Government
Designatory Letters:	NA		Avenue, Yateem Center,
Administering Body:	Accounting and Auditing		Manama, Bahrain.
	Organization for Islamic	**Telephone:**	973-1724-4496
	Financial Institutions	**Fax:**	973-1725-0194
Profession:	Accounting/Auditing	**E-mail:**	aaoifi@batelco.com.bh
Membership:	--	**Web:**	www.aaoifi.org
Established:	1990		

BANGLADESH

Designation:	NA	**Address:**	Chartered Accountant Bhaban, 100
Designatory Letters:	NA		Kazi Nazral Islam Avenue,
Administering Body:	The South Asian		Kawran Bazar, Dhaka-1215,
	Federation of		Bangladesh
	Accountants (SAFA)	**Telephone:**	327017/317521/819399
Profession:	Accounting	**Fax:**	814087
Membership:	--	**E-mail:**	--
Established:	1984	**Web:**	--

BELGIUM

Designation:	NA	**Address:**	4 Rue Jacques de Lalaing, B-1040
Designatory Letters:	NA		Bruxelles, Belgium
Administering Body:	The European Federation	**Telephone:**	32-02-736-8886
	of Accountants and	**Fax:**	32-02-736-2964
	Auditors for SMEs	**E-mail:**	info@efaa.com
Profession:	Accounting	**Web:**	www.efaa.com
Membership:	--		
Established:	--		

Designation:	NA	**Address:**	Rue d'Egmont 13, B-1000
Designatory Letters:	NA		Brussels, Belgium
Administering Body:	European Accounting	**Telephone:**	32-2-511.9116
	Association (EAA)	**Fax:**	32-2-512.1929
Profession:	Accounting	**E-mail:**	eaa@eiasm.be
Membership:	--	**Web:**	www.bham.ac.u/EAA/
Established:	--		

Designation:	NA	**Address:**	Pl. Chasseurs Ardennais 20, 1030
Designatory Letters:	NA		Brussels, Belgium
Administering Body:	European Marketing	**Telephone:**	32-2-942-1780
	Confederation (EMC)	**Fax:**	32-2-742-1785
Profession:	Marketing	**E-mail:**	infodesk@emc.be
Membership:	17	**Web:**	www.emc.be
Established:	1960		

CANADA

Designation:	NA	**Address:**	150 Metcalfe Street, Ste 800,
Designatory Letters:	NA		Ottawa,Ontario K2P, 1P1,
Administering Body:	International Actuarial		Canada
	Association	**Telephone:**	613-236-0886
Profession:	Actuarial Science	**Fax:**	613-236-1356
Membership:	--	**E-mail:**	IFAA@inasoc.ca
Established:	--	**Web:**	www.actuaries.org

FRANCE

Designation:	--	**Address:**	Palais de la Bourse, Place de la
Designatory Letters:	--		Bourse, 75002 Paris, France.
Administering Body:	European Federation of	**Telephone:**	49-6103-5833-48
	Financial Analysts	**Fax:**	49-6103-5833-35
	Societies (EFFAS)	**E-mail:**	cluadia.stinnes@effas.com
Profession:	Investment Management	**Web:**	www.effas.com
Membership:	--		
Established:	--		

Designation:	--	**Address:**	20, rue d'Athenes, 75442 Paris,
Designatory Letters:	--		Cedex 09, France
Administering Body:	European Associations of	**Telephone:**	33-01-4281-9841
	Corporate Treasurers	**Fax:**	33-14-280-1890
Profession:	Treasury Management	**E-mail:**	secretary@eact-group.com
Membership:	--	**Web:**	www.eact-group.com
Established:	--		

GERMANY

Designation:	NA	**Address:**	Hoheustaufenring 47-51, 50674
Designatory Letters:	NA		Cologne, Germany
Administering Body:	European Actuarial	**Telephone:**	49-0-221-912554-21
	Academy (EAA)	**Fax:**	--
Profession:	Actuarial Science	**E-mail:**	contact@actuarial-academy.com
Membership:	--	**Web:**	www.actuarial-academy.com
Established:	2005		

GHANA

Designation:	NA	**Address:**	PO Box 4268, Accra Central,
Designatory Letters:	NA		Ghana
Administering Body:	Association of	**Telephone:**	666-954/5; 669 591/2
	Accountancy Bodies in	**Fax:**	233-21/669-594
	West Africa	**E-mail:**	info@icagh.com
	(AABWA)	**Web:**	www.icagh.com
Profession:	Accounting		
Membership:	10		
Established:	--		

INDONESIA

Designation:	NA	**Address:**	Malaysia c/o Ikatan Akuntan
Designatory Letters:	NA		Indonesia (IAI), Jl.
Administering Body:	ASEAN Federation of		Sisingamangaraja
	Accountants		No. 59 Kebayoran Baru Jakarta
Profession:	Accounting		12120 Indonesia
Membership:	15	**Telephone:**	62-21-7222-989
Established:	1977	**Fax:**	62-21-724-5078
		E-mail:	iai-info@akuntan-iai.or.id
		Web:	www.afa-central.org

JAMAICA

Designation:	NA	**Address:**	6 Lockett Ave., Kingston 4,
Designatory Letters:	NA		Jamaica
Administering Body:	Institute of Chartered	**Telephone:**	876-922-3223
	Accountants of the	**Fax:**	876-948-6610
	Caribbean (ICAC)	**E-mail:**	icac@cwjamaica.com
Profession:	Accounting	**Web:**	www.icac.org.jm
Membership:	--		
Established:	1987		

JAPAN

Designation:	--	**Address:**	5F Tokyo Stock Exchange Building, 2-1 Nihonbashi Kabutocho, Chuo-Ku, Tokyo 103-0026, Japan
Designatory Letters:	--		
Administering Body:	Asian Security Analysts Federation Inc.		
Profession:	Investment Management	**Telephone:**	81-3-3666-7866
Membership:	--	**Fax:**	81-3-3666-5845
Established:	1979	**E-mail:**	asaf-manager@saa.or.jp
		Web:	www.asaf.org.au

KENYA

Designation:	NA	**Address:**	2nd Floor, Hughes Building, Kenyatta Avenue, Nairobi, Kenya
Designatory Letters:	NA		
Administering Body:	Eastern and Southern African Federation of Accountants	**Telephone:**	254-20-2191-51
		Fax:	254-20-22-9284
Profession:	Accounting	**E-mail:**	ecsafa@afriocaonline.co.ke
Membership:	--	**Web:**	www.ecsafa.org
Established:	1990		

MALAYSIA

Designation:	NA	**Address:**	No. 3 Dewan Akauntan No. 2, Jalan Tun Sambanthan 3, Brickfields, 50470 Kuala Lumpur, Malaysia
Designatory Letters:	NA		
Administering Body:	Confederation of Asian and Pacific Accountants (CAPA)	**Telephone:**	60-3-274-5055
Profession:	Accounting	**Fax:**	60-3-274-9949
Membership:	--	**E-mail:**	--
Established:	1957	**Web:**	--

NEW ZEALAND

Designation:	NA	**Address:**	c/o New Zealand Institute of Chartered Accountants, Level 2, CIGNA House, 40 Mercer Street, Wellington, New Zealand
Designatory Letters:	NA		
Administering Body:	Global Accounting Alliance		
Profession:	Accounting	**Telephone:**	64-4-474-7840
Membership:	Comprising nine of the world's leading accounting bodies representing over 700,000 members	**Fax:**	64-4-460-0394
		E-mail:	garry.muriwai@nzica.com
		Web:	www.globalaccountingalliance.com
Established:	2005		

SERBIA AND MONTENEGRO

Designation:	NA	**Address:**	Njegoseva 19, 11000 Belgrade,
Designatory Letters:	NA		Serbia & Montenegro
Administering Body:	SEEPAD (South Eastern	**Telephone:**	--
	European Partnership	**Fax:**	--
	on Accountancy	**E-mail:**	seepad@yubc.net
	Development)	**Web:**	www.seepad.org
Profession:	Accounting		
Membership:	11		
Established:	--		

SINGAPORE

Designation:	Certified Professional	**Address:**	APMF Education Headquarters, 51
	Marketer (Asia Pacific)		Anson Road, #03-53 Anson
			Centre, Singapore 0207
Designatory Letters:	CPM (Asia Pacific)	**Telephone:**	65-6221-7788
	(Certified Professional	**Fax:**	65-6223-8785
	Marketer (Asia	**E-mail:**	--
	Pacfic))	**Web:**	www.apmf.org.sg
Administering Body:	Asia Pacific Marketing		
	Federation (APMF)		
Profession:	Marketing		
Membership:	16		
Established:	1991		

SOUTH AFRICA

Designation:	NA	**Address:**	101101 Sanwood Park, 379 Queen
Designatory Letters:	NA		Crescent, Lynwood Road,
Administering Body:	Eastern and Southern		Pretoria, South Africa
	African Association of	**Telephone:**	--
	Accountants General	**Fax:**	--
Profession:	Accounting	**E-mail:**	lindi@esaag.co.za
Membership:	--	**Web:**	www.esaag.co.za
Established:	1976		

SOUTH KOREA

Designation:	NA	**Address:**	South Korea
Designatory Letters:	NA	**Telephone:**	admin@iiakorea.or.kr
Administering Body:	Asian Confederation of	**Fax:**	www.iiakorea.or.kr
	Institutes of Internal	**E-mail:**	--
	Auditors	**Web:**	--
Profession:	Internal Auditing		
Membership:	--		
Established:	--		

SWITZERLAND

Designation:	Certified International Investment Analyst	**Address:**	Feldstrasse 80, Buelach, Zurich, CH-8180, Switzerland.
Designatory Letters:	CIIA (Certified International Investment Analyst)	**Telephone:**	41-44-872-3543
		Fax:	41-44-872-3532
		E-mail:	info@aciia.org
Administering Body:	Association of Certified International Investment Analysts	**Web:**	www.aciia.org
Profession:	Investment Management		
Membership:	28 national and regional associations of investment professionals		
Established:	2000		

UNITED KINGDOM

Designation:	NA	**Address:**	PO Box 433, Chartered Accountants' Hall, Moorgate House, London EC2P 2BJ, England
Designatory Letters:	NA		
Administering Body:	Consultative Committee of Accountancy Bodies Ltd. (CCAB)		
		Telephone:	020-7920-8100
Profession:	Accounting	**Fax:**	020-7920-0547
Membership:	6 leading U.K. accounting bodies	**E-mail:**	admin@ccab.org
		Web:	www.icaew.co.uk
Established:	1976 (Became a limited liability company in 1986)		

Designation:	NA	**Address:**	Napier House, 4 Worcester Street, Oxford OX1 2AW, England
Designatory Letters:	NA		
Administering Body:	Groupe Consultatef des Associations d'Actuaires des Pays des Communautes Européennes	**Telephone:**	44-01-1865-268218
		Fax:	44-01-1865-268233
		E-mail:	groupeconsultatif@actuaries.org.uk
		Web:	--
Profession:	Actuarial Science		
Membership:	--		
Established:	--		

Designation:	NA	**Address:**	16 Park Crescent, London, W1N 4AH, England
Designatory Letters:	--		
Administering Body:	International Corporate Governance Network	**Telephone:**	44-020-7580-4741
		Fax:	44-020-7323-1132
Profession:	Corporate Governance	**E-mail:**	--
Membership:	--	**Web:**	www.icgn.org
Established:	1995		

Designation:	--	Address:	UK
Designatory Letters:	--	Telephone:	32-2-645-4816
Administering Body:	International Group of	Fax:	--
	Treasury Associations	E-mail:	honsec@igta.org
Profession:	Treasury Management	Web:	www.igta.org
Membership:	--		
Established:	--		

UNITED STATES

Designation:	NA	Address:	545 Fifth Avenue, 14th Floor, New
Designatory Letters:	NA		York, NY 10017, USA
Administering Body:	International Federation	Telephone:	212-286-9344
	of Accountants	Fax:	212-286-9570
Profession:	Accounting	E-mail:	julissaguevara@ifac.org
Membership:	163	Web:	www.ifac.org
Established:	1977		

Designation:	NA	Address:	Fointainebleau Executive Center,
Designatory Letters:	NA		275 Fountainbleau Blvd., Ste #
Administering Body:	Asociación		245, Miami, Florida 33172, USA
	Intermaericana de	Telephone:	305-225-1991
	Contabilidad (Inter-	Fax:	305-225-2011
	American Accounting	E-mail:	oficina@contadoresaic.org
	Association -IAA)	Web:	www.contadoresaic.org
Profession:	Accounting		
Membership:	--		
Established:	1949		

Designation:	NA	Address:	150 Fourth Avenue North,
Designatory Letters:	NA		Nashville, Tennessee 37219-
Administering Body:	National Association of		2417, USA
	State Boards of	Telephone:	615-880-4200
	Accountancy	Fax:	615-880-4290
Profession:	Accounting	E-mail:	dcostello@nasba.org
Membership:	55	Web:	www.nasba.org/
Established:	1917		

Designation:	NA	Address:	c/o W.J. MacGinnitie,
Designatory Letters:	NA		Tillunghast/Towers Perrin, One
Administering Body:	International Association		Atlanta Plaza, 950 East Paces
	of Consulting		Ferry Road, Atlanta, GA 30326-
	Actuaries (USA)		1119, USA
Profession:	Actuarial Science	Telephone:	404-365-1602
Membership:	--	Fax:	404-365-1663
Established:	--	E-mail:	--
		Web:	--

Designation:	NA	**Address:**	449 Lewis Hargett Circle, Suite
Designatory Letters:	NA		290, Lexington, Kentucky
Administering Body:	National Association of		40503-3590, USA
	State Auditors,	**Telephone:**	859-276-1147
	Comptrollers, and	**Fax:**	859-278-0507
	Treasurers.	**E-mail:**	kpoynter@nasact.org
Profession:	Auditing/Accounting	**Web:**	www.nasact.org
Membership:	--		
Established:	--		

Designation:	NA	**Address:**	12208 Mount Vernon Avenue,
Designatory Letters:	NA		Alexandria, Virginia 22301-
Administering Body:	International Consortium		1314, USA
	on Governmental	**Telephone:**	703-562-0035
	Financial Management	**Fax:**	703-548-9367
	(ICGFM)	**E-mail:**	ICCF@yahoo.com
Profession:	Government Financial	**Web:**	www.icgfm.org
	Management		
Membership:	--		
Established:	1947		

Designation:	--	**Address:**	8531 Utica Avenue, Suite 200,
Designatory Letters:	--		Rancho Cucamonga , California
Administering Body:	International Institute of		91730, USA
	Municipal Clerks	**Telephone:**	909-944-4162
Profession:	Local Government	**Fax:**	909-944-8545
Membership:	--	**E-mail:**	Hq@iimc.com
Established:	1947	**Web:**	www.iimc.com

Designation:	NA	**Address:**	858 Longview Road, Burlingame,
Designatory Letters:	NA		California 94010-6974, USA
Administering Body:	International Council of	**Telephone:**	650-342-2250
	Management	**Fax:**	650-344-5005
	Consulting Institutes	**E-mail:**	icmc@icmci.org
Profession:	Management Consulting	**Web:**	www.icmci.org
Membership:	45		
Established:	1987		

Designation:	Certified Project Manager	**Address:**	Renaissance Square, 426 Main St., #360, Spotswood, New Jersey, NJ 08884, USA [Chapters in India, Turkey, Canada, UK, China, USA, Jordan, UAE, Egypt, Libya, Kuwait, Iraq, and Lebanon]
Designatory Letters:	CPM (Certified Project Manager) (The Association advises that they are working on a Certified Project Auditor designation to be introduced in 2008)	**Telephone:**	732-421-2306
Administering Body:	International Association of Project and Program Managers	**Fax:**	--
		E-mail:	info@iappm.org
		Web:	www.iappm.org
Profession:	Project Management		
Membership:	3,500		
Established:	2003		

Designation:	NA	**Address:**	USA
Designatory Letters:	NA	**Telephone:**	--
Administering Body:	International Federation of Purchasing and Supply Management	**Fax:**	--
		E-mail:	--
		Web:	www.ifpmm.org
Profession:	Supply Chain Management		
Membership:	--		
Established:	--		

Designation:	NA	**Address:**	12100 Sunset Hills Road, Suite 130, Reston, VA 20190, USA
Designatory Letters:	NA	**Telephone:**	703-437-4377
Administering Body:	National Association of Corporate Treasurers	**Fax:**	703-435-4390
		E-mail:	nact@nact.org
Profession:	Treasury Management	**Web:**	www.nact.org/
Membership:	--		
Established:	--		

INDEX BY PROFESSION

INDEX BY DESIGNATIONS

INDEX BY COUNTRY AND ADMINISTERING BODIES